Film as Religion

Film as Religion

Myths, Morals, and Rituals

John C. Lyden

NEW YORK UNIVERSITY PRESS

New York and London

NEW YORK UNIVERSITY PRESS
New York and London

Library of Congress Cataloging-in-Publication Data
Lyden, John, 1959-
Film as religion : myths, morals, and rituals / John C. Lyden.
p. cm.
Includes bibliographical references and index.
ISBN 0-8147-5180-6 (cloth : alk. paper) —
ISBN 0-8147-5181-4 (pbk. : alk. paper)
1. Motion pictures—Religious aspects. 2. Motion pictures—
Moral and ethical aspects. I. Title.
PN1995.5 .L89 2003
291.1'75—dc21 2002153769

New York University Press books are printed on acid-free paper,
and their binding materials are chosen for strength and durability.

Manufactured in the United States of America
10 9 8 7 6 5

To Liz, Karl, Grace, and Clara
my favorite film critics

Contents

Introduction   1

PART I   A Method for Viewing Film as Religion   9

    1   Existing Approaches to Religion and Film   11

    2   The Definition of Religion   36

    3   Myths about Myth   56

    4   Rituals and Morals   79

    5   The Religion-Film Dialogue as Interreligious Dialogue   108

PART II   Genre and Film Analyses   137

    6   Westerns and Action Movies   141
       Die Hard (1988)   146

    7   Gangster Films   153
       The Godfather (1972) and *The Godfather, Part II* (1974)   156

    8   Melodrama, Tearjerkers, and "Women's Films"   164
       Titanic (1997)   171

    9   Romantic Comedies   179
       When Harry Met Sally . . . (1989)   183

    10   Children's Films and Fantasy   191
       E.T., The Extraterrestrial (1982)   194

11 Science Fiction   202
    The Terminator (1984) and
    Terminator 2: Judgment Day (1991)   207
    The Original *Star Wars* Films (1977, 1980, 1983)   216

12 Thrillers and Horror Movies   226
    Alfred Hitchcock   230
    Psycho (1960)   232
    The Silence of the Lambs (1991)   240

    Conclusion   246

    Notes   251

    Bibliography   269

    Name and Subject Index   279

    Film Index   285

    About the Author   289

Film as Religion

Introduction

In recent years we have seen a surge of interest in religion and film studies. The study of religion and film is not exactly new, but there are a few reasons why the field is currently growing. For one thing, the availability of inexpensive VCRs has made classroom showings of movies much easier than it was in the days when one needed a 35 mm film projector and access to films in order to study them in a college classroom. Now anyone can walk into a video store and, for a few dollars, rent any of hundreds of movies made over the last seventy years. Religion professors, like teachers of many subjects, have noticed how easy it is to incorporate the discussion of films into their courses, and students obviously appreciate such use of popular media.

But there is obviously more to it than that. The growing interest in film also indicates a growing appreciation for the role that technological media play in our lives, from television to computers. We are beginning to realize that we cannot understand or interpret our society except in its relation to these unavoidable additions to it. Some welcome them and some fear them, but they are here to stay.

Scholars of religion are also more interested in interdisciplinary study than they used to be, when they were more comfortable to remain in their isolated fields. Today, there is a greater awareness of academic fields that study the surrounding culture, including popular culture studies such as those regarding film. The study of popular culture itself has also evolved in recent decades, so that there is more for this newer field to share with the older areas of academic study.

Given the fact that film has now been recognized as part of the modern culture with which religions will inevitably interact, a wide range of approaches has been suggested, all of which seek, in one way or another, to relate the study of religion to that of film. There is no real consensus about what approach religion scholars should take to film, but almost all agree that the question involves the relationship between those cultural phenomena we recognize as "religions" and other, "nonreligious" cultural phenomena. As such, it becomes a form of the classic "problem" of "religion and culture." What is taken for granted in these discussions is that we pretty much know what religion is, and what culture is, and we can distinguish them without too much difficulty.

In this book I take a different approach. It is my contention that there is no absolute distinction between religion and other aspects of culture, and that we have a tendency to label certain sorts of activities as "religious" chiefly because they fall into the patterns that we recognize from religions with which we are familiar. As a result, we have a tendency to limit what we view as religion to that which is recognized as such by us in our own culture. The result is that we can find ourselves shortsighted when we encounter a diverse form of religion—as, for example, the European colonists who came to America did. For a long time, they refused to even grant the name "religion" to the activities in Native American culture that paralleled those undertaken by Europeans under that name. In time, they came to see that the "otherness" of American beliefs did not disqualify them from performing the same functions for Native Americans that Christianity did for most Europeans, and therefore these beliefs might be considered equally "religious." Perhaps they feared to give such practices the label of "religion" because doing so might require an acknowledgement that these practices are as valid or true as their own. In fact, it merely required them to acknowledge that they exist.

It may be that we experience a similar form of shortsightedness when we encounter aspects of our own culture that we view as opposed to religious values or beliefs. We fail to acknowledge the extent to which modern people base their worldviews and ethics upon sources we do not usually label "religious." Though we may see the powers of the new media, we often fear them and do not wish to recognize them as sharing in the same functions that historically have been accorded to religion. There may, of course, be good reasons to fear some of the values and worldviews projected in popular culture, but this does not mean that it deserves absolute rejection by those who have found its flaws. Like any other aspect of culture, including every religion, popular culture is likely to have aspects with which each of us might agree and others that we would reject. We will not all agree on which aspects to accept and which to reject, but probably we would all admit that there are aspects we like as well as aspects we dislike. We cannot make a fair assessment of popular culture unless we seek to understand it and its appeal, even when we do not agree with its messages. We need to be able to analyze the relationship between our traditional values and these new values without simply falling into a defensive posture that cannot even see the "other." Although there are religious groups that have chosen to live without movies, television, computers, and telephones, most of us have not taken that option. We therefore need a critical method for relating to the culture that allows for genuine engagement with it.

It is my hypothesis that such engagement will be most readily accomplished by granting that certain aspects of popular culture have a "religious" side to them. This is not to say that everything in culture is "religion." Rather, it is to argue that what we have always called "religion" is identified by its function in society, and that this function can be met even by cultural phenomena not normally called "religions."

I am not, of course, the first person writing about religion and film to observe that there is a "religious power" present in the cinema. However, no one has systematically and thoroughly developed this insight as a basis for developing a method for religion and film studies. Some authors have recognized the religiouslike quality of cinema even as they dismiss it for its lack of depth in comparison with "real" religion. Such an approach fails to take film (or popular culture in general) seriously enough to provide a measured assessment of it. This book seeks to address this problem by developing a method for understanding film as performing a religious function.

In my first chapter I consider past and present work in the field of religion and film, assessing the methods that have been proposed and their advantages and disadvantages. Most of the approaches can be understood as falling into one of two categories (or a combination thereof) that I would define as "theological" and "ideological." The latter is more characteristic of film studies in general, seeking to critique the aspects of films that perpetuate racial, gender, or class hegemonies. The former is more interested in finding parallels between Christian (or other traditional religious) doctrine and the ideas conveyed in films. It is not my intention to suggest that such methods should cease or be replaced by my own, but I hold that these methods have certain limitations that prevent them from fully addressing how films function for their audiences, apart from their parallels to traditional religions or their ideological functions.

Chapter 2 will develop the functional definition of religion we will use, based primarily on the work of Clifford Geertz. This definition includes the three aspects noted in this book's title: a "myth" or story that conveys a worldview; a set of values that idealize how the world should be; and a ritual expression that unites the two. This chapter will also suggest some preliminary considerations about how Geertz's definition can be applied to film, in particular, how it (like religion) offers methods for dealing with suffering and injustice, and how it presents an alternate reality in which we participate during the viewing experience. The viewer may be well aware of the artificial nature of this filmic reality, and yet it still has the power to affect the way we think and act in the reality that exists outside the cinema.

Chapter 3 will consider the concept of myth and how it might profitably be applied to film. Although a number of people have looked at films as "modern myths," this term signifies different things for different people, depending on what they mean by "myth." Following some of the leading contemporary myth theorists, I will argue for an understanding of the term that does not reduce it to a psychological projection or an illogical hegemony-promoting falsehood, but rather views it as a story that expresses the worldview and values of a community. Myth has often been a pejorative term, and we must transcend this sense of it if we are to fairly assess the religious power of the stories of film (or of any religion, for that matter).

Chapter 4 deals with the nature of rituals and the ways in which films offer ritualized experiences with religious power for the viewer, as well as the ways in which these express the realization of a set of moral values. Films offer a vision of the way the world should be (in the view of the film) as well as statements about the way it really is; the ritual of filmgoing unites the two when we become a part of the world projected on screen. We often hope and wish for a world like the one we see in the movies even though we must return to a very different world at the end of the show; in this way, films offer an entry into an ideally constructed world. This does not mean justice is always done to characters, but that when injustice is done, characters (and the audience) have the opportunity to learn from injustice and so experience redemption from it. This chapter will also discuss rituals of sacrifice and scapegoating, which allow catharsis through offering opportunities to participate vicariously in redemptive suffering, and rituals of liminality, which create situations in which normally forbidden behavior is permitted as a means of questioning as well as reinforcing societal norms.

Chapter 5 will develop the analogy between religion and film further, arguing that the dialogue between the two can and should be understood according to a certain understanding of the norms governing interreligious dialogue. In practice, religions have often either demonized all others as incomprehensible in their difference and hence evil, or they have ignored the differences as they attempt to view the other as simply an alternate form of the self. The latter approach tolerates others only on the condition that they relinquish their otherness, so that we can say "we all believe the same thing, really." That is, we can only accept them if they believe what we do. The former simply rejects other religions as without value or use as they are viewed as too different from us. The most profitable form of interreligious dialogue, however, is one that does not seek to eliminate such difference in an attempt to make others "just like us," but also recognizes that difference can be good, even when it means that others view things differently than we do. Too often, films are either demonized as irredeemable from a traditional religious viewpoint, or they are "baptized" via an interpretation that would ignore their difference in an attempt to read our own religious views into them. By allowing films to have their own religious voice, and seeking to discern it, we will be on a better path to hearing what the films actually have to say, and perhaps gain some understanding and appreciation of them in the process.

Part II, chapters 6 through 12, will apply this method to the study of film genres and individual films. Genres have varying conventions and expectations they provoke, even though genres are not quite as monolithic as film genre critics once believed. We will examine the conventions of seven genres: westerns/action movies, gangster films, melodrama, romantic comedies, children's films (especially those involving fantasy), science fiction, and thrillers/horror movies. In each case, I will give a more extended study of at least one film and seek to show how such films function religiously according to my definitions.

The interpretations of the individual films may not always seem to go beyond what the average filmgoer might discover in a film. This is intentional. This method does not seek to uncover hidden meanings in the films that can be detected only by the scholar who is trained in abstruse methods of analysis, but to point to the ways people's beliefs, values, and feelings are affected by films. Ideological analysis often looks at how people may be affected in ways they do not realize, which is extremely valuable, but it can overlook some more obvious ways in which films may influence our attitudes and beliefs. *Gone With the Wind*, for example, is certainly a political apology for the South and an indirect defense of slavery and racism, but it is also often appropriated as a story with a message about how to survive adversity, quite apart from its political agenda. My interpretations, then, in looking at how films function for their audiences, are not attempts to read content into them so much as to read the response of viewers to them.

By way of concluding this preface, I should mention my own subjective relationship to this project. Film, by its very nature, invites subjective responses, and I have found myself at certain points in this project having to admit my personal biases and how they affect my taste in films. This is a crucial part of the task of viewing religion as film; to acknowledge that multiple interpretations are valid and that we cannot pretend that there is a privileged reading of the "text." Although postmodern scholars are supposed to know this, there is still a certain authority that goes with many of the scholarly pronouncements on film that would seem to derail the possibility of allowing for multiple views. In my own study of film, I have tried to listen to all views and to understand why certain people like certain films. I have done this because I have noticed that some people can argue about the interpretation of a film with more vehemence than they may argue about anything else, and I find myself in this category. I have always loved movies, but this is a critical love that makes distinctions between good and bad films. This does not mean that I do not allow for the possibility of being wrong about a movie, or that I regard my view as the only defensible one. One reason I have undertaken this project is to understand better my own relationship with the movies, as they have affected me in powerful ways. A key question to emerge in this study is, How shall we determine what is good and what is bad in films? Although viewers will not agree on the criteria for such determination, we need to take into account the situation of the individuals who are assessing the film and how their own values interact with it. People may come up with entirely "legitimate" but different responses to a film, based precisely on the differences between their values and worldviews.

It is because I have wished to avoid a narrow or prejudicial view of film or popular culture that I have viewed film as having an independent religious significance and have not simply made it into a dialogue partner for theology. As my own training is in the area of theology, the latter would have been a natural move for me. However, I have looked beyond the field of theology to insights from anthropology, the history of religions, and sociology of religion in developing this approach, precisely because I believe that this view will give a broader and more accurate understanding of popular culture. My own discipline has not always proved helpful in providing this larger view, and it is for this reason that I have turned to other fields within religious studies for approaches more amenable to the task of gaining understanding of film in its religious aspects.

I would like to thank all those who made this book possible. Dana College granted me a sabbatical leave for the writing of it, and Willard and Leitha Richardson gave generous support to a fellowship that allowed me additional release time from teaching. Jennifer Hammer, my editor at NYU Press, took an interest in the project from the outset and has provided crucial assistance and advice. Two anonymous reviewers gave encouragement and helpful suggestions for revisions. Colleagues and friends have given me numerous ideas on the manuscript and various films. The students of my 2002 class on Religion and Film also read and reviewed the entire manuscript and "field-tested" its use in the classroom. Input from all of them was immensely helpful, which requires me to name each one: Toni Ahrendt, Mara Bartlett, Chris Bertschinger, Allison Botkin, Owen Day, Derek Fey (who also assisted with the index), Beth Garber, Theresa Harrison, Lisa Grasso, Chris Headley, Tony Knuppel, Emily Neve, Janai Robinson, Wendi Sieh, Sara Smit, Erin Sorensen, Justin Wiese, and Michelle Young. But most of all, I must thank my wife Liz, whose support and encouragement were invaluable. Her love of movies matches my own, and her opinions on them have often shaped my own. In my viewings and discussions of countless films with her and with our three children, Karl, Grace, and Clara, I have been constantly reminded of the need to recognize the experience of average moviegoers, and not simply scholars of film and religion.

PART I

A Method for
Viewing Film as Religion

1

Existing Approaches
to Religion and Film

Some years ago I taught a class on ethics and society in which we discussed the impact of media, especially violent media, on our values. I invited students to bring in a videotape of a violent film to share with the class, and to perhaps speculate on the effect such violent films exert on viewers. I had expected class members to engage in ideological critiques of such films by looking at the ways they celebrate violence, in contrast to what most of us regard as an "ethical" framework. I was surprised, then, when a young woman—who had all semester clearly stated her morals were based on her Christian values—volunteered to show us part of *The Silence of the Lambs* (1991), which she told us was her favorite film. At the time, I had not yet seen the movie, and I knew little about it except that it featured Anthony Hopkins as a cannibalistic serial killer in an Academy Award–winning role. My student proceeded to show to the class the scene in which Hopkins's character, Hannibal Lecter, escapes from the authorities through a combination of intelligence and brutal violence. I found it so graphic and horrifying that I had to urge her to turn it off. When I asked her why she liked this film, she seemed unable to offer an explanation; she also couldn't say how her enjoyment of such films could harmonize with her professed Christian values.

Faced with this puzzle, I might have concluded that the film was an unholy glorification of violence and that she had failed to see this because she believed it was "only a movie" and as such not a challenge to her values. This is often how students respond to such questions, by suggesting that movies are "not real" and so have nothing to do with the rest of life other than providing a meaningless escape from it. I might have agreed with her, or I might have insisted that the film was having a deleterious effect on her values whether she knew it or not. But I chose to see the film, to see what the professed attraction to such films might be. By so doing, I came to believe not that the movie had no effect on viewers other than entertainment, nor that its effect was wholly negative. Instead, I speculated that the film was functioning as a way for her to deal with her fears and in some ways master them, as the heroine of the film does. I even came to appreciate the film as one that deals exceptionally well with the depiction of evil and its relationship to all of us. (My own analysis of the film is found later in this book.)

This experience and others like it have convinced me that, in order to understand how films function for audiences, I must be willing to broaden the ways in which I look at them as a religion scholar.

In order to attempt to give popular films this fair hearing, I have developed a method that views them as phenomena analogous to religions. This approach is certainly not the only way in which one might seek to get at the distinctive qualities of popular film or its functions in culture, but it has certain advantages in its ability to call attention to aspects of film that might otherwise be missed. Some religion scholars have already noted this approach, as when Darrol Bryant suggested that "as a popular form of the religious life, movies do what we have always asked of popular religion, namely, that they provide us with archetypal forms of humanity—heroic figures—and instruct us in the basic values and myths of our society."[1] But he also seems suspicious of this popular religion, associating it with a "secular" culture that can be distinguished from traditional religion. "The difference between a 'religious' and a 'secular' culture is that a religious culture seeks to mediate a transcendent order, whereas a secular culture has no referent beyond itself and consequently worships itself."[2] This definition seems an unsupported generalization, based in certain theological assumptions that may prejudice the study of film as religion before it ever begins. Conrad Ostwalt, on the other hand, avoids such pejorative conclusions when he suggests that "the movie theater has acted like some secular religion, complete with its sacred space and rituals that mediate an experience of otherness."[3] Rather than asserting that popular culture's influence suggests a victory of secularization over religion, Ostwalt argues that religion is not fading away but "being popularized, scattered, and secularized through extra-ecclesiastical institutions."[4] He seems more open to a positive assessment of this "secular religion," though he has not developed the ramifications of this assessment in any great detail.

The majority of religion scholars writing about film, however, have not viewed film as analogous to an independent religious tradition so much as they have viewed it as part of the nonreligious culture with which religion engages. They have taken two main approaches, the theological and the ideological, and each of these deserves brief consideration.

Approaches to Theology and Culture: Niebuhr and Tillich

Many of the attempts to relate religion and film have essentially sought to relate Christianity, and more specifically Christian theology, to popular film. Their approaches have been governed by theological attempts to define the relationship between Christianity and "culture," where the latter term indicates the popular milieu in which religions find themselves in any particular place and time. Two theologians of the twentieth century stand out as perhaps the most influential among those who have sought to define the relationship between Christianity and culture, and their work on this point has also been most influential in religion and film studies: H. Richard Niebuhr and Paul Tillich. As both of these men were (broadly considered) among the "neo-orthodox" theologians who sought to get beyond classic liberal and conservative positions of Protestant theology, they were seeking a new way to relate Christian concerns to those of the wider society. Each set forth a typology of ways in which theology can relate to culture.

In his book *Christ and Culture* (1951), H. Richard Niebuhr set forth a fivefold typology of ways in which Christians can choose to engage the larger culture. The five types are Christ rejecting Culture, the Christ of Culture, Christ above Culture, Christ and Culture in Paradox, and Christ Transforming Culture. The first describes those who have chosen to reject the wider culture in the name of their faith, essentially setting up a separate culture that largely ignores and does not interact with the larger society.[5] This approach is often associated with members of the Anabaptist tradition, such as the Amish who do not even utilize much of modern technology. It could also apply to conservative Christians who believe one should not participate in popular culture, rejecting its media altogether. Most people, however, do not find this approach viable as it requires almost complete isolation from the larger society and disallows any possibility of finding value in films or any other aspect of popular culture.

The "Christ of Culture" approach goes to the opposite extreme, essentially appropriating the norms of the society and defining them as Christian. There is no problem relating one's faith to the society in this view, as the larger society is allowed to define how Christianity is to be understood. Niebuhr believed that late nineteenth-century Protestant liberalism fell into this category, and that this approach sacrifices what is distinctive to Christianity in its effort to accommodate itself to the larger culture. It is worth noting that Protestant liberals certainly did not see themselves as making such a sacrifice, and those who have been associated with this type would almost certainly see themselves in one of the other three categories.[6]

Niebuhr's last three approaches all seek a middle path between the two extremes of completely rejecting the wider culture or capitulating to it entirely, and, as such, they comprise for him the main alternatives for those who are seeking a way to relate their religious faith to the culture. The synthetic approach, also known as "Christ above Culture," Niebuhr associates with high medieval Roman Catholic thought such as that of Thomas Aquinas. This approach views culture as good and valuable, but incomplete. Christianity completes the fulfillment of culture through adding revelation to reason, grace to nature, church to secular society. There is a harmony between the two, such as was sought by medieval Christendom and the Roman Catholic Church at the height of its power.[7] (It might be fair to say that most of those whom Niebuhr categorizes under the "Christ of Culture" position probably viewed themselves as holding this view of synthesis, as they would not have believed themselves to be capitulating to culture so much as seeking harmony with it.)

Fourth, the approach of "Christ and Culture in Paradox" is typified, in Niebuhr's view, by Martin Luther. Rebelling against the Catholic synthesis, Luther believed that the attempt to marry the "two kingdoms" of Christ and the world inevitably resulted in a corruption of both. The Church would become like the kingdoms of the world, focused on power rather than the Gospel, and the secular state would seek to control religion. Although Luther's view was not identical to that of the early American architects of the United States Constitution in arguing for a complete separation of church and state, he did believe that the state should not be in the business of religious coercion and that the freedom of the religious conscience must be respected. This "dualistic" approach, as Niebuhr calls it, puts forward two parallel moralities and systems of norms such that, for example, as a private citizen, the Christian must live a life of nonviolence, but as a public member of society he may take up arms to defend his country. These moral worlds should not interfere with each other but exist side by side as the two forms of our God-given lives.[8]

Finally, the "conversionist" view of "Christ Transforming Culture" suggests that the two realms can interact in such a way that the Christian tries to transform the larger culture to be more "Christian" in its values. This approach is more typical of the Reformed heritage of Calvin, and as such seems closest to the view of Niebuhr himself as he came out of that tradition. This approach differs from the classic "Catholic" model of synthesis in being more dynamic, not viewing the society as already in relation to Christ but as having the potential to become so. It is more suspicious of culture than the synthetic view, but it does not reject the culture or relegate it to a realm unrelated to Christian values. It seeks a dynamic interaction of the two, but one governed by the norms of Christian faith rather than the society (thus avoiding the supposed mistake of Protestant liberalism).[9] Parallels to each of these three types can be seen in some theological approaches to popular film, as will be seen below.

The other typology regarding Christianity and culture that has been highly influential in the field of religion and film is that of Paul Tillich. In a 1919 essay entitled "On the Idea of a Theology of Culture," Tillich set forth his classic distinction between autonomy, heteronomy, and theonomy in regards to the relation of faith to culture. Those aspects of culture (such as the arts) that do not see themselves as expressing a religious element view themselves as autonomous, responsible only to their own norms. If the Christian church accepts this view of them, it will leave them alone, and not seek to correct or guide them. (This resembles Niebuhr's "Christ of Culture" position in that it undertakes no criticism of the culture at all, and it also resembles "Christ and Culture in Paradox" in strictly separating church and world.) On the other hand, heteronomy seeks to impose an alien law on culture, such as when the Church tries to control what art is "acceptable" via censorship. (This might be akin to Niebuhr's "Christ Rejecting Culture," or perhaps even "Christ Transforming Culture.")

Tillich favors neither of these views, but rather argues for a third approach, which is a Hegelian-style synthesis of the other two: theonomy. If one focuses solely on the form of cultural functions, one will see them autonomously, but if one focuses on the content they express, one will understand them "theonomously."[10] This is to say that art may appear to have nothing to do with religion, but in fact the content of great art is the same as the content of religion, here defined as "directness towards the Unconditional."[11] Tillich views the Unconditional not as a higher thing or being nor the sum of all beings, but as a "reality of meaning," the "ultimate and deepest meaning" that "shakes the foundation of all things and builds them up anew."[12] The Unconditional is not a thing within the world, but the depth of meaning present for all things in the world. This depth of true meaning is the religious substance expressed in cultural/artistic forms, and it is the job of the theologian of culture to interpret these forms to find this substance—without, however, falling into either heteronomous or autonomous interpretation. The challenge for a theology of culture is to avoid condemning culture as "other" than religion (as it in fact has the same substance) and also to avoid severing the connection between culture and religion so as to miss the deeper significance of culture. (This view in some ways resembles what Niebuhr calls the "synthetic" approach of "Christ above Culture.")

We shall see both Tillich's and Niebuhr's typologies operative in the various approaches to religion and film which have been taken—and although they will be critiqued in that context as well, a few preliminary observations can be made. Both view the relation of religion to culture in the prophetic mode in which the primary task of a theologian of culture is to critique the culture in the light of one's own religious tradition. Religion (specifically, Christianity) is viewed as being in opposition to the culture, for even though it is part of culture it gives itself a privileged position as its critic. In Tillich's view, the theologian can decide what is good or bad art based on how well it conveys an iconoclastic sense of "horror," critiquing the culture that religion wishes to correct.[13] In Niebuhr's view, "Christ" is defined as distinct from "culture" in all five types, even though he acknowledges separately that Christianity (and indeed all religion) is part of culture. By speaking of "Christ" rather than Christianity or religion, Niebuhr gives the impression that the theologian can gain the divine position of "Christ" outside of culture, and so observe and critique it. He admits the relativism of the theologian's position, and that we cannot know for certain where truth lies, but the structure of his typology belies this point; it appears that Christianity can distinguish itself sufficiently from its cultural matrix to make judgments on it.

I would not deny that we can and should make judgments, or that the "postmodern turn" makes it impossible to do so. But, I would argue that as we make judgments we should be more honest about their sources and admit that we are creations of multiple cultural influences beyond what we explicitly identify as our religious backgrounds. Scholars of religion or theologians cannot pretend to the sort of Promethean theological vantage point that Niebuhr and Tillich seemed still to believe was possible (even with their recognition of the nonabsolute and uncertain character of their own judgments).[14] If there are judgments to be made about culture by those who study and/or profess religious viewpoints, they cannot be so monolithic as to suggest that there are entities corresponding to "religion" and to "culture" that can clearly be defined as distinct. The realms of religion and culture overlap to a much greater extent than many of the studies of religion and popular culture seem to admit, and theology cannot stand outside culture any more than any other aspect of human religion or culture can do so. It is for this reason, in part, that I would suggest the classic distinctions between "religion" and "culture" must be put aside for a more nuanced view that sees all features of culture as having religious aspects that cannot be separated from their nonreligious aspects. Although we can distinguish the religious aspects in all of culture to a certain extent, those aspects cannot be restricted to those portions that identify themselves as "religious"; they must instead be seen as echoed in most (if not all) portions of the culture. The dialogue between "religion" and "culture" is really a dialogue between various religious views expressed within culture, many of which we may share. No religion exists in a historical vacuum and each is shaped by its interaction with others.

In what follows, we will examine the ways in which various authors have conceived the relationship between religion and film. Some have intentionally made use of Tillich's or Niebuhr's categories regarding how religion (or Christianity, or theology) should relate to culture, and others can be defined as fitting within one or another of these categories even though they have not always identified their positions in this way. Not all the approaches fit within these categories, but most of them share with Tillich and Niebuhr the idea that culture and religion can be distinguished fairly clearly. Also, while it would certainly be possible to have a "theological" position based in almost any religious tradition, in practice most of the approaches have been explicitly Christian in basis.

Theological Approaches to Film

To consider Niebuhr's typology first: which of his five categories are found among approaches to popular film? The two extreme positions (Christ Rejecting Culture, and the Christ of Culture) seem the least viable to most

Christians today, because one disallows any contact with the culture, and the other sacrifices religion to the culture. This leaves the three intermediate positions. The conversionist approach (Christ Transforming Culture) can be seen in the creation of Christian popular media in recent years, including Christian rock, Christian movies, and Christian popular novels. Conservative evangelicals have shifted from a strategy of rejecting popular culture to remaking it in their own image; for example, rock 'n' roll is no longer "the devil's music" if it can be given lyrics focused on God rather than sex and drugs. This approach has been enormously successful for the subculture it addresses, and it has affected the larger culture as well. But while this approach can help in designing separate Christian popular media, it is not too often used as a method for interpreting existing popular media. This may be because it would require the interpreter to view non-Christian films as if they were Christian in content, which may wrongly assume that the content of popular culture is the same as that of Christian culture—much as the "Christ of Culture" position does. Niebuhr applauded this approach for its efforts to bring Christian values to bear on the culture, but as a method of interpreting preexisting cultural phenomena it seems to fall short.

The other two approaches have been the most accepted theological methods for interpreting popular culture. In general, and not surprisingly, the synthetic approach (Christ above, or Completing Culture) has been used more by Roman Catholics, and the dualistic approach (Christ and Culture in paradox) has been used more by Protestants. Let us consider the latter approach first.

The Protestant-Dialogical Approach to Theology and Film

The dualistic approach, also sometimes referred to as a dialogical or dialectical approach, assumes the independence of religion and culture and seeks to bring them into dialogue in order to gain from that interchange.

One of the first studies to attempt to find religious value in film in this way was *Celluloid and Symbols* (1970), edited by John Cooper and Carl Skrade. Changes in the culture at this time were taking the Christian churches by storm in the United States, and there was much discussion about how to make Christianity relevant to the younger generation. They propose a "dialogue" with modern film, but one that does not seek to "baptize" the filmmaker or impose a theology on the film.[15] In other words, one does not need to pretend that the film is more Christian than it is, but instead one should look both for points of contact and points of dissimilarity in vision. They invoke Tillich's method of correlation, in the idea that the culture asks questions that (we hope) Christianity can answer.[16] In this way, popular media can express the search for meaning, and theology can point toward its resolution. James Wall, longtime editor in chief of *The Christian Century*, articulates a similarly dialogical view in his *Church and Cinema* (1971). He realizes that we need to understand a film's vision of reality, whether or not we share it, and that we should not reject it without understanding it.[17] He also points out that a filmmaker may not condone all that the characters in the story do, and so there may be an implied moral criticism of the characters by the filmmaker at the "presentational" level beyond the merely "discursive."[18] Christians should therefore not simply dismiss films because they are offended by the actions of the characters in them, for a deeper point may be made.

More recently, biblical scholar Robert Jewett has written two books initiating a "dialogue" between St. Paul and popular film. In *Saint Paul at the Movies: The Apostle's Dialogue with American Culture* (1993) he argues that, just as Paul engaged his culture in dialogue in order to "preach the Gospel" more effectively, so should modern Christians confront their culture with the biblical materials of their tradition.[19] Jewett states that he wishes to let the films speak for themselves rather than force them into "ecclesial servitude" by reading theological meaning into films where it does not exist.[20] Paul's voice can be related to current cultural situations through an "interpretive arch" that links his time to ours.[21] In all this, however, Jewett makes it clear that Paul's voice will speak (for the Christian) with a canonical authority that the film lacks, and so his view will be "primus inter pares" ("first among equals").[22] In practice, Jewett tends to be most critical of those films that uphold the efficacy or redemptive power of violence (e.g., *Star Wars*, *Red Dawn*, *Pale Rider*), which fly in the face of Christian biblical ethics and their basic pacifism. In his second volume, *Saint Paul Returns to the Movies: Triumph over Shame* (1999), Jewett seeks to find a harmony with Christian beliefs and values.[23] He analyzes films that make a more clear use of Christian themes, such as *Babette's Feast* and *The Shawshank Redemption*. He also likes the basic moralism of standard Hollywood films such as *Mr. Holland's Opus* or *Forrest Gump*, which show that good deeds are rewarded. But if one only looks for how a film differs from the Christian view, or how it is like it, one may overemphasize either similarities or differences and fail to hear what the film itself has to say.

Bernard Brandon Scott, another biblical scholar, also seeks to construct a dialogue or "conversation" between biblical material and contemporary popular films, in his *Hollywood Dreams and Biblical Stories* (1994).[24] Scott structures his remarks on popular films by viewing them as "myths," which he defines, following Claude Levi-Strauss, as stories that "mediate the fundamental problems of life" in a hidden and unacknowledged manner. Myths seek to overcome the contradictions present in our experience and values, a task that is ultimately impossible. This does not stop myths from being effective, however, provided that their existence remains hidden. But to reflect on the presence of a myth is to cut off its power; one will see the illusion it presents and its inability to reconcile the tensions it seeks to resolve.[25] Scott acknowledges that not all films work as "myths," and that there are "antimythical" films that work to "subvert" the myths of society. He focuses on mythic films, claiming that if we do not gain some understanding of how these myths operate on us, religion will risk becoming a casualty of the electronic media that will govern how religion is conveyed and understood.[26]

The dialogue, according to Scott, is not a neutral conversation but one that will expose the nature of myth so that it might lose its power. This does not completely mesh with what Scott says about the norms governing the "conversation," as when he quotes David Tracy's remark that conversation is "not a confrontation. It is not a debate. It is questioning itself. It is a willingness to follow the question wherever it may go."[27] Elaborating on this, Scott writes that "conversation allows a dialogue in which each is mutually enlightened by the other's horizon" and that "as part of the rules of conversation, we outlaw the Bible's standing in judgment on postmodern culture or our culture's standing in judgment on the Bible." Although Scott avoids heavyhanded heteronomous judgments on the culture, he clearly has an ax to grind in his analysis, in that he wants to show the often malevolent influence of popular culture in contrast with certain biblical ideals.

Still, Scott's analysis of the ideologies present in films is quite thorough, and it is generally not marred by the importation of Christian judgments into this analysis. He focuses especially on action movies, from westerns to *Dirty Harry* (1972), and deftly exposes the ethic of violent revenge that underlies them—contrasting it to the ethic of New Testament pacifism (as with Jewett's critique of similar films). Scott admits that the Bible has used myth as well, and that it can sometimes be tarred with the same brush with which he wants to paint popular film. For example, in his chapter dealing with sexism in film, he points out that the Bible has been instrumental in supporting women's subordination, the same as the texts of popular culture. He comes closest to a genuine conversation here, where he admits that films have both perpetuated the myth of "female embeddedness" as well as critiqued it, and that biblical texts have done the same.[28] He also admits that the use of apocalyptic in both film and in the Bible has a negative effect in its tendency to separate humanity into the chosen and the rejected. This dualism is an option "we no longer can afford." We must see beyond the demonization of the other to a recognition of "love as the solution to chaos," which is also acknowledged by both biblical apocalyptic and films with apocalyptic themes.[29] In his willingness to see both good and bad in popular culture and in the Bible, Scott sometimes moves beyond a simple rejection of culture to a genuine dialogue with it.

The greatest limitation to Scott's method is his rather narrow definition of myth, which really only allows him to see the mythological power of film in a negative light. Insofar as films have good things to say, in his view, it is because they transcend the mythic structure and critique it. But myths need not only be viewed as fruitless attempts to reconcile oppositions, which ultimately fail when exposed to analysis; one can define myth far less pejoratively, as we will discuss in a later chapter. It is also questionable whether a myth loses its power as soon as it is revealed as "myth" in Levi-Strauss's sense. Although we may view the resolution of certain conflicts as historically impossible, an awareness of this may not cause us to give up the myth that promotes such resolution; it may be an eschatological ideal that we choose to follow and allow to govern how we live and see the world, even if it is not realizable in our current experience. The myths of male-female unity or peace on Earth need not only be seen as ideological constructions that obscure the true nature of our unjust world—they may be ideals we want to work toward. Slaves who sang Christian spirituals about "freedom" were not just singing about the next life, but were expressing the hope that things could change in this world, as impossible as the realization of that hope may have seemed at the time. They were certainly not simply singing the words to express an irresolvable tension between the ideal of freedom and the reality of slavery, nor did their hope disappear when confronted with the apparent impossibility of its actualization.

Clive Marsh has also defended the dialogical approach in *Explorations of Theology and Film* (1997). Marsh invokes Niebuhr's typology but simplifies it into a threefold structure of Christ in opposition to culture, in agreement with culture, and in dialectical relationship with culture.[30] Marsh clearly prefers the latter, and also connects it with Tillich's theology of correlation. Marsh does find three problems with Tillich's approach, however: Tillich did not always listen to the voice of the arts themselves, he read culture as homogeneous, and his judgments on culture betray an elitist bias.[31] In contrast, Marsh believes that theology should seek a dialogue with all aspects of culture, high and low, hearing all voices, and that the dialogue should not seek to impose a theological interpretation on culture in the process. Marsh's own work tends to follow this approach by frankly admitting both the similarities and the differences between a Christian worldview and the worldview of a particular film. His stated purpose is to find ways in which "church" and "world" may relate, making Christianity more "relevant" to modern people.[32]

Most recently, Robert K. Johnston has defended a dialogical approach in *Reel Spirituality: Theology and Film in Dialogue* (2000). He offers a fivefold typology of ways in which Christians can engage popular culture that differs somewhat from the typology of Niebuhr: avoidance, caution, dialogue, appropriation, and divine encounter.[33] Johnston believes that Christian approaches to film have generally progressed through these stages to increased engagement with popular culture, and an ability to see God at work in it. This view is actually closer to the classic Roman Catholic view of synthesis with culture than the Protestant view of distinction and dialectic.[34]

Roman Catholic–Synthetic Approaches to Theology and Film

Roman Catholic approaches to popular film have not always been open to seeing a harmony between the values of movies and those of Christianity. Even before the advent of sound films, Roman Catholic leaders had been among the most vocal in the denunciation of popular films. They had a crucial role in the founding of The Legion of Decency, which policed cinema, and they aided in its censorship during the decades when the Hays Code ruled. In the 1960s, however, the Roman Catholic Church realized that the days were past when it could or should try to engage in this sort of heteronomous critique. After the Second Vatican Council, there was a new openness to culture that, in part, helped to open up possibilities for seeing the cinema in a fresh light.

Neil P. Hurley, S.J., developed an approach that could be seen to fit Niebuhr's model of "Christ above Culture" according to which culture is affirmed in the values it conveys, but these values ultimately need Christianity to fulfill and complete them. This "synthetic" approach of classical Catholicism usually supports a kind of "natural theology" that looks for a generalized sort of religiosity in all cultures and religions. In *Theology through Film* (1970) Hurley expressed his belief that "religious transcendence" is a universal constant in human culture.[35] As a part of culture, films can express this "humanistic" form of general revelation, even if they do not speak of specifically Christian themes. In *The Reel Revolution: A Film Primer on Liberation* (1978) Hurley developed this view by asserting that film is "the new humanism . . . [that] can tease out of us a sense of greater possibilities, alternate selves, and new horizons."[36] Film has a positive benefit, then, in that it forms a kind of natural theology or "humanism" that proposes values according to which we can live. These are not a substitute for Christian values, but rather a preparation for them; Christian beliefs and values can complete the process of moral development begun by humanism. There is thus no need to reject the values as "unChristian" (as with "Christ Rejecting Culture") nor to transform them (as with "Christ Transforming Culture") before we can consider their value. The values of film have been defined as preparatory to Christian revelation, and not in conflict with it, as they speak of general "humanistic" values of which all religions and philosophies can approve.

Hurley avoids demonizing popular cinema, seeing its value, even when this "value" is not the same as Christian "values." Hurley may overrate the potential of popular films to make significant moral statements, but he certainly is willing to look for and hear such statements when they are made. Where his approach may fall short is in its reduction of the significance of films to their "moral" messages. Moreover, he only looks for moral messages of a certain sort. He is interested in films that convey the type of messages he is looking for, and does not look at the sort of films that might convey messages he could not see as preparatory to Christian revelation.

We can also question whether there actually is such a thing as a generalized sense of transcendence that can be conveyed without reference to a particular religion. Today, theologians are more suspicious of the whole notion of a "natural theology" that allegedly exists apart from particular religious traditions. There is no such thing as a universal understanding of reason, or morality, unconditioned by a cultural perspective, as traditional "natural theology" would have us believe. If film helps connect us with what it means to be "human," it will always be in specific ways, not a generic way that exists apart from particular religions. This is one reason why I maintain that films should be examined as expressing a religion in their own right, rather than as a generic form of "religiosity" that does not as such exist. Christians, for example, who claim that a cultural phenomenon represents a generic religiosity often seem to view it as a veiled form of their own religion, and so covertly "baptize" it as Christian after all. Hurley himself seems to engage in this Christianization of film in his analysis of *On the Waterfront*, the story of one man's stand against union domination by criminals. Because Terry Malloy (Marlon Brando's character) fights for what he believes and is beaten up and bloody before the triumphant ending, Hurley sees him as a Christ-figure enacting a crucifixion and resurrection motif. In addition, the character of his girlfriend Edie "will complement him, refurbishing the faded image of God latent within his boorish personality."[37] If every bloodied hero becomes a Christ figure and every female lead a symbol of Eve, it will seem that we can find Christianity in every action film—but this may stretch the interpretation of such films to the breaking point and do an injustice both to Christianity and to the films in question.

Probably the most significant Roman Catholic writer on religion and film is John May, who has edited or coedited a number of volumes on the subject. In *Religion and Film* (1982), May's own essay, "Visual Story and the Religious Interpretation of Film," presents his approach. Evoking Tillich's categories of autonomy, heteronomy, and theonomy, he criticizes heteronomous approaches for their tendency to either condemn films for the apparent absence of religious themes in them, or to read religious themes into a film.[38] In either case, May claims, the film is not allowed to speak its own message, and we fail to hear what it has to say. May holds up a form of interpretation that respects the autonomy of the art. Rather than insisting on reading a meaning into it, one can see that "certain films are open or not to a religious world view." One can then look at "those dimensions of the formal structure of the film that represent the visual analogue of religious or sectarian questions." For a list of basic religious questions, May paraphrases the three basic ones outlined by Huston Smith in *The Religions of Man*: Is the universe indifferent or friendly, are humans independent or interdependent, and does liberation come via wisdom or compassion?[39] By allowing it to speak its own message before we look for connections to Christianity this approach seems to avoid imposing a Christian view on the film to a greater extent than Hurley's view. But May is still primarily interested in such connections, and so may read Christian themes into the films he is analyzing in spite of his stated principle to avoid doing so.

May also draws on the work of biblical scholar John Dominic Crossan in making a distinction between "myth" and "parable" as types of religious stories. According to this typology, myth "establishes" world, and parable "subverts" it. Myth seeks to resolve tensions, but parable emphasizes the absence of resolution. Whereas myths satisfy their hearers through visions of vindication and wholeness, parables convey a challenging vision of the world that stresses risk-not-security, weakness-not-strength, and death-not-life.[40] May shows that both myth and parable are found in films and gives examples of each, although he seems to have a preference for the filmic parables insofar as they parallel the form of Jesus' teachings as represented in the New Testament.

In the same volume, Michael Bird's essay on "Film as Hierophany" takes a basically Tillichian view that film, as an aspect of culture, can point beyond itself "toward the transcendental dimension."[41] The experience of anxiety and emptiness drives culture to this beyond, placing us in a "condition of openness" to the Unconditioned. Bird accepts Tillich's concept of a "belief-ful realism" that looks for the ultimate in the concrete, in distinction from all forms of idealism that try to escape the real world via fantasy.[42] He connects this concept with the filmic realism of scholars Andre Bazin and Siegfried Kracauer insofar as they viewed the task of film to be the disclosure of "reality" rather than the creation of an alternate world of fantasy to which the viewer retreats to escape the real. They eschewed the excessive artistry of the formalists, who would call attention to the artificial nature of film, for an understanding of film as the medium that most directly records the nature of reality.[43] This school of filmic realism, then, has affinities with Tillich's notion that art should not create an artificial view of reality but instead provide an opening to seeing the depth of reality, especially through focusing on the negative, the void and emptiness of our experience. Films can provide a "spiritual realism" not by attempting to directly portray the holy (which cannot be portrayed) but by a simple realistic style that conveys the real emotions of characters in all their anxieties. This realistic style serves to point up genuine questions about meaning and purpose, or their loss, and so encourages the viewer to look at a deeper level of reality and meaning. The infinite cannot be filmed, but the finite can be, and when portrayed realistically it will express its true longing, in all its misery and imperfection, for the infinite.[44]

Bird's approach is strikingly similar to that developed by Paul Schrader in *Transcendental Style in Film* (1972). Schrader, who later went on to be a well-known screenwriter and director of feature films himself, came from a rigid Calvinist religious background that he later rejected. The book develops the thesis that a certain style of film, notably the realistic style of directors Yasujiro Ozu, Robert Bresson, and Carl Dreyer, creates a sense of "absence" through a sparse technique that limits editing, camera movement, and plot action to a minimum. In this way, according to Schrader, these films evoke a sense of "transcendence" by pointing beyond the emptiness of the "everyday" to a higher reality. In fact, this style is not properly speaking "realistic" in that its ultimate purpose is to "knock down" the everyday sense of reality through a technique that shocks the viewer into stasis.[45] Although Schrader suggests some parallels between this notion and Zen Buddhist philosophy, he admitted he found it in his own Calvinistic background. In particular, Schrader suggests that the goal of Calvin's theology was, like that of filmic transcendental style, to ascetically deprive one sensually in order to make the window to the transcendent so narrow that the light of faith becomes "blinding."[46] Calvinist theology, which has insisted that "the finite cannot contain the infinite," has long been suspicious of arts that claim to "capture" the transcendent—but Schrader uses the Calvinist insight to develop an aesthetic theory of sparseness, according to which the infinite is never "in" the arts, but the arts can point beyond themselves to the infinite by indicating their own lack. This has clear connections to Tillich's view, as well as Bird's appropriation of it.[47]

Ernest Ferlita, who has also worked with May,[48] expresses similar views. Quoting William F. Lynch, he goes so far as to suggest that by a "descent" into the depths of reality, expressing all its pain and suffering, film ultimately can "ascend" to God. As an example, he discusses how Lina Wertmuller's *Seven Beauties* (1976) provides a story about how one man sacrifices all his values to save his own life during the Second World War, even to the point of killing his own friend, effectively losing his soul in the process. As a story of the loss of self, according to Ferlita, it points beyond itself to its converse, that to save one's soul one must be ready to sacrifice one's own life.[49] In this sense, it does not matter if directors like Wertmuller or Ingmar Bergman claim to reject religion, because their films finally make religious points. When Wertmuller says she hopes to express her "great faith in the possibility of man becoming human," she is really expressing a religious hope for the transformation of humans.[50] Films can express a "search for meaning" that characters may find through deeds, suffering, the experience of being loved, or all three.[51] In this way, films can encourage us to hope in the face of suffering—for without hope, we lose faith, religion, and all ability to find meaning.[52] Quoting Mircea Eliade, Ferlita states that all filmic quests for meaning point us toward the quest for God.[53]

Roman Catholic approaches like those of May, Bird, and Ferlita find religious themes "in" film not explicitly, but implicitly in that the negative images of human life expressed in film point beyond themselves to a divine resolution. Theology is invoked as the meaning-making activity to be annexed to film narrative in order to interpret the "theonomy" it expresses. This meaning may not be intended by the filmmaker, but that is not so important as long as the work can inspire a religious vision. In fact, this method does not exactly read religious themes "into" films so much as it reads them "onto" films—in other words, the religious interpretation fulfills and completes the secular cry of pain and suffering. One can see how this accords with Niebuhr's model of synthesis insofar as religion is here viewed as the completion of culture that discloses its content. This approach thus does risk falling into heteronomy, in spite of its concerted efforts to avoid it, by only seeing the significance of films through the ways they prepare the audience for the Christian message of grace and hope. And although May, Bird, and Ferlita prefer challenging "parabolic" narratives to simply "mythic" ones, the parables seem to serve only as prolegomena for a Christian myth of reassurance that may supplant the challenge the filmmaker wished to make. Undermining the autonomy of the film risks losing its voice, as May himself asserted.

Ideological Approaches to the Study of Religion and Film

Many religion scholars do not study film in order to establish a connection to a theological agenda. Instead, they analyze its ideological content, and in this way they mirror many of the approaches used within film studies generally speaking. Their religious training is chiefly relevant insofar as it gives them the ability to recognize when and how religious themes are used in the service of ideological purposes.[54]

The most significant effort by a religion scholar to develop an ideological method may be Margaret Miles's *Seeing and Believing: Religion and Values in the Movies* (1996). She utilizes a cultural studies approach, drawn from film studies, which focuses on the "social, political, and cultural matrix in which the film was produced and distributed."[55] She intends this approach to reduce the emphasis on "text" associated with approaches that arose out of literary studies. She suggests that this focus will allow the interpreter to be more aware of the ideological dimension of films, and the ways they perpetuate conventional notions of race and gender in particular. This approach is used by Miles to examine, first, films that have represented western religious traditions, and second, how values related to race, gender, and class are portrayed in popular films.[56]

Miles's approach is intended to reveal how films are actually understood by viewers, by paying attention to how a viewer's social situation within a group determines what one "sees" in the film. "Social location, race, class, sexual orientation, gender, education, age" are among the sociological variables that exist in the viewer and may affect his or her perceptions. Oddly enough, however, most of Miles's conclusions about the ways viewers perceive films are not based on any actual studies of different groups but instead are based on a priori assumptions about how certain groups will perceive a film. This is a problem endemic to cultural studies' film analyses, as they have tended to neglect audience reaction and ethnographic study in their focus on the processes that produce the films as cultural products—in particular, how they are marketed.[57] But the factors that govern a film's production do not completely determine viewer reaction; for example, a film that is intentionally designed to conform to conventional notions of race and gender (out of the financial concerns of its backers) may still be perceived as challenging those conventions by its viewers. In contrast to the view of Miles, feminist scholar Lisa Taylor has argued that we cannot assume that cultural products that appear to reinforce women's servitude actually have such an effect on them. She points to evidence that suggests that women's reading of romance novels and even viewing pornography can be used by them as activities that liberate rather than enslave. Conclusions about the effects of cultural products on a group must be based on studies of how they are used and perceived, not on the untested assumptions of the researcher.[58]

Miles's analyses of individual films also tend to be based on her own assumptions about audience reactions rather than any study of such reactions. When she reviews *Jesus of Montreal* (1989) and *The Last Temptation of Christ* (1988), she concludes that these films raise religious issues but fail to "act religiously" because "both films fail to inspire imitation of their protagonist, or even to communicate clearly what such imitation might look like or feel like."[59] Although they failed to create such inspiration in her, it seems premature to conclude that such inspiration is impossible for all viewers. Again, ethnographic study is needed to support such assertions. My own showing of *Jesus of Montreal* to a class of traditional college-age students affected some of them rather deeply, especially women who were also committed Christians, apparently to a greater extent than the average church service. The film concerns a man who begins to act like Jesus after playing him in a passion play, so that his story becomes similar to the one he performs—complete with persecution by the religious authorities, in this case the Roman Catholic Church. It raised a number of questions about the extent to which Christianity has fallen away from its original religious vision, none of which are taken very seriously by Miles. She does admit that these films could be read "against the grain" so as "to act religiously," but in this case "their ability to do so would have more to do with the spectator than the films."[60] This remark seems to imply, against Miles's own cultural studies assumptions, that meaning rests first of all in the film rather than in the spectator—but that some spectators may effectively *mis*read the film and so come up with subversive understandings that are not "there" in the text of the film. Not only does Miles thus assume without evidence that her reading represents the experience of most spectators, but she claims that spectators who would disagree have not really understood the film. This stance seems to be a return to those forms of ideological criticism that believe that the critic can find the "meaning" of the film apart from any real analysis of what viewers themselves say they found in the film.

Many of Miles's other analyses also make assumptions about films that seem ill-warranted. *The Mission* (1986), made with the participation of radical Roman Catholic priest Daniel Berrigan, purports to tell the story of the Jesuit mission to the Guarani tribes of Paraguay, though it distorts the facts of history in a number of ways (as Miles correctly observes). The director, Roland Joffe, claimed that the film was really intended to speak to contemporary debates between the Vatican and Central American churches involved in political struggles of liberation. But Miles believes that the film actually neutralizes social protest, rather than encouraging it, because it identifies social protest with gifted and unique individuals rather than collective action. "Ironically, films that may be intended as radical protest become conformist by representing collective action as individual rebellion."[61] Again, she has no real evidence for this claim but simply asserts it; it would seem in her estimation that every film with *characters* (who are by nature individuals) is doomed to be socially regressive. Miles makes the same claim about *Romero* (1989), the first film to be made in the United States by a Roman Catholic organization (Paulist Pictures). Ultimately, this account of Bishop Romero's life and martyrdom in El Salvador, she claims, is merely "a cautionary tale about the futility of protest" because "heroic individual struggle is presented as the only model of social protest." Miles also calls attention to the political murder of the character of Lucia in the film, after which the camera "lingeringly retreats from her body with a long tracking shot of her crotch and leg." This she views as exemplifying a "titillating emphasis on women's bodies" that is out of place in a film that claims to "sensitize and inform." Despite the noble intentions of the filmmakers, *Romero* cannot overcome its use of "Hollywood conventions that fetishize women's bodies and display violence and suffering for pleasure." In Miles's view, "a film that employs an adventure film's scenes of sex and violence cannot communicate anything but voyeuristic exploitation of suffering people. The pain of the oppressed is ultimately used for the entertainment of comfortable spectators."[62]

This interpretation exemplifies Miles's willingness to draw strong conclusions based on little or no evidence outside her own viewing experience. It seems almost bizarre to suggest that a viewer of *Romero* could come away from the film with the same sense of voyeuristic pleasure as someone who just saw a James Bond movie. Viewers obviously make distinctions among films and the ways they represent sex and violence, which is why viewers were more disturbed by *Saving Private Ryan* and *Schindler's List* than *Raiders of the Lost Ark* and *Jaws*, even though all these films were made by the same director. Steven Spielberg utilized different techniques, including more handheld camera and a more realistic depiction of violence, in his "serious" films in order to unnerve and disturb the viewer rather than indulge the viewer's sense of pleasure in the images. Filmmakers and audiences are well aware of the differences between films made for "fun" and those made to "enlighten," though Miles does not seem to acknowledge this distinction. In any case, there is no reason to automatically assume that films designed to challenge people normally fail in their aim simply because most people do not make radical, life-changing decisions after viewing them. One might just as well assume that the Bible cannot be challenging because most people who go to church and hear the Sermon on the Mount being read do not become pacifists or give all their money to the poor afterwards.

Miles's approach differs from many of the others we have examined in that she has more thoroughly appropriated the methods and ideological assumptions of much of contemporary film theory and criticism. It is no coincidence if it seems that this has made her ultracritical of popular film. Many approaches within the field of film studies continue to be governed by the assumption that popular films represent conservative ideology and little else. This idea can be traced to the influence of "mass culture" theorists Theodor Adorno and Max Horkheimer, who believed that the American film industry offered one of the primary ways for capitalism to propagandize the masses with its values. There can be no such thing as a "good" popular film, in their view, as popular cinema is packaged so as to make a profit and therefore is "already implicated in the maintenance of ideological and economic domination."[63] Although later film theory departed from many of their beliefs, such as the notion that audiences are entirely passive and will receive whatever "message" the filmmakers wish to convey, the idea that popular films function primarily as ideology continues to be the dominant paradigm for feminist film theory, leftist political film theory, psychoanalytic film theory, screen theory, genre studies, and cultural studies.[64]

Ideological criticism of popular film is essential because one of the major ways in which cultural hegemonies involving gender, race, or class are promoted and perpetuated is through the images of popular media, including film. To conclude, however, that films can function only in this way is to neglect other ways in which films can be analyzed, including aspects of the films as "texts" and the ways in which these texts are read by audiences. Many, perhaps most, popular films perpetuate stereotypes about race and gender, but this is not all they do. Similarly, one can (and should) engage in ideological critiques of literature or religion, but it would surely impoverish the study of those fields if ideological critique were the only sort of analysis utilized. If popular films do function as religion, as this study claims, then it is critical that approaches beyond the ideological be developed.

The suspicion with which popular film is viewed by those within the field of film studies has rubbed off on those religion scholars, like Miles, who have made use of the methods of film studies. Yet the same cultural critics who practice film studies would probably include religion (and many other cultural activities) within the range of those phenomena that they consider primarily as purveyors of ideology. If religion scholars are to bring the insights of film studies into their own filmic analyses, they should realize that the field of film studies may represent a Trojan horse out of which could pour an army of hostile soldiers who are just as happy to reduce religion to ideology as to view film in this way. While ideological analysis of film and of religions is an essential tool for understanding certain aspects of these cultural phenomena, we must be aware of and make use of other approaches as well.

It is ironic that leftist critics of culture may find themselves in harmony with right-wing conservatives in their wholesale denunciation of popular culture. Both sides seem to believe that nothing good can come out of Hollywood. Yet, to make assumptions about the evils of popular film without looking at the details of the films or their audience reception is to draw conclusions based on ideological bias rather than sound analysis. This approach also ignores the specifics of individual genres or films, which is akin to generalizing about "all religions" and what they believe. Local knowledge of individual phenomena must precede any attempt at generalizations, which must in any case be offered tentatively and with the understanding that our conclusions are scholarly constructions rather than statements about the nature of reality. Postmodern thought has certainly indicated the need for such suspicion of generalizations and greater caution about globalizing conclusions.

An Alternative to Theological and Ideological Approaches

Both theological and ideological approaches to the study of film are very valuable, but each has blindspots in regards to what they are able to see in films. If we only see ideology, or materials for our own religious tradition's theology, we may be missing a great deal that is in films—especially in regard to how they may function religiously for their viewers. The rest of this book is an attempt to develop a method for viewing film as in some ways being like a religion in its own right.

There has been some effort to develop such a method in the recognition that films have a "mythology" all their own. In Joel Martin and Conrad Ostwalt's *Screening the Sacred: Religion, Myth, and Ideology in Popular American Film* (1995), Martin proposes a threefold typology to describe the study of religion, which can then be applied to the study of religion and film as well. The three approaches he identifies are the theological, the ideological, and the mythological. His definitions of the first two are similar to mine. Theology, he states, studies religious texts and thinkers, especially those of Western religions (in particular Christianity); "theological scholars tend to equate religion with Judaism and Christianity." Their focus is therefore limited, but valuable to the discussion of these traditions. Second, ideological criticism of religion focuses on "religion in its historical, social, and political contexts," especially in relation to "how religion legitimates or challenges dominant visions of the social order." Third, Martin uses the term "mythological" study to refer to comparative religious studies and the history of religions approach, which asserts that "religion manifests itself through cross-cultural forms" including myth and ritual. This approach views religion "as a universal and ubiquitous human activity."[65]

Martin holds that all three forms of religious analysis are legitimate and necessary, and so are also useful when applied to the study of religion and film. Each approach, however, has its limitations. Theological approaches may be ill-equipped to understand or recognize religious beliefs outside the Western paradigm, and so may fall into ethnocentric conclusions; ideological critics may view religion only as "the opiate of the people" that reinforces regressive politics; and mythological approaches tend to ignore historical context and the differing specifics of religions, proposing that religious ideas are ahistorical archetypes universally present in the human unconscious. A good scholar, however, will balance all three approaches and not rest content with one, avoiding to some extent the dangers of reductionism.[66]

I would agree with Martin's basic summary of the advantages and limitations of theological and ideological approaches. In his summary of the mythological approach, however, I believe he has reduced much of the study of non-Christian religions (e.g., the fields of the history, sociology, and anthropology of religions) to the study of mythology, and a rather restrictive understanding of it. His conflation of comparative religious studies with the mythological studies of Jung, Campbell, and Eliade makes it seem as if all comparative studies assume that religion is made up of universal archetypes that make details of difference unimportant. Such approaches have been superseded by those that stress the importance of difference in religion and seek to avoid reductionistic simplifications about its nature: for example, Jonathan Z. Smith, Clifford Geertz, and Wendy Doniger (whose views will be discussed in later chapters). In developing my own approach, I take into account a wider range of ideas about myth, as well as theories regarding other aspects of religion such as ritual that can also be profitably applied to the study of film.

In sum, there are a number of ideas that have been advanced in the discussion of religion and film that point toward an understanding of how film itself functions as a religion, but there has been little attempt to develop this understanding and all its ramifications. If such an approach is to be developed, it will provide an alternative to both theological and ideological interpretation of film, which have been the two dominant approaches in religion and film studies. If the religious dimensions of film were better understood, we might see both how film's views may parallel those of various religions and how film functions religiously in its own right. Like any religion, the "religion of film" will borrow from other religions as it develops its own distinctive forms of myths, morals, and rituals, and so attention to the use of materials from various religions will remain appropriate. At the same time, we need to transcend the tendency to limit the discussion of religion and film to the connections with the history of religion that we notice. Instead, we need to see how this new religion operates on its own terms. Only then can we really understand the religious power and dynamics present within it.

Such an approach might also provide an alternative to some of the tendencies toward eisegesis and heteronomy present in both the theological and the ideological interpretations of film we have examined. If we impose our own theological or ideological framework on the film we may fail to understand how it conveys its message to its viewers and how it functions religiously or filmically. Whether past approaches have applauded or critiqued particular films, they have often looked only for what they wanted to see, and so found only either what fits with their views or what can provide a convenient straw man to oppose. In neither case is the film properly understood. My own approach cannot claim to be free of bias or error, but in attempting to find the religious voice of the film itself, it seeks to free the interpretation of film (from a religious studies vantage point) from some of the conditions that have been imposed on it such as limiting the dialogue of film and religion to dialogue with a *particular* religious tradition.

Seeking to find the "religious" voice of the film before critiquing it does not preclude judgment of the film; I am not arguing that complete "objectivity" that would allow us to analyze films without importing our prejudices is possible. In this respect, I agree with Marsh in his recognition that we must admit the ideological and theological biases that affect our interpretation.[67] This recognition, however, should not prevent us from seeking a method of dialogue that allows the voice of the other to be better heard. Interreligious dialogue and study have progressed to the point that scholars seek to understand the other religion as it understands itself, even though they know they cannot fully achieve this goal. They seek to overcome narrow types of interpretation that have imposed alien understandings on religious traditions. I will argue that this same approach needs to be taken in regard to popular-culture studies. We must seek to understand the message of popular-culture products before we can identify areas of agreement or disagreement with them. First, however, we need to analyze further the ways in which film might be defined as a religion, and to begin that task by defining what we mean by "religion."

2

The Definition of Religion

Limitations of Theological and Social-Scientific Definitions

Religion is not an easy thing to define. It is hard to list the requisite characteristics of any cultural phenomenon, given the diversity of cultures and
the inevitable variations in their expressions. Defining religion offers special challenges, however, in that it is an area of culture that involves basic
beliefs about the ultimate nature of reality, our purpose in the world, and
how we find meaning in it. Thus the scholar's own subjective religious
worldview affects the study of the subject matter from the outset, and the
judgments imported into our analyses will unavoidably influence how we
define "religion."

Moreover, as Jonathan Z. Smith has pointed out, "There is no data for
religion. Religion is solely the creation of the scholar's study."[1] By this he
means that the scholar chooses what to call religion, and that it therefore
"exists" only as the product of the scholar's effort. Smith reminds us that
the "map is not territory," that our understanding of religion is not equivalent to the actual cultural phenomena described. "Religion" is a construct
we have invented as a label for certain sorts of activities that we classify
under this rubric. But this does not mean that there is no such thing as the
subject matter we classify as religion, or that we cannot say anything about
those things we call religions—it is simply a recognition that whatever definitions we favor, they represent an interpretation from a particular viewpoint.

In the last chapter, I suggested that viewing film as religion would provide an alternative to both theological and ideological approaches and
their tendency to narrowly interpret film only through its connections
with Christian thought or in its ideological functions. Definitions of religion have suffered from similar problems in being too closely identified

either with theological or ideological agendas. Christian theologians who have offered definitions of religion have tended to use Christian theological concepts as the basis for their views, and so have sometimes limited what can be called religion to that which echoes Christian ideas. Social scientists, on the other hand, have often identified religion with ideology, or have held that religion can be fully explained by reference to the psychosocial processes that are its causes. Each of these problems should be briefly examined in order to point us toward the definition that best avoids them.

Early attempts by Christian thinkers to define the essence of religion unwittingly imported Christian categories into the definition, often assuming that all religions focus on a transcendent being such as the Christian God. Friedrich Schleiermacher (1768–1834) defined religion as "the feeling of absolute dependence" on that which the Christian calls God, so that "to feel oneself absolutely dependent and to be conscious of being in relation with God are one and the same thing."[2] Although Schleiermacher's definition was broader than that of most Western thinkers before him in that he did not equate religion with belief in God as such, the general feeling he postulates still has as its referent the Western or even the Christian concept of God. A century later, Rudolf Otto (1869–1937), on the basis of more study of world religions than Schleiermacher had undertaken, asserted that religion is the feeling that arises when we encounter the "holy" or "numinous," that which transcends us so totally that it inspires a mixture of fascination and fear. It evokes an experience of being a creature "submerged and overwhelmed by its own nothingness in contrast to that which is supreme above all creatures."[3] Otto claimed to have found this experience of radical transcendence in all the world religions he encountered in his travels, but he seems to have neglected those aspects of religions that would not fit his view—for example, the radical this-worldliness of certain forms of Chinese religions or Buddhism.[4] In spite of a genuine effort to understand other religions on their own terms, Otto still based his analysis on a concept of divine transcendence based in a particular Western theological understanding of God. Otto influenced other thinkers in turn; Mircea Eliade defined religion by its relation to "the sacred" in distinction from "the profane," and although he defined sacrality more broadly than Otto (as religions may have numerous sacred realities, not just one), he still understood religion as always entailing relationship to a transcendent reality that is radically distinguished from empirical reality.[5] Among philosophers of religion, John Hick has made the same claim that religion is defined by a relationship with a transcendent reality.[6]

The definition of religion offered by Paul Tillich in his later theology sought to overcome many of the shortcomings of previous theological definitions, and his view has probably been the most significant one for modern theology. As we have seen, Tillich's thought also has had a very significant effect on theological approaches to film and culture, so his definition warrants somewhat closer consideration. Tillich defined religion as "ultimate concern," meaning that each of us has something that receives our highest devotion and from which we expect fulfillment. It demands the total surrender of all other concerns to it as the primary concern of our being.[7] Even if one denies the existence of any transcendent reality, one will still hold something as being of greatest concern for one's being, that which one finally values more highly than anything else. Even the cynic takes his cynicism with "ultimate seriousness," and so his cynical philosophy becomes his ultimate concern.[8]

But Tillich also insisted that there is a criterion that can be used to evaluate the validity of the various ultimate concerns one might have, and so to arrive at some judgments about the relative "truth" of religions. If one takes something that is nonultimate (finite or nontranscendent) as being of ultimate significance, one is guilty of idolatrous faith, or of attributing ultimacy to that which is not ultimate. The consequences of this include radical "existential disappointment" because the finite object cannot fulfill the promise of ultimate satisfaction that the believer expects it to fulfill. This does not prevent people from viewing finite things as ultimate, but in such a case they have made a grave error in falsely viewing the finite as the infinite. A truer faith is one that remains focused on the ultimate itself rather than on any finite reality. The difficulty with achieving this goal, Tillich explains, is that we can never apprehend the ultimate in itself but only through symbols. The trick of avoiding idolatry is then to look beyond the symbol and to see it as a medium for the ultimate rather than the ultimate itself. If we fail in this and view the symbol as itself being the ultimate, we have given our ultimate devotion to that which is not really ultimate. We can never know for certain whether we have given our devotion to the true ultimate or to a penultimate form of it, and so faith requires commitment and courage in the face of this uncertainty.[9]

Tillich's definition is more comprehensive than many others, in that through it he can view as "religious" a wide range of phenomena, even some not normally considered religious, which have the element of intense devotion involved with them. It is not coincidental that many of the theological approaches to film examined in the last chapter made use of

Tillich, for his definition does not narrowly exclude the religious significance of apparently secular phenomena (such as politics or the arts). But one may still ask whether he has isolated the actual feature shared by all religions, or whether he has imported a Western bias into his definition. He considers it axiomatic that everyone must have some ultimate concern to which all other concerns are subordinate, but this may not be the case. In practice, we all have many shifting areas of concern. Although one or another of these may take precedence at a particular moment that does not mean that it is that which we take with "ultimate seriousness," that which promises "total fulfillment" or demands our complete obedience. These terms are relevant to biblical monotheism, as Tillich shows, but they may not illustrate the religious character of polytheists, who turn to different gods for different purposes, or for that matter religions like Confucianism or Taoism, which rarely speak of subjecting all principles to one. Taoists go so far as to say that there is no right or wrong, good or bad, but that each thing has value when its proper use is found. It's questionable whether there is one "ultimate concern" in this sort of system.

Of course, Tillich might regard this sort of relativism as itself a kind of ultimate concern, which subjugates absolutist systems of value to its own relativizing framework. The relativist who says there is no ultimate has made relativism his ultimate; the skeptic who says there is no truth has made skepticism his truth; the nihilist who rejects the task of finding a concern has made lack of concern into his concern. But one has to suspect a linguistic sleight of hand here on Tillich's part. If we are to say that anything one might believe—even a failure to take the question of the meaning of life seriously—has been taken with "ultimate seriousness" simply because there is nothing one takes more seriously, we may be misdefining "ultimate concern" by effectively reducing it to whatever the content of consciousness is, even if it seems to lack any concern or direction toward ultimacy. If any belief at all is an "ultimate concern" simply because there is nothing higher believed in, this usage would seem to distort the normal sense of the term and the meaning implied by it. It effectively negates the difference between the person who is truly devoted to something as an ultimate and the person who has no such devotion, so that it appears they are equally religious when in fact they are not.

In addition, in distinguishing between types of ultimate concerns, Tillich sneaks value judgments on some ultimate concerns into an apparently value-free definition. He claims that one who is devoted to the nonultimate as if it were an ultimate has committed idolatry by giving ultimate status to that which he should not. In this way a judgment is implied upon those religions that do not focus on a single ultimate concern, as they commit idolatry in their failure to properly conceptualize their ultimate. The insistence upon a transcendent is still present here, albeit in veiled form.

In spite of the Christian biases present in his definition, Tillich made it clear toward the end of his life that Christianity is not to be viewed as the "absolute" religion that effectively discredits the validity of others. No religion can fully express the ultimate, as all must use symbols, and there is always a gap between the symbol and that which it symbolizes. The best symbols are those that point beyond themselves, like the cross—but this is not the only valid symbol of the ultimate, even though it provides the criterion for Christians.[10] Still, his view defines religion in such a way as to make it seem that all valid religion must have a relationship with a unitary transcendent principle, defined according to the norms of the biblical understanding of covenant ("demand and promise"). Those that lack this focus on the transcendent (or its unity) are viewed as less adequate forms of religion.

Just as such theological definitions have narrowed the understanding of religion by their use of Christian categories, so also the ideological definitions of social-scientific approaches have tended to reduce religion to its psychological or sociological function. Most famously, Karl Marx reduced religion to a by-product of social oppression, the "opiate of the people" which they use to cope with intolerable economic conditions; Freud, on the other hand, reduced religion to a by-product of our neurotic attempts to deal with the absence of an omnipotent father. In both cases, religion is viewed as harmful and unnecessary, as well as explicable wholly through the categories of either sociological or psychological analysis based on an examination of its empirical nature. Although the pejorative and simplifying definitions of Marx or Freud are not used as widely as they once were, many social scientists still believe that in their efforts to "explain" the causes of religion in observable social forces they effectively preclude the truth of religion. Rodney Stark and William Bainbridge, for example, write that religion is "a purely human phenomenon, the causes of which are to be found entirely in the natural world. Such an approach is obviously incompatible with faith in revelation and miracles."[11] The transcendent or other-worldly referents of religion cannot be real on such a view, as religion is merely a product of this-worldly forces that can be examined and understood by social science. Such reductionism commits the so-called "genetic fallacy" of believing that a this-worldly explanation for the cause of religion discredits any other-worldly explanation, and hence transcendent referent, for religion. In opposition to this view, I would claim that it is possible to believe that religion(s) might be true, even when we believe we have adequately explained their "causes" naturalistically. After all, a believer can hold that God works through natural processes such as evolution, so why can't one also allow that God creates faith and religion through sociopsychological processes? Even if people can be said to believe in God "because" of such processes, that does not negate the possibility that God "exists." Nonetheless, it has been widely held that religion must have either a theological (i.e., belief-based) or a psychosocial "explanation," as these two approaches are held to be incompatible.[12]

In contrast, I would argue that social-scientific approaches do not need to accept the reductionist view that religion can be fully explained naturalistically or that such explanation necessarily discredits the beliefs of religious people. Similarly, religion need not be viewed solely as an ideological construct that supports cultural hegemonies, as the social-scientific study of religion has sometimes held.[13] Although religion is this, it is not only this—just as I have argued that film may be ideology, but not only that. We need to be able to understand the workings of religion in ways that transcend the purely ideological. Luckily, many social scientists working in fields such as anthropology and sociology have recognized that their analysis of religion does not require them to adopt reductionist views of religious behavior that suggest it can be fully understood solely as a product of societal or cultural forces. Religion may be seen not merely as a byproduct of society, a sort of cultural dross thrown off by social forces, but as a cultural force in its own right that contributes to and shapes society.

Clifford Geertz's Definition of Religion and Its Application to Film

I have found the definition of religion put forward by the anthropologist Clifford Geertz to be the most helpful and comprehensive one for analyzing religious phenomena. Geertz defines religion by its function in human society, rather than by theological content (e.g., belief in a transcendent being), but he also avoids the reductionism of many social-scientific definitions. Part of the reason for this is that he views anthropology as essentially an interpretive science rather than an explanatory one. Geertz believes that we should attempt to "describe" rather than "explain" religion, as one cannot fully analyze the causes of human cultural activities in the same way that the natural sciences examine physical phenomena. One cannot assert "scientifically tested and approved" hypotheses about religion in general; the diversity and particularity of human experience and culture make it impossible to come to general conclusions about the nature of religion in the same way that one might about chemistry or physics.[14] Although his views are firmly based in the observation of actual religions, Geertz does not reduce the data of religion to the mere recording of religious behavior, as he believes some social-scientific accounts have attempted to do. Rather, utilizing a semiotic approach, he insists that one must understand the meaning intended by a religious behavior in order to understand its function in a religion. A nervous twitch and a wink may look the same, but one has no intended meaning while the other does—a meaning, furthermore, defined by its context and the set of assumptions that accompany it.[15] Geertz is interested in the set of meanings implied in religion, and his definition of religion reflects this.

Geertz's definition of religion is found in his 1966 essay, "Religion as a Cultural System," which defines it as consisting of five aspects: "1) a set of symbols which acts to 2) establish powerful, pervasive and long-lasting moods and motivations in men by 3) formulating conceptions of a general order of existence and 4) clothing these conceptions with such an aura of factuality that 5) the moods and motivations seem uniquely realistic."[16] He then unpacks each of these five aspects to spell out his conception of religion and how it functions.

First, as a set of symbols, religions provide both models "of" reality and models "for" reality. The difference is reflective of that between worldview and ethos, that is, the way the world is believed to be and the way it is believed the world ought to be. Models "of" reality describe the way we think the world really is, while models "for" reality describe how we would like it to be. We might also say that religions provide both beliefs and ethical values.[17]

Second, these symbol systems establish both moods and motivations in us. Motivations incline us to doing certain things in certain situations, and so are a cause of our actions, while moods do not incline us to act so much as indicate our emotional reactions to certain situations.[18]

Third, these moods and motivations are based in "conceptions of a general order of existence." Here Geertz specifies how religious feelings or inclinations differ from other sorts of feelings and inclinations: they are "directed toward the achievement of an unconditioned end" and are "symbolic of some transcendent truths." By this he does not seem to mean that a "belief in spiritual beings" is the central characteristic of religion, but that something greater than the ordinary is referenced. (Note that he also does not assume that there ought to be a single transcendent referent, as Tillich does.) Religion involves conceptions of the "all-pervading" that affects all of life and not just a part of it. Geertz even whimsically allows that golf might be a religion to some, but only if it points to some higher truths for the player and not merely because he is passionate about it.[19] It is not then that religion is simply one's highest concern, but that it relates to one's view of life's purpose and meaning grounded in a general concept of reality.

In elucidation of this point, Geertz suggests that the primary purpose of religious symbols is to deal with the encroachment of chaos on our lives and to offer a sense that life is meaningful and orderly in spite of the challenge of chaos. In three fundamental areas are we threatened by chaos: at the limits of what we can explain intellectually; at the limits of what we can endure in suffering; and at the limits of morality, with the need to deal with the injustice of life.[20] Although all three may be related to what is sometimes called the "problem of evil," they are distinct in that they deal with different mental faculties and the different challenges posed to each by chaos. It is worth noting that, in Geertz's view, religion does not "explain away" the problems of life as if they did not exist; rather, in response to the very natural suspicion that the world has no order or coherence, religion offers

> the formulation, by means of symbols, of an image of such a genuine order of the world which will account for, and even celebrate, the perceived ambiguities, puzzles, and paradoxes in human experience. The effort is not to deny the undeniable—that there are unexplained events, that life hurts, or that rain falls upon the just—but to deny that there are inexplicable events, that life is unendurable, and that justice is a mirage.[21]

Religion then recognizes "the inescapability of ignorance, pain, and injustice on the human plane while simultaneously denying that these irrationalities are characteristic of the world as a whole."

Fourth, religion also clothes these conceptions with an "aura of factuality." This means that religion deals with the "really real" in asserting that its conceptions are not fictions but are descriptive of (or, in the case of ethics, normative for) the actual nature of the world. This assertion of reality is not achieved simply by an act of faith, but is expressed in religious life through ritual—the third key component of religious experience, alongside worldview and ethos. Rituals unite the conception of how the world is with the conception of how it ought to be, for "in ritual, the world as lived and the world as imagined, fused under the agency of a single set of symbolic forms, turn out to be the same world."[22] For religious people, rituals are "not only models of what they believe, but also models for the believing of it. In these plastic dramas men attain their faith as they portray it."[23]

Geertz gives an example of this in the Balinese ritual dramatization of the mythic battle between the evil witch, Rangda, and the benevolent and comical monster, Barong. Members of the audience participate in the drama by attempts to restrain Rangda or (sometimes) through being possessed by demons and actually entering into the performance. The ritual is therefore "not merely a spectacle to be watched but a ritual to be enacted. There is no aesthetic distance here separating actors from audience and placing the depicted events in an unenterable world of illusion."[24] In this way, the enacted myth becomes real to the participants; as Geertz observes, "To ask, as I once did, a man who has *been* Rangda whether he thinks she is real is to leave oneself open to the suspicion of idiocy."[25]

Fifth, this aura of factuality makes the "moods and motivations seem uniquely realistic." This point actually explicates the previous one, noting that religious assertions utilize a different set of assumptions from the commonsensical perspective, effectively introducing a new "language game" (in the Wittgensteinian sense).[26] Having moved into the ritual context and then back to the commonsensical again, there is a slippage from one context to the other so that the ordinary world is now seen "as but the partial form of a wider reality which corrects and completes it."[27] The man who played the part of Rangda, for example, realizes he is no longer she after the ritual, but having played that part and having felt the reality of it affects how he sees himself and the world, for example, involved in the struggle between good and evil in the world, or in himself.

Can each of these aspects of Geertz's definition be found in the religion of film? First of all, films do provide a set of symbols, both visual and narrative, which act to mediate worldviews as well as systems of values—and, in accordance with Geertz's second point, these establish both certain moods (e.g., of reassurance or hope) as well as motivations (to "do the right thing," for example, to be true to yourself, or to love your family).

When films are called modern "myths," I take this (in part) to refer to a set of stories that represent the two functions Geertz calls "models of" and "models for" reality. (In the following chapter, the concept of myth and its applicability to film will be examined in greater detail.) That film narratives act this way should be clear; the world is claimed to be a certain way, and it is simultaneously claimed that it should be that way. The world is believed to be a place where good conquers evil, for example, as it tends to in all but the darkest of motion pictures (at least, those made in Hollywood). And if films do diverge from this convention, audiences may find themselves annoyed and even upset.

As one example of this, when I showed Woody Allen's *Crimes and Misdemeanors* (1989) to one of my classes, most of the students seemed to think that Allen was somehow saying that Dr. Judah Rosenthal (played by Martin Landau) deserves to get away with murder because he is never caught and even overcomes the tortures of his own conscience for having arranged the death of his mistress. They were incensed that Allen should make a film showing the wicked going unpunished, even though Allen's point was not that this is the way things should be but rather that this is the way things are. Allen wanted audiences to reflect on the lack of justice in the world and how this creates an existential situation in which people must choose good or evil even though it appears that good things happen to bad people and bad things happen to good people. I was surprised that my class seemed so reluctant to accept this viewpoint. The worldview they expect to see in films, however, is one that reassures them that justice will be served—even if life experience contradicts this. The model of and for reality that Allen proposed was not one they were accustomed to see in films, nor one they particularly wanted to see.

This clearly relates also to the third aspect of Geertz's definition: that religions formulate conceptions of a general order of existence that include the attempt to deal with experiences of chaos—the uncanny, pain and suffering, and injustice or evil. Most people go to the movies claiming the need to "escape" from their daily lives, but to what do they escape? The world presented by films tends to be neater, more orderly, and has satisfactory endings (usually) in which vice is punished and virtue rewarded, families are reunited, and lovers mate for life. Although the narratives can introduce considerable conflict and tension, it tends to be resolved within the time limit prescribed by the film-going experience. However bad the situation of the characters may be at various points in the story, by the end all will be tidy and we will be reassured that all is well with the world. This does not mean that every film invokes a banal "happy ending," as not everything may work out perfectly for all the characters in every respect. But, as Geertz said about religion, it can provide a sense that justice and order exist, even though particular events remain unexplained or seem unfair. There are films that are exceptions to this (such as some of Woody Allen's work), but they tend not to represent the norm, nor do they do as well at the box office. At the same time, such films could still be considered "religious" for the intelligentsia that enjoys them in the same way that atheistic existentialism can be said to be a "religion"—it simply offers a rather different way of dealing with chaos. In this way, even "alternative" or "art" films might be viewed as having a religious function for those who like and watch them, and we should realize that to speak of the "religious" qualities of film is not simply a way of issuing ideological judgments on "popular" cinema and its audiences.

This brings us to the fourth aspect of Geertz's definition of religion: the aura of factuality provided through the ritualization of the mythic world-view and its values. Although the worldview and ethics of films have been examined by some scholars, there has been almost no examination of the rituals of filmgoing by which the worldview and ethos of films are religiously appropriated by the viewer. It might even be alleged that there is no real religious ritual involved in film viewing, as it need not be communal and does not require the viewer to participate in the same way as in a religious service. However, I would claim that this view of filmgoers as passive receptacles, doing nothing but imbibing the film's values in isolation from one another, is a remnant of the discredited "hypodermic needle" model of cinema propounded by the Mass Culture theorists—according to which filmgoers were "injected" with the ideology of the filmmakers in the theater, and their response could only be that of unquestioning acceptance.[28] In fact, filmgoers are very involved in their own appropriation of a film, and they do not passively accept whatever it says. They are often highly critical and spend much time discussing films before, during, and after the viewing. People are involved in the film especially while viewing it, whether they are screaming in a horror movie, laughing in a comedy, or applauding the hero at a key moment. This is one reason why people still go to the movies instead of just renting a movie at home; it creates an "aura of factuality," to use Geertz's term, a sense of reality in a darkened room with an enlarged screen that encompasses all attention. Furthermore, a good audience can make a difference in how well one likes the movie—whether they laugh, cry, scream, or applaud enough to invite one to join in the communal experience of enjoying the film.

Geertz himself does not seem to see how Western popular cultural experiences might have the sort of ritual dimension he depicts as part of Balinese religion. He notes that the Balinese drama, because of its participatory aspect, is more "like a high mass, not like a presentation of *Murder in the Cathedral*," which presumably does not invite the audience to join in.[29] But popular films do often invite audience participation—more than live theatrical performances like *Murder in the Cathedral* in some ways, though (oddly enough) the film actors are not "there" to appreciate it. (Perhaps films even invite more audience participation precisely because audiences don't need to fear upsetting the actors by their heckling!) Had Geertz done an ethnographic study of a midnight showing of the film *The Rocky Horror Picture Show*, for example, he might have had some appreciation for the ways in which Western popular culture creates the sort of ritual experience that the Balinese have in their religious drama. As the audience flick their lighters on, throw toast at the screen, or respond verbally to the cues in the film, they become part of the story. This no doubt explains also why people would go to the film over and over again, as if to a church service, for this ritual experience. In fact, filmgoers routinely go multiple times to a film they like, and then buy the film on video so that they can watch it over and over again.[30] And the experience of watching the film on video is often communal, too, as friends are invited over, popcorn is made, and a discussion of the film surrounds its viewing. Many people memorize dialogue from movies that they can repeat with their friends as a sort of "in joke" that defines their own groups. Clearly, the communal nature of film viewing and its ritual aspects are linked.

Much more ethnographic study needs to be done on the ways films are experienced, as the tendency has been to treat the film as a "text" in need of interpretation rather than describing the event of film viewing and its attendant symbolisms. Films are understood and interpreted only in the context of their actual viewing, a point that has been almost entirely missed in the analysis of the religious import of popular films. Instead of pretending we "understand" the meaning of a film because we have watched it ourselves and intellectually analyzed its meaning for *us*, we need to allow for the possibility that to "understand" the "meaning" of the film involves understanding how the average viewer sees it, what she liked about it, where she saw it, why, and with whom. Only by answering these sorts of questions can we have any idea what the film might represent to those who have seen it. Within the field of film studies, some scholars are beginning to move in this direction, but scholars of religion who write about film have not yet really picked up on this trend.

Geertz's fifth point reinforces the idea that religious rituals create a sense of reality that points to a different way of viewing the world from that provided by ordinary experience. Although people clearly know that films are not "real" in the commonsensical sense of the term, the films take on the dimension of reality within the context of the viewing. Geertz himself seemed unwilling to admit the extent to which works of art can create this alternate sense of reality. In distinguishing art from religion, he accepts Suzanne Langer's view that art deals with illusion and appearance, imagining how the world could be, whereas religion claims to represent the world as it really is.[31] But religion also imagines how the world might be, and as Geertz's own theory indicates, religion links together what "is" and what "ought" to be in its ritual structure. Religion does not simply describe the world, and art does not simply provide imaginary illusions—both are involved in the complex relationship between the ideal and the real, in that both offer a worldview as well as an ethos. The way in which films, and religion, represent a version of "reality" has been a point of much debate that deserves further attention.

Film (and Religion) as Illusion or Reality

From the beginning of cinema in the late nineteenth century, it was already clear that film had a dual nature in its ability to "reproduce" reality but also to distort it. Louis Lumière made films that depicted events in ordinary life, such as *Baby's Breakfast* and *Workers Leaving the Lumière Factory*, and he did not intend to create art so much as to capture events on film that could then be reproduced for an audience. *Teasing the Gardener*, in which a boy turns on the hose just as the gardener examines it, featured a point-of-view shot that caused viewers to jump with the expectation that they, too, would be hit by the water. *Arrival of a Train* is a more familiar example of a film said to have provoked some shock, as the train appears to be heading into the audience. Lumière's popularity waned quickly as the novelty of his method wore off, because he was not very interested in story development or artistic details—but he had established the ability of the moving picture to film a "real" scene, or at least one that appeared to be real.

On the other hand, George Méliès made films that were clearly fantastic in both theme and appearance, such as *A Trip to the Moon*, which features the moon as a "man" hit in the eye with a rocket ship. He was the first to utilize "special effects" which could seem to make objects appear or disappear (by stopping the camera at key moments), and he also discovered multiple exposure and superimposition of images. People enjoyed the obvious lack of realism in his films, as they were designed to entertain through the evocation of an imaginary world that no one could mistake for reality.[32]

A debate soon began among filmmakers and theorists as to whether films should seek simply to reproduce what lies before the camera, or attempt to alter reality through the filmmaker's artistry. The formalists, who dominated during the silent era, took the latter view. Theorists such as Sergei Eisenstein and V. I. Pudovkin defended the art of film against those who defamed it by arguing that the filmmaker made decisions about how to depict reality and did not simply set up a camera in front of an event. In particular, editing (or "montage") provides the means whereby distinct images filmed at separate times can be joined together so as to appear connected. The filmmaker can manipulate images through editing so that the viewer will link the images in his mind, creating the sense of meaning desired by the filmmaker. In this way, he can create the desired emotional or intellectual response in the viewer, and so the filmmaker is a genuine artist.

When sound pictures were developed, many (including the formalist Rudolf Arnheim) thought that now the medium would become too "realistic" in its depiction of action and that it would lose the artistic, visual qualities that had dominated silent films. Realists such as Andre Bazin, however, celebrated the new use of sound and its ability to capture a better sense of reality on film. He argued that films should use less editing and more long shots that allow the viewer the freedom to see the scene as it is, rather than as cut up by the filmmakers. He did not completely eschew editing, however, as he liked the "invisible" editing technique of popular Hollywood films that gave an appearance of reality without calling excessive attention to the technique. Siegfried Kracauer took realism further than Bazin in his rejection of the unrealistic details of Hollywood films; he favored the Italian neorealist films (such as *The Bicycle Thief*) that sought to depict ordinary people in ordinary situations.[33]

In spite of their differences, formalists and realists shared the notion that films are artistic insofar as they prompt viewers to reflect on reality in new ways. In this sense, neither school embraced the idea that films are primarily escapist entertainment. But even escapist films, we might note, give the viewer some kind of sense of reality, albeit a reality that differs from his own. One escapes to the world of film in order to return better equipped to this world, and so even the "idealist" aspect of film serves a "realist" function. In addition, even the most "realistic" films do not simply reproduce reality as they involve the filmmaker in the decision of what to film and how to film it. Even documentaries or films such as those of Lumière involve choices that are designed to elicit certain responses in the viewer—as indeed Italian neorealism also intended a certain effect on the audience through its attempt at verisimilitude. There is no pure realism possible in film, due to the fact that an artist is involved who processes reality through his or her own subjectivity. Likewise, no art form (including film) can be completely devoid of relationship with reality, not even surrealism or abstract art, as these too represent the artist's response to the reality he or she lives in. Film is both realistic and artistic at the same time, and so involves the elements both formalists and realists attributed to it.[34]

Debates have continued, however, as to whether this combination of realism and artistry is properly understood by the viewers. Ideological critics such as Colin McCabe have argued that the ostensible "realism" of film causes viewers to overlook the fact that it is a constructed work, and so to take it as a representation of reality rather than an ideologically motivated artifact.[35] The appearance of reality depicted in the film is actually a cover for its ideology, as what it presents is not reality but an illusion. Only films that discomfort or alienate the viewer, or which radically challenge the normal structure of narrative, can hope to make an effective attempt to bring reality to him or her. Other theorists have similarly claimed that film viewers cannot distinguish the illusion of film from reality. Jean-Louis Baudry has argued that film viewing is akin to dreaming in providing an experience of regression (psychoanalytically understood) in which the viewer finds the self reflected rather than an outside reality, as there is no distinction between reality and self in the primitive, infantile state. In Baudry's view, viewers believe they are experiencing an outside reality even though they are merely having an experience of self; like the poor prisoners in Plato's cave, film viewers see only shadows but take them for the real thing.[36] Jean Baudrillard has gone even farther than Baudry in asserting that reality does not exist anymore in postmodern society, as we have been entirely absorbed into the "hyperreality" created out of pop culture and media images that permit no perspective on a world outside themselves.[37]

Not all film theorists, however, have accepted these dire pronouncements. Tom Gunning has pointed out that the often-told anecdote about viewers screaming and running for the exit during the first showing of Lumière's *Arrival of a Train* is itself a "myth" without historical basis. Film theorists continue to tell this myth, he suggests, as it supports their own agenda according to which audiences cannot tell a film from the real thing—even if we have become more sophisticated in our reactions. Gunning suggests that film viewers were never that naïve, and are not so now. Rather, their delight at the illusion of the train's motion was based in a reaction of astonishment at the ability of the apparatus to produce such an illusion—which was never mistaken for reality. At this time in the early 1900s, as the new creations of technology provoked both fear and confidence, audiences reacted with both fascination and horror at the abilities of these technologies. Amusement parks began to feature roller-coasters with simulated collisions that were averted at the last possible moment. Audiences sought new thrills even as they quickly tired of them and had to seek new experiences to shock and amaze them. The excess of special effects and horror movie "shockers" today should show that we are still in quest of such experiences in film, not to mention the new fascination with virtual reality technology. In all of this, however, Gunning contends that audiences maintain their sense of the illusion of the media being exploited for emotional affect.[38]

Noel Carroll has also critiqued the idea that film viewers cannot separate film from reality and, more specifically, Baudry's thesis that film viewers experience regression and a dreamlike state in the cinema. Viewing a film is not like dreaming, Carroll points out, in that we are well aware of where we are and can move or even get up and leave at will; to be more obvious still, we are not asleep when we are watching a film. Although Baudry admits this difference, Carroll believes he has made too much of the analogy between film viewing and dreaming in order to establish a psychoanalytic model for understanding the film-viewing experience. After all, films are not private like dreams, as they can be experienced and discussed with others, even during the viewing; I can also go back to see the same film again, and I cannot control my dreams in this way. Nor is the film the product of my own mind, like dreams are, but a product of the filmmakers' efforts—and these may produce a vision in harmony with my own, or not. The film need not affect me as powerfully as my own dreams do.[39]

Richard Allen concurs with Carroll's view that film viewers are well aware of the unreality of cinema, but differs from him in choosing to revise rather than discard the psychoanalytic account of the nature of film viewing. He describes the experience of seeing a film as an experience of "projective illusion" that we enter into willingly and knowingly, not unconsciously, but which still affects us powerfully in its impression of reality. Like a conscious fantasy into which we willingly place ourselves, films offer a "fully realized world" we can accept via a certain suspension of disbelief.[40] We can be aware at the same time of the fictitious nature of the film, and our desire to believe in it. Allen offers an analogous experience: one can look at a drawing that presents an image of a duck when viewed one way and a rabbit when viewed in another way, and even cause oneself to see one and then the other, but not both at the same time.[41] In the same way, we can be drawn into a film such that we "forget" its unreality, but as soon as our attention is diverted we recall its illusionary nature. We are never really fooled, but we do not constantly reflect on the fact of its unreality while we are entertaining a fictitious piece of work—like a daydream. Allen argues that we are much more in control of our filmic experience than most psychoanalytic theories would allow; for example, he rejects what he sees as the overemphasis such theories place on the voyeuristic aspects of film, in that we can choose to identify with the characters portrayed and not only the perspective of the camera that views them.[42]

If film viewers do have some sense of the unreality of cinema, as these latter theorists propose, the power of film is not in its ability to erase or displace our sense of the real world but in its ability to provide a temporary escape from it. And yet that escape is not simply a matter of illusion, but a construction that has the "aura of factuality" about it that Geertz associates with religious ritual. We willingly enter another world in the cinema, one that we realize is not the empirical world, but one that has power over us nonetheless. It may be argued that the spiritual world referenced by religions is believed to be more "real" than the imaginary world we enter in films; but in both cases, the participant enters into such ritual space in order to experience an alternate reality. The man who played Rangda had no problem distinguishing himself from Rangda once he was outside the ritual; but in the ritual space and time, that distinction was not observed. In a similar way, a viewer who entertains the fictitious world of the film as "real" during its viewing does not lose connection with the fact that she is in a theater viewing a constructed work, but she will not dwell on this fact if she is enjoying the film and is sufficiently absorbed in it.

Sometimes a film will even remind the viewers of its artificiality. In *E.T., The Extraterrestrial* (1982), there is a moment when Elliot's brother's friends first see the alien that they have thought to be a figment of Elliot's imagination. As Elliot matter-of-factly tells them, "He's a man from outer space, and we're taking him to his spaceship," one of the boys asks, "But can't he just beam up?" Elliot answers with exasperation (and somewhat condescendingly), "This is reality, Greg." Audiences laughed at that line because they realized that the film is not our reality, but it is for the characters in the film, and for that reason we can enter its world temporarily in order to discover a reality different from our own which is somehow connected to us as well. It is not less "relevant" to us for being recognized as imaginary.

It is also the case that film viewing, like religion, affords a link between the alternate world it imagines and the empirical world of everyday life. Were there not such a connection, the illusion would not be powerful or relevant—or even desired. We desire alternate worlds because we find our own imperfect; but such desires to flee also entail a desire to return, renewed and refreshed, to the everyday. One who wishes only to live in ritual time, or in the virtual reality of a film or computer game, has fallen into pathology in his preference of the imaginary world over the empirical world—and will soon have difficulties living in the empirical world, as he may begin to neglect duties and relationships that are necessary for survival. Modern technology has spawned this sort of obsessive behavior, such as that found in the person who surfs the Internet nonstop, but this is not the norm for all experience of the alternate realities offered by religion or modern media. Those who are less pathological will find a way to relate the two worlds more effectively, so that "real" life may be enriched rather than impoverished by media consumption. Some may find this hope overly optimistic, but we have no reason at the outset to conclude that it is impossible to go back and forth between the two worlds without ultimately losing the distinction between them (as Baudrillard insists).

If film does operate as a religion according to Geertz's definition, as I contend, then like religion it offers a connection between this world and the "other" world imagined in offering both models of and models for reality. These two aspects—worldview or mythology, and ethos—together express a vision of what the world really is, and what it should be. There is some confusion between these two, in that the ideal world imagined by religion is represented as the goal toward which empirical reality should reach, but it is also taken as a description of the way "true" reality really is. The imagined world is taken not as an invention of our minds, but as a true representation of reality precisely because it depicts the way things really should be. In the same way, films offer near-perfect worlds that do not correspond exactly to reality as we experience it, but we often believe they are models of (and not only models for) reality as we would like it to be so. This need not be taken simply as wishful thinking, as the desire to view models for and models of as identical is based in our desire to realize a unity of the two, to cause utopia to come to pass. This is not mere escapism, but a real desire to change the world to be more like the way that the "religion" in question thinks it already is, at a "higher" level.

In addition, the fact that a cultural phenomenon—like religion or film—is humanly constructed does not take away from its power to express another reality, even when people are aware of the constructed, "imaginary" nature of the phenomenon. Just as people can be affected by stories that they know are fictitious and even change their views of the world as a result, so also constructed religious artifacts can connect people with other realities even when they know that they are human "inventions." Sam Gill, for example, has argued that the masks used in Native American religious rituals are not disguises but are symbolic re-presentations of spiritual realities. Those who wear them are not "masquerading" as deities to fool the audience, but are portraying in dramatic form beings that they believe to be real. Like Geertz, Gill argues that the performer who wears the mask takes on the identity of the character he portrays. Even when children are initiated into the masking process, so that they realize it is their own relatives who wear the masks, this does not mean the gods portrayed are now recognized as unreal or that the ritual is viewed as a sham. Rather, Gill suggests that the new knowledge of the initiate is that gained by looking through the mask from the inside, to realize not its falsity as a way of portraying the spiritual, but rather its truth. The performer who looks out of the mask to see reality through it identifies with the character portrayed and so "knows" its reality in a clearer sense even than the audience that sees him. The mask does not hide truth; it reveals it.[43] Filmgoers, too, know that films are not "real," but the imaginary constructions within them can still serve to convey real truths about the nature of reality and how it is believed to be.

The question may still arise as to whether or not there "really" is a referent for religious beliefs, or whether the religious person only thinks that the world imagined by religion is real. Some of those who define religion by its function in human life have been reductionist in claiming that it has no referent beyond its cultural function, that its referential claims are illusionary. This is not my view, or that of Geertz, who, as we have seen, avoids reductionism. Questions about the "truth" of religious beliefs must be bracketed by the religion scholar as they can never be definitively answered. This does not, however, prohibit religious people, including some scholars of religion, from believing particular truth-claims of particular religions, or from making such claims; it simply means that it is impossible to prove whether such claims have an external reality referent or not. What we can do is examine the faith of those who hold to such claims to see the differences it makes for them in terms of worldview and ethos. Thus we can seek to understand the beliefs of Christians, which have a meaning whether or not God or Jesus really exists, and we can seek to understand the filmic religion whether or not the visions of reality it presents are "true." Even if good guys don't always win and not all romances are happy, those who enjoy films may believe justice and love will ultimately triumph, in part because this is presented as the nature of reality in many movies. And, as such claims are not subject to definitive verification or falsification, filmgoers may choose to believe such things even when some evidence seems to count against them—for example, it is believed that in the end justice will be served, even though we do not always see this happen.

Films, then, can be taken as illusions in one sense, but can also have the force of reality by presenting a vision of how the world is as well as how it might be. In the ritual context of viewing a film, we "entertain" the truth of its mythology and ethos as a subject of consciousness even as its "entertains" us. It presents a reality that differs from that experienced in ordinary profane time and space as the reality depicted in religious myth and ritual differs from the empirical world of our everyday lives—and yet, that alternative reality is still integrally connected with the world of the everyday, and hence its vision is relevant to it. To understand this more fully, we will examine how the notions of myth, ethos, and ritual apply to film.

3

Myths about Myth

Rehabilitating the Notion of "Myth"

The term "myth" is so laden with negative connotations that it is practically unserviceable for the study of religion. But its use persists, and it also continues to be used in reference to films, largely due to their narrative form. It may be helpful to rehabilitate the term by uncovering the ways in which it might be usefully applied to religion or film. To do so, we must first purge it of some of its unfortunate associations and acknowledge the ways in which the concept has been used to oppress or condemn as well as romanticize religious and cultural phenomena. We will also critically examine certain scholarly approaches to myth that have been helpful in giving insight into religious phenomena. As with definitions of "religion," every definition of "myth" is a construction of the scholar's imagination and as such cannot provide total objectivity about the phenomena it seeks to delineate. Nonetheless, some definitions seem more helpful in giving us genuine understanding of religion, and certain characteristics of these definitions can be applied to the phenomenon of film as well. The definitions of myth are themselves myths, created by scholars of myth, but these myths about myth may help us understand the stories we are trying to hear.

From its origins through the present day, the word "myth" has often been held to mean "a story that is not true." The Greek philosophers who began to doubt the myths as providing literal histories of their gods sought to find some meaning hidden beneath the obviously false surface details, often either accepting the allegorical view that the stories were really about natural phenomena hypostacized as personal beings, or the euhemeristic view that the stories were historical accounts about humans that had been exaggerated to divine proportions and they may have sought some ethical content in them as well. They applied the term "myth" to those stories they no longer believed as history, or they invented new myths (which were not believed literally either), as Plato did.[1]

In modern Western usage, however, the term "myth" has usually been reserved for the stories of religions other than one's own, as few wanted to allow the connotation of falsehood to the stories of their own religion. Those who did analyze biblical stories as myths, like David Friedrich Strauss in his *Life of Jesus Critically Examined* (1835), incurred the wrath of Christians who felt that the truth of their religion was being attacked by this method—and, in fact, Strauss and others did dismiss the historical truth of many biblical stories, although they sought (like their Greek forebears) to find some "deeper" truth within them. Early Christian allegorical interpretation had done the same thing, of course, but not to such an extent or in such a way as to suggest the primitive nature of the biblical authors. Christian allegorists like Origen had held that some things are false as literal statements in the Bible because God wished us to look deeper than the surface to find an allegorical truth; modern mythological interpreters of the Bible, on the other hand, held that the biblical authors used mythic language because they lacked the modern sophistication to express the same meaning in demythologized form. They believed not only that the factual details of the stories were literally false, but that the authors of them were too primitive to know how to express their ideas in the "proper" philosophical form.

Yet those who were uncomfortable viewing biblical stories as myths were often happy to view stories of other religions in this way. Friedrich Max Müller (1823–1900) was among the first scholars to extensively examine other religions through this concept, essentially claiming that myths were allegorical accounts of natural phenomena that were erroneously accepted as referring to historical beings. The idea that myth was an "error" to be dispelled by a more "scientific" understanding was reiterated by Edward Tylor (1832–1917) and James Frazer (1854–1941), both of whom viewed mythic ideas of supernatural beings as "primitive" and finally dispensable. In this way, they assumed an evolutionary framework for the history of religion, according to which earlier ideas were displaced by more sophisticated forms of rational monotheism, and ultimately by a scientific worldview. It is now commonly recognized that such an evolutionary schema oversimplifies history and falsifies data (e.g., ignoring the fact that monotheism often precedes polytheism in cultural development), and also is obviously prejudicial in its judgments on cultures that hold with ideas of magic and myth.[2]

Another aspect of early myth theory was its association with cultural chauvinism and racism. Even though Müller was not enamored of the mythological worldview and basically viewed it as one left behind by Christianity, he did hold that the Indo-European or "Aryan" languages were much richer in myths than the Semitic languages of the Bible—and this view was utilized by those who came to celebrate Aryan culture and denigrate "Semitic Jewish" culture in Germany and elsewhere. Ernest Renan (1823–1892) exalted Aryan culture over the Semitic to the point that he held even Jesus was not really part of Jewish culture; this attitude finally led to books like Hans Hauptmann's *Jesus the Aryan* (1931), which claimed Jesus was crucified by "Semitic Jews." The so-called German Christians who supported the racist ideology of national socialism even wanted to replace the "Jewish" Old Testament with more suitable "Aryan" mythology as a background to the Christian New Testament. "Mythology" came to be associated with fascism and extreme nationalist politics, as right-wing groups sought to establish a religious basis for their claims of racial superiority.[3]

In this way, the study of "mythology" underwent a not-so-subtle shift as it moved from being a negative method that rejected the historicity of religious stories to a positive method of exalting particular religious stories for their cultural value. The odd thing about this transition was that it still basically associated "myth" with nonbiblical religion, although it was now held to be good rather than bad. Few people considered that there might be more similarity than difference between the miraculous stories of the Bible and the stories of other religious traditions.

Psychological Interpretations of Myth: Carl Jung and Joseph Campbell

Today, many people who have overcome the scientifically motivated denigration of myth as "false history" have come to appreciate it not as a source of political or racist ideology but as an expression of a healthy psychological need for stories that define our identities and values.[4] This development can be traced in part to Carl Jung (1875–1961), who as a psychologist departed from Freud's ideological critique of religion as he came to see its positive benefits. He believed that mythology utilized a series of universal, archetypal figures (e.g., the wise old woman, the brave hero, the mother-goddess) that reappear in stories around the world, expressing the experience of the "collective unconscious" of humanity.[5] Whereas Freud believed that individuals suppress details of their personal histories which then emerge in the activity of the individual's unconscious (e.g., in dreams), Jung believed that there are many symbols in consciousness that cannot be explained simply as a result of the individual's history. For this reason he asserted the existence of a "collective unconscious" that preexists all individuals and societies and so has the character of an a priori part of human nature. This approach is in effect an attempt to overcome Freud's reductionist view of religion by admitting that it refers to something bigger than the individual psyche and its neuroses.

But Jung's understanding of religion still has reductionist elements to it. Although the collective unconscious and its archetypes transcend individuals, they are still understood through psychological categories that confine religion to internal experience—albeit internal experience of our species as a whole. Although myths may seem to be about external realities, they are in fact "symbolic expressions of the inner, unconscious drama of the psyche . . . mirrored in the events of nature."[6] Even the story of Jesus is ultimately not about a historical individual so much as it is the exemplification of a psychological archetype.[7] Jesus represents the fully integrated "Self," the ideal of the mature and "whole" person we all seek to be; the details of his external historical life are unimportant to Jung, for Jesus is only of real importance as he exists in the inner religious experiences of believers who encounter him as an archetypal ideal. He serves as a means to our own realization of complete selfhood, so his existence independent of us is irrelevant. "The self of Christ is present in everybody a priori," although in unconscious form, so that it can only become real to us "when you withdraw your projections from an outward historical or metaphysical Christ and thus wake up the Christ within."[8]

Jung has also been accused of basically reducing God to an element of consciousness, an accusation he attempted to refute by invoking the Kantian philosophical distinction between things as they truly are ("things in themselves," or noumena) and things as we experience and know them (phenomena). We can only know the archetypes as we know them as objects of consciousness (phenomena), and this applies to God as much as any other archetype. But Jung holds that this does not mean that God only exists within our minds, for we can know nothing about the existence or nonexistence of God independent of us (as noumenon)—therefore, he argued, we cannot reduce God to a by-product of consciousness as Freud did.[9]

This argument, however, does not completely refute the charge that Jung has reduced religion and God to internal psychological realities. Although he allows for the possibility of a transcendent God, he also asserts that we can know nothing about this God (not even whether it exists independently of us), so that God's external existence is basically as irrelevant as the external historical existence of Jesus. What Jung says about God is entirely shaped by his psychological categories and his understanding of how they apply to God—for example, how God mirrors all aspects of human consciousness by modeling for us the integrated "Self," as well as the male and female aspects of it (Animus and Anima) and its Shadow side.[10]

Jung's approach remains a popular one in many circles and has been used by some scholars to analyze the mythological symbols in cinema, especially science fiction films.[11] It is not my intention to suggest that these studies are illegitimate, but to indicate that such a Jungian approach to myth is limited in its focus due to its reductionist tendencies. This approach imposes general psychological categories on all cultures, insisting that the details of the individual myths are less important than their conformity to archetypal psychological patterns, alleged (without real evidence) to be universal in all cultures. Because myths are understood to be representative of the struggle for integrated wholeness or "individuation," they tend to be seen as a function of this unconscious drive for self-discovery rather than an attempt to deal with the external encroachment of chaos on our lives (which Geertz identified as the fundamental task of religion). In Jung's view, myths help us embrace and integrate our own Self in all its aspects (Shadow, Anima, Animus), but this is basically understood as an internal struggle rather than one that is related to our lives in community and world.

The approach of Joseph Campbell, who made use of Jung's ideas, illustrates these problems even more clearly. Campbell probably did more to popularize mythology than any other modern scholar, thanks in part to Bill Moyers's television series on him. Few people realize, however, the biases built into his approach. More so than Jung, Campbell simplified the nature and diversity of mythology by insisting that there really is only one myth (the "monomyth"), endlessly reproduced in cultures across the world, which exists as a model for the human journey of self-discovery. In

The Hero with a Thousand Faces Campbell describes the structure of this myth as including a series of characteristic events: the hero is called to the adventure/quest; he initially refuses the call; he is convinced to go with the help of a figure who gives him supernatural aid; he passes the threshold of home and must survive combat with the monster; he enters the "belly of the whale" and is symbolically killed and reborn; he passes through a series of ordeals and tests of his character; he rescues the mother-goddess; he is reconciled to his father; he destroys the monster and is united with the divine.[12] Not all myths conform to this pattern, but Campbell works hard to make it seem as if they do, emphasizing those features that seem to fit and ignoring those that do not.[13] He seems to have been influenced here by his early studies of medieval European literature, with its stories of chivalric romance, heroic knights battling dragons, and damsels in distress, so that he desired to find this the universal structure for all myths. He also claims that this myth is really about an internal struggle within ourselves, rather than any struggle with external realities, to a greater extent than Jung. He even belittles the problem of external suffering, claiming that the only problem exists within ourselves in our inability to deal with it; we deserve everything that happens to us, for (in an existentialist sense) we make our own universe.[14] We can decide whether to suffer or not, in other words, so it does not really matter what goes on outside of our heads.

This complete reduction of the subject of myth to our internal psychological universe is abetted by Campbell's philosophical monism, his belief that all reality is one and that there is ultimately no distinction between our selves and the divine; this allows him to reduce all our experience of the world to an internal psychological matter. In his monism, it is not a transcendent reality with which we unite (as in Vedantic Hinduism), but rather all of reality is reinterpreted as an aspect of the self, as in Friedrich Nietzsche's philosophy; the individual realizes he himself is the absolute, the creator, the center of his own universe.[15] Campbell also rejects any resistance to this monism in the history of religion, such as the insistence of Western biblical religion on a transcendent God.[16] In general, he prefers Eastern to Western religion, and he reserves particular venom for the Jewish claim to be the chosen people who have received a unique revelation from God.[17] That this denigration of Judaism is tied to Campbell's own anti-Semitism has been well documented by Robert Segal and Maurice Friedman, among others.[18]

By reducing myth to a product of the unconscious and a series of universally present archetypes, both Jung and Campbell risk losing the distinctiveness of individual myths as well as the meanings attributed to them by those who tell them. Myths seek to state something about the world, not just something about the psychology of those who tell them. Furthermore, such psychological interpretations are often largely fanciful, being based in speculations about the mindset of peoples rather than any real empirical study, and they tend to impose one culturally specific set of psychological categories onto all cultures and religions.

Clifford Geertz on Myth and Sociological Reductionism

Many theorists of myth have avoided psychological reductionism but may fall prey to sociological reductionism instead. I have previously noted how Clifford Geertz sought a nonreductionistic anthropological method (which I am attempting to mimic), and he sometimes criticized his predecessors and their understandings of religion and myth—most notably Emile Durkheim, Bronislaw Malinowski, Lucien Lévy-Bruhl, and Claude Lévi-Strauss. These sociologically oriented theorists tended to view religion and myth as expressions of social integration or social conflict, and so effectively reduced myth to a by-product of social forces, not unlike Marx. Durkheim, the main founder of sociological analysis of religion, essentially equated religion and society, but in such a way that religion is reduced to a role of societal maintenance. This approach can admit that society shapes religion, but not that religion can shape society as an independent cultural force, as Geertz claims it does.[19] As for Malinowski and Lévy-Bruhl, Geertz finds them engaged in opposed forms of reductionism. Malinowski essentially reproduces Durkheim's view, that myth is a "common sense" pragmatic strategy for societal maintenance, hence ignoring any transcendental function for myth in its purported connection to a mystical, extramundane reality. On the other hand, Lévy-Bruhl reduces the myth to the mystical only, claiming it has no relevance to pragmatic everyday matters because it involves a way of thinking that is totally alien or incomprehensible to outsiders, and for this reason myth is essentially impervious to logical analysis.[20] In contrast, Geertz insists that myth must function both pragmatically and mystically, and that in so doing it can be reduced neither to merely a strategy for societal maintenance nor an irrational and inexplicable mystery. In his view, myth connects the everyday (empirically real) world of social matters and "common sense" with the mystical (ideal, or ultimately real) world of religion, even as it connects a view of how the world is with a moral vision of how it ought to be. There is considerable slippage between the two, as the myth portrays a model *of* how the world is believed to be but this also corresponds to a model *for* how people would like it to be. We should then neither reduce myth to its sociological function in the everyday world nor to being a fundamentally incomprehensible phenomenon that deals with an imaginary fairyland but not our real (societal) lives.[21] If Geertz is right, religion and myth connect the real and the imagined, the everyday and the ideal, as I also argued in the last chapter, in which I also argued that films do the same thing.

Geertz's efforts to utilize sociological analysis in a nonreductive way also contrast with the methods of Claude Lévi-Strauss, who expanded the sociological approach through the use of structuralism and linguistics. Geertz found Lévi-Strauss to be influenced by Jean-Jacques Rousseau's idea of the "noble savage," a romantic construct of "primitive" life as more moral and natural than life in our modern industrial society.[22] This effort to romanticize and idealize pretechnological societies fails to understand individual cultures as it reduces them all to forms of the primitive archetype within ourselves, which Lévi-Strauss would like to see modern society recover.[23] This reduction of all myth to a universal, "primitive" archetype has resonances with Campbell's view, and shares the same problems. We have also noted (in chapter 1) Bernard Scott's use of Lévi-Strauss's view of myth in relation to popular film and some of its problematic aspects. Specifically, Scott views myths as essentially irrational attempts to unite contradictory views, which reveal themselves to be untenable when exposed to analysis. The alleged irrationalism of so-called "primitive" societies, which Lévi-Strauss and Lévy-Bruhl regard with romantic nostalgia, is applied to popular culture by Scott in such a way as to indict and ultimately reject it as a repository of contradictions it cannot resolve. What Scott does not see is that his definition of myth has already prejudiced him against it, so that he cannot see the myths of popular films as anything but fruitless attempts to escape the contradictions of life. He cannot allow that myths may actually empower people to work to overcome or deal with contradictions in positive ways.

It is apparent that we need a better definition of myth than many of these views, one which avoids romanticizing or defaming it, which is neither sociologically nor psychologically reductionistic in viewing it merely as a by-product of social or psychological forces, and one that views myth as neither irrational falsehood nor a basis for racist and fascist ideology. Geertz's view points the way in his notion that myths unite the ideal and the real, a notion of how things could be with a pragmatic understanding of how they are. Myths can help people deal with life's problems and also provide hope for a better day. Several other thinkers have offered significant ideas about myth that may help in developing a more positive and useful notion of the concept; four of them will now be considered, as well as the possible application of their views to popular film.

Mircea Eliade

It would not be an overstatement to suggest that Mircea Eliade (1907–1986) has had a greater affect on the academic study of comparative religions than any other twentieth-century figure. He based much of his own understanding of mythology on a stark contrast between the Western "historical" view of time and the cyclical view of time found in other (especially archaic) religions. Mythology, to Eliade, is primarily cosmogony in that it gives an account of creation in a distant primordial time. This time of creation, however, can be accessed ritualistically through the retelling and reenacting of the myth of creation, in that such reenactment brings one outside of ordinary time and space to the sacred realm in which creation can once again occur.[24] Eliade found that people whose lives are closely linked with nature (e.g., via agriculture) see the repetitious patterns of life and death in the seasons, and believe that they can effect new life and so the new season by tapping into the power of creation. Through the myth of sacred origins, one can be returned to that time in order to bring its power to bear in the present of ordinary time. In such religions, time is viewed as cyclical rather than as linear. Even rites of passage have this cyclical character, in that each new generation must pass through the same stages of development in life as the previous generation and so make use of the same sacred power of new life.[25]

This cyclical view of time differs from that found in Western religions in that the latter find the sacred not in the constant repetition of creation outside of ordinary time, but rather in ordinary historical time. God comes into history in biblical religion, making it possible to speak of a linear progression toward a fulfillment of history as God has planned it. History drives toward its completion, whether it is understood as the return of Israel to the Promised Land or the return of Jesus as the Messiah. There are elements of repetition in Western religion, of course—for example, the Jewish reenactment of the Exodus experience at the Passover Seder or the Christian reenactment of the death and resurrection of Jesus in Holy Communion. But these rituals always have an eschatological component in that they point forward to final liberation in a distant future, rather than backward to creation in the distant past. It is not through returning to origins but through anticipating the end of history that meaning is found in biblical religion.[26]

This drive toward the fulfillment of life within rather than outside of history has now been secularized, according to Eliade, in political movements such as communism or fascism that seek to bring their own visions of societal perfection into the present. These movements are dangerous in that they have lost all connection with the sacred, so that while the historicism of Western religion was still linked to a transcendent reality, the secularized form of it believes that perfection is attainable here and now.[27] In practice this means that historicism is now linked with political ideologies that seek to subordinate all culture and society to their own vision of the future, often through violent means. Eliade therefore seems to favor the mythic (cyclical-repetitious) view over the historical (linear-progressive), in spite of the link between historical thinking and Christianity. His preference is for a "cosmic Christianity" such as that practiced by the peasants of his youth in Romania, which viewed Jesus more as lord of nature than of history, and which emphasized the cyclical nature of seasons continually renewed by the divine power of Christ more than a final transformation of history to his kingdom.[28]

Eliade has also applied his understanding of myth to Western popular culture, albeit in a limited way. He notes the mythological aspects of the Superman comic books, as the man of steel represents a modern hero in disguise (as mild-mannered Clark Kent) with whom readers can identify. "The myth of Superman satisfies the secret longings of modern man who, though he knows that he is a fallen, limited creature, dreams of one day proving himself an 'exceptional person,' a 'Hero.'" Detective novels also offer a modern version of the battle between good and evil, so that the reader, "through an unconscious process of projection and identification . . . takes part in the mystery and drama and has the feeling that he is personally involved in a paradigmatic—that is, a dangerous, 'heroic'—action."[29] Whether reading or going to the movies, modern people escape from ordinary profane time and enter a "sacred" space and time.[30] But

even though the modern person is unavoidably and perhaps unconsciously religious, Eliade laments the fact that modern people deny the sacred, believing that they "make themselves" without any reference to a
transcendent reality (as existentialism puts it).[31] Their religiosity is therefore a diluted and desacralized faith that seeks fulfillment in the world
rather than beyond it, in his view; here we see the criticism of popular culture for its supposed lack of a transcendent referent that has also characterized some of the other religious analyses of culture and film (as I noted
in the first chapter).

Eliade's analysis of myth is possibly more comprehensive than any that
preceded him, and it has much to commend it—but it has also been criticized for romanticizing the "primitive" as other theories have, and for
overemphasizing the contrast between Western "historical" religion and
the more "mythical" religions that allegedly have the cyclical notion of
time so crucial to Eliade's analysis. Perhaps myth is not primarily or only
about creation and its repetition.[32] Must mythology be understood as ef-
fecting an "eternal return" to the time of origins, outside of history, or can
it sometimes be understood as incorporating a historical dimension?
Francisca Cho has pointed out that Chinese "mythology" does not fit Eliade's criteria, as the dichotomy between historical and mythical time does
not exist in Chinese thought. Rather than define myths as stories that nar-
rate a creation story in order to help us escape history, she suggests that we
understand myths as providing archetypes that are models for "creation in
the present." In this way, "the creation *narrative* can be traded in for a creation *function.*" The basic purpose of all types of myths is to "provide patterns for living a life," and this can be done with or without a rejection of
the historical.[33]

Discarding the dichotomy of myth and history might also help us to see
the mythic dimensions of Western religion, not only in its attempts to escape history but also within its historically presented stories. We have seen
the tendency to separate myth from Western religion, which may serve either to protect Western religion from mythological analysis (where myth
is viewed as bad, or false) or to critique Western religion as less "true" than
the more "mythological" religions (where myth is viewed as good). Such
dichotomies have served the value judgments of those who made them,
but they have not necessarily served the goal of better understanding religion. This is not to say that Eliade engages in the sort of simplistic judgments on Western religion that mark the less scholarly work of, for example, Joseph Campbell; in contrast to Campbell's anti-Western bias, Eliade

criticizes Western secular historicism (communism, fascism) but not religious historicism as it is found in Judaism or Christianity.[34] Still, Eliade demonstrates a tendency to exalt those cultures that differ from the Western in their view of time, or at least exalts the nonhistorical (i.e., mythical) aspects of Western religion as more effective in relating the sacred to human life. He also tends to assume that all cultures use basically the same cosmogonic, cyclical notion of myth—a generalization that may be unwarranted, as some other scholars have claimed.

One thing for which Eliade deserves credit is his effort to avoid reductionism, as he was just as concerned as Geertz to provide a method that does not reduce religion to being an expression of psychological or sociological forces. In order to do this, Eliade relied on a concept of the sacred as the transcendent (as in Rudolf Otto's studies) more than as an expression of society (as in Durkheim's studies). In practice, this means that his method does not work as well with those religions that lack a radical concept of transcendence, as we have seen. Geertz, to a greater extent than Eliade, avoided reductionism without such a "theological" concept of the sacred as the radically transcendent, but both of them understood the dialectical relationship between the sacred and the profane as one in which neither term can be reduced to the other, and there is considerable interaction between the two in both of their theories. Just as Geertz held that there is slippage between the commonsense worldview and the religious worldview, so Eliade finds the profane can be a vehicle for the sacred even as there is a continual alteration between the profane worldview and the sacred worldview. Myth gains its relevance, for both thinkers, by providing a connecting link between the ideal world of the sacred and the ordinary world of the profane—even as I have suggested that films make a similar connection between the ideal and the real.

Jonathan Z. Smith

Jonathan Z. Smith is one of those religion scholars who admits his debt to Eliade even as he provides some criticisms of him. Smith finds Eliade's dichotomy of "archaic" and "modern" religion problematic, especially insofar as it may imply a periodization that is artificial. Smith believes that the two forms of religion Eliade characterizes as mythic-cyclical and historical might be better referred to as "locative" (place-centered) religion and "utopian" (future-centered) religion—although here too one must be wary of implying a development from one to the other, as both appear throughout the history of religions. More significantly, Smith calls attention to the "dark side" of religious myths, which do not always deal with a cosmogonic unity and harmony that is to be reproduced as a source of order and new life. Instead, many myths deal with unresolved conflicts and tensions in life between good and evil, order and chaos. It is not that chaos is repeatedly overcome by creation, as Eliade would have it, but that chaos itself is a continual source of power, just as sacred as its converse. Smith finds myths to be more dualistic, especially in those stories that deal with outsider figures (like tricksters) that challenge the normal way of seeing or doing things.[35] In addition to calling attention to such dualism and conflict in myth and ritual, Smith has focused on the importance of the particular in his studies of religion, and so is suspicious of the sort of generalizations about "the sacred" that characterize the work of Eliade or other scholars.[36]

Smith's own view of myth is, not surprisingly, rather different from Eliade's. He criticizes those views that make it seem as if nonliterate peoples have a "primitive" and, to us, incomprehensible understanding of myth, or which romanticize the "pristine" nature of this worldview as one that lacks skepticism, the ability to make distinctions, or critical thought. In such views, according to Smith, the "primitive" is viewed as incapable of "those perceptions of discrepancy and discord which give rise to the symbolic project that we identify as the very essence of being human."[37] In contrast, Smith believes that every culture, modern or not, reflects on the incongruities of its experiences and develops ways of dealing with those incongruities and tensions. For this reason, Smith insists that "there is no pristine myth; there is only application." Myths exist as particular strategies for dealing with particular situations, and so there is no single form for all myths (e.g., Campbell's "monomyth," or Eliade's cosmogony), nor a pure myth that exists apart from the social context in which it is lived. As a strategy for dealing with incongruity in life, myth is "a self-conscious category mistake. That is to say, the incongruity of myth is not an error, it is the very source of its power." Myths do not seek to overcome incongruity, but (like jokes, or riddles) they delight in the incongruous fit of disparate elements.[38]

Smith gives some examples to illustrate his view of myth. The story of Hainuwele from the Wemale tribe of Ceram (near New Guinea) deals with a girl who is born in a supernatural manner and who has the ability to excrete valuable items, "cargo" from other lands such as porcelain dishes and golden earrings. Her tribesmen kill her out of jealousy, and her dismembered body is buried, out of which grow various new plant species. The classic interpretation of this myth, by Adolf Jensen, viewed this as an example of the "pristine" myth of the origin of vegetation, death, and sexuality, which has been "corrupted" in its application by reference to modern items. But Smith points out that the story is not about origins at all, as death, agriculture, and sex all exist at the beginning of the story. Instead, it is a story developed to deal with the arrival of outsiders who have "cargo" which the Wemale do not. As the white outsiders did not share these goods equally with the Wemale (as Wemale morality dictated they ought), the Wemale developed this story to explain that the cargo came from their own people, who made it their own by assimilating (i.e., killing) its source and transforming cargo into the local food. Even though this myth does not result in the desired equalization of wealth, it speaks of a fully intelligible desire for such equality that is not incomprehensible to the outsider. In other words, the myth does not express a worldview that is totally alien to our own.[39]

Smith also discusses the Enuma Elish, the ancient Babylonian text that was understood by Eliade and others as a prime example of a cosmogony. According to the cosmogonic interpretation of this myth, it reinacts the creation and guarantees new life through a symbolic death and resurrection of the king. Smith, however, argues that the myth is not primarily about creation, death, or resurrection to new life, but is rather about the founding of Babylon and its divine kingship by the god Marduk. As such, it is a more political and historically conditioned text than is sometimes realized, as it acts to establish the legitimacy of the current rulers of Babylon. The associated ritual of the Akita festival involves a staged slapping and humiliation of the king, who is stripped of his royal garments and who engages in a negative confession (claiming he has done no wrong) before being restored. This is no symbolic death and resurrection that reenacts the cosmic cycle of life and death, but an implied threat of what will happen to a poor ruler. Unless one rules wisely and protects Babylon, as the king claims he has in the ritual, he will be judged and destroyed. This ritual had particular relevance during the time when it was written, a period during which Babylon was occupied by the Seleucids—so that it acts as "a ritual for the rectification of a foreign king." In other words, Babylonians could accept a foreign ruler as long as he promised to comport himself as a native ruler would, and this ritual enacted both the threatened judgment (if he ruled poorly) and the promised acceptance (if he ruled well). The myth is used to deal with the tense situation of foreign occupation and provides a means to legitimize it.[40]

Smith then wants us to understand myths in their local sociopolitical context, and not homologize them to a single idea or concept. To understand a myth, we must understand its cultural and historical situation and how it speaks to the people who tell it in that place and time. This does not mean that he reduces myths to simply being political strategies, but he insists that we deal with the context in which they have meaning, and this point is well taken. Smith's emphasis on the importance of understanding the particular details of religions and myths is perhaps his most significant legacy as a scholar of religion.

It may be, however, that Smith insists too much on incongruity, to the point that myths cannot possibly resolve the conflicts with which they deal. One may hear some echoes of Lévi-Strauss's notion of myth as involving an attempt to resolve a fundamental conflict that is doomed to fail. For Lévi-Strauss, this functioned as part of his romanticized concept of the mythic and illogical "savage" whose worldview loses credibility as soon as it is exposed to analysis. Smith has made it very clear that he does not wish to turn the myth teller into an alien and illogical creature, but it is sometimes unclear how he can avoid viewing mythological cultures in this way, given his assumptions.

One can also ask if the incongruity is as all-encompassing as he believes, and whether the myth actually goes farther toward resolving the tension than he allows. The Enuma Elish, for example, may actually succeed in its effort to legitimize a foreign ruler. The Hainuwele myth, too, does not fail in its efforts to view foreign cargo as equivalent to native products; it simply did not convince the whites to share equally with the Ceram, which may not have been its purpose. Myth is a strategy for dealing with a situation, and the measure of its effectiveness may not be in the objective political changes it makes but in the attitudes it evokes in those who tell it. Such attitudes may bespeak more reconciliation and "wholeness" than incongruity and tension, as people generally tend to seek wholeness rather than conflict. Smith holds that by playing with incongruities, myths provide "an occasion for thought"—but it is not altogether clear what one is supposed to think in such a situation of incongruity.[41]

For example, he discusses how the Aranda of Australia are initiated into the mystery of the "bull-roarer," which they have thought to be the voice of Tuanjiraka, a monster responsible for all pain and suffering, but which is in fact a piece of wood whirled at the end of a string to produce a frightening sound. Initiates are told that they should not believe in this monster, as it does not really exist; Smith concludes that it is "the incongruity between the expectation and the actuality that serves as a vehicle of religious experience."[42] But it is hard to see how this in itself is very enlightening to the initiates. One could instead conclude that they are being taught that suffering does not come from any supernatural being but that it is simply the nature of life—a lesson we might all find intelligible, and even helpful, in learning to view pain as a part of normal existence and not as a punishment. This message could help people deal with the conflicts created by suffering rather than simply observing or enshrining such conflicts and the incongruities related to them.

Wendy Doniger

Wendy Doniger is yet another contemporary scholar who has written a great deal about myth, especially from her viewpoint as a scholar of Hinduism. A myth, in her view, is a story with "religious meaning," in other words, a story that deals with "the sorts of questions that religions ask" about "such things as life after death, divine intervention in human lives, transformations, the creation of the world and of human nature and culture—and basically, about meaning itself." This is not meant as a terribly precise definition, as Doniger does not want to limit what might be considered "religious," although she assumes we all have some idea of what is to be associated with that term. A myth also has no author, as by the time it becomes a myth its origins are always placed in the distant past; it is a story that has always been and so cannot, properly speaking, ever be heard "for the first time." But myths are not isolated in a distant past, as they are retold because they are perceived as remaining relevant to subsequent ages. "Myths encode meanings in forms that permit the present to be construed as the fulfillment of a past from which we would wish to have been descended." A myth must also be part of a mythology, a set of myths with overlapping characters and events. In this way, the myth and its themes are reinforced in the memory of the group.[43]

Doniger has also insisted that there is no "monomyth." It is not the case that there is one myth endlessly repeated with variations in the world's cultures. She is well acquainted with the tendency of myth scholars to overgeneralize about the content of myths and to ignore the details of individual stories. At the same time, she does not wish to give up the task of cultural comparison, as there may be some similarities that can be found among myths from diverse cultures and religions. If myths deal with basic questions about the meaning of life, it may be because they deal with basic human experiences such as "sexual desire, procreation, pain, death," which are universal, although understood in different ways in different cultures.[44]

Words like "true" and "false" do not apply very well to myths, Doniger notes, as the historical referent for such stories is perhaps the least important measure of their value for a culture. Even cultural stories that include "impossible" situations such as a reversal of gender roles or the absence of death serve to demonstrate the undesirability of such situations and thus the necessity and "truth" of the actual order of things. "They preserve for us the cultural 'truth' that women should *not* work in the fields and men should *not* keep house, or the philosophical truth that we *must* die." We are "better off" with the way things are, according to such myths, as they show us how the world would be less perfect if it were different. Myths in general might be considered "true," she allows, not in the historical veracity of the events described but in the fact that they represent a culture's understanding of the central questions of life.[45]

The Western tendency to distrust the value or truth of myths, Doniger holds, is related to our tendency to discount alternate "realities" such as those experienced in dreams. From Plato to Freud, dreams have been viewed in Western thought as expressing our "lower" desires but not an objective reality.[46] In Hindu thought, in contrast, the line between waking and dreaming and between reality and illusion is blurred, as is shown in numerous myths; Doniger gives two examples from the text of the Yogavasistha. King Lavana dreams that he is an untouchable for sixty years, with a full set of memories of this time, then wakes up only moments after he fell asleep in his original body; but he is unable to dismiss it as complete illusion as he finds the place where he "lived" and the other people from his "dream," who are able to verify all the details of his life there. The Brahmin Gadhi likewise dreams he is an untouchable who becomes king, but when he is discovered to be an untouchable he kills himself—only to awaken as himself once again. He, likewise, is able to verify the "reality" of his dream by visiting the place where he was king.[47] Both stories are interpreted within the Hindu text as demonstrating the fact that all of life is an illusion or dream from the point of view of the ultimate, and in this way to show that the distinction between "dreams" and "reality" is itself an illusion. The rigid duality between reality and unreality that characterizes Western thought is absent in Hindu thought, according to Doniger, as there are many kinds of "reality" that include concrete experience, visions, dreams, memories, past lives, and fantasies, all of which "would have to be set out at various points on a spectrum that has no ends at all."[48] All types of stories have value, then, and not only those that deal with what we normally regard as "real."

One can see that Doniger's view of myth might apply well to film, as film also trades in the confusion between reality and ideality, suggesting that there might be "truth" even in narratives that do not deal with historical events insofar as they have the appearance of reality during the viewing experience. Films are also "true," following Doniger, in the sense that they deal with the central questions of our culture about gender roles, sex, love, child raising, purpose in life, and death. Indeed, they deal with all the concerns of our culture and its struggles to define its worldview, morals, and identity through various stories. It might be questioned whether the filmic myths get repeated as much as traditional myths, as the stories change from one film to the next. However, as we have already noted, people do view films multiple times in some cases, and also there is a certain sameness and predictability to some films, namely those that conform to the patterns of a certain genre, so that audiences can expect something like the same story, or at least one that is part of a general "mythology." This does not mean that the differences are unimportant or that they negate the ability of films to tell meaningful stories (as early film genre theorists held), but that these exist as variations on certain well-known themes, such as the romance, the adventure, the tearjerker, and the horror film, which we will examine in part II of this book.

Doniger does note the parallels between popular culture and traditional mythology, especially in science fiction and children's literature (which often utilizes the forms of fantasy). She also allows that "great films have mythic dimensions and often become quasi-myths in our culture."[49] But she also claims that modern Americans who have rejected their traditional religious cultures are left with "an emasculated mythology of atheism and solipsism, a degraded mythology that is found not in churches but in films and children's books." She admits that even this secular mythology has a community of sorts, in, for example, Star Trek conventions and online groups, but holds that "there is no group that will hold them responsible to live in a certain way because of these myths."[50]

Doniger's judgments on popular culture reflect a certain amount of prejudice that may be groundless. There is no reason to assume that people who practice the "religion" of Star Trek follow its dictates any less regularly than American Roman Catholics follow the dictates of the pope, or that their community is less (or more) able to enforce its strictures. All religious communities show the remarkable ability of humans to avoid their own rules as well as sometimes to follow them. There seems no reason to dismiss the religion of popular culture out of hand because it is alleged without evidence to lack morality, commitment, or community, though this judgment is common.[51]

William Doty

William Doty is one scholar of myth who avoids making blanket judgments on popular culture, and who sees the mythic dimensions present in a range of human activities outside of what is normally called "religion." In particular, he rejects the common rationalistic dichotomy between myth and science, as he believes science itself has become a modern myth through which we understand the world. We believe that we have left myth behind, and so entertain the "myth of mythlessness" when in fact we have simply invented a new, scientific myth based in the rejection of transcendence (just as traditional myth was based in its acceptance). In either case, an untestable assumption based in a particular worldview determines what conclusions one will reach about the reality or unreality of the transcendent.[52]

Doty questions the common dichotomy between biblical stories and myths, as the biblical authors themselves used mythological materials to develop their understandings of, for example, the divinity of Jesus.[53] We cannot so rigidly distinguish "our" stories from "theirs," nor distinguish "history" from "myth" as neatly as some scholars would like. All our understandings of events are already colored by a particular mythology; but this does not mean that myths are "false" distortions of history. They are "fictional" in the sense that they are *made* and represent an interpretation of events, but "fictional need not mean unreal and certainly not non-empirical" or incomprehensible, as "the most statistically driven science is shaped by the values of the underlying mythical orientations of cultures."[54] In our history and science as much as in religion, we cannot directly reproduce the object of study without importing our interpretations of it into our analyses; there is no pure objectivity in any discipline, and so all modes of knowing are "fictions" created by us to help us understand the world. We should not denigrate the religious interpretation in relationship to the scientific or historical, as we need a variety of languages and methods to express our varied understandings of reality.

In addition, Doty recognizes the mythological dimensions of popular culture. Aided by postmodernism, he points to the "shattering of a coherent worldview" in Western thought that has brought about a radical "decentering" in our experience.[55] No longer are we able to naively assume that we know what "reality" is or that our systems of thought can reproduce it. Deconstructive criticism looks for multiple meanings rather than a single one in a narrative, and does not assume that there is a single "reality" referred to by it; the various meanings in a text are released and critiqued. In Doty's view, "To deconstruct the mythic text would similarly be to expose the structures by which it works, to lay out the possible alternative futures to which its gestures might lead, to show how its expression is molded and shaped by its cultural contexts."[56] Although Doty thus uses deconstruction as a method of ideological critique, he does not propose abolishing myth altogether as some more reductionist forms of criticism have, largely because he realizes that myth will always be with us in one form or another. He does not then approach myth either totally negatively, or in a "value-neutral" fashion, but via a "progressive, pro-humanistic" method that argues we can re-vision "those oh, so rewarding mythical resources of our common inheritance." Doty makes it clear that he is "not interested in merely sustaining a conservative status quo that represses the mass of our population" but rather hopes "to stimulate ethically involved forays into the possible futures toward which mythological materials give us hints and promises."[57] His utopianism allows him to realize the value and necessity of a mythic worldview in constructing a new future, and makes him willing to look in a variety of places for materials to re-envision it.

Conclusions

These four theorists all offer ideas about myth that can be fruitfully applied to the study of film as religion. With Eliade, we can see that films are mythological in the sense that they create an alternate world, a sacred apart from the profane, and that we enter into a separate space and time when we view a film; this relates to the idea that film offers a sort of alternative reality experience, as noted in the previous chapter. On the other hand, Eliade's tendencies to view most myths as cosmogonies, and to rigidly distinguish myth from history, have been found limiting in the study of religion—just as his assumption that all "real" religion has a transcendent referent may be questioned. He views the myths of popular culture as generally degenerate forms, inferior to traditional religions, and this assumption too must be questioned if we are to have a more objective understanding of film as religion.

With Smith, we can see how myths often involve a fundamental tension or conflict in a situation that is not resolved via the myth so much as laid out for us to observe. Films also deal with conflicts between basic values (e.g., family versus career, or moral conviction versus wealth), usually suggesting that the conflict is illusory, and we can really "have it all" (e.g., be perfect parents and have great jobs), at least in the mythological universe. The fact that a tension remains between the myth and the reality we know in our daily lives indicates that Smith may be right in asserting that the conflict remains unresolved (at least after we leave the theater). But myths, and by extension films, may also be more successful at providing resolution than he is willing to admit. Even if we cannot be *perfect* parents and *perfect* career women/men at the same time, as our filmic counterparts manage to be, the model proposed in the film can serve as an ideal to which we aspire, however inadequately, and one that helps us partially resolve the conflict in our daily lives. Similarly, the Christian ideal of self-sacrificial love is seldom if ever realized adequately, but the story of Christ serves as a model Christians seek to follow; for even though they know they cannot achieve it, it may inspire them to do more than they would otherwise. Smith's understanding of the basic incongruities involved with religion will be discussed again in the next chapter, in relation to the concept of ritual, and there I will have occasion to say more on this point.

Doniger's view of myth can also be applied to films, for although she, like Eliade, views them as degenerate forms of traditional mythology, her analysis of myth applies quite well to films. They are narratives that express some of our culture's understandings of the basic experiences of sex, love, pain, death, and so on, and how we construct meaning in the conflicts surrounding such experiences. Films are also like the Hindu myths described by Doniger that conflate the "reality" of dreams with that of everyday experience, suggesting that the line between the "imaginary" world of myth and our own world is fluid—for films also trade in the "slippage" between the world of the film and the world outside the theater, ever seeking greater "realism" in the viewing experience. In both cases, an alternate reality is proposed that is distinguished from the everyday even while it is related to it, providing a different view of reality that can "correct or complement," as Geertz puts it, our view of the everyday.

Doniger is only really able to denigrate the myths of popular culture through her assumption that they lack the ability to enforce a moral vision. But as I have observed, few American religions can truly enforce their moral visions anymore, unless they are part of isolated communities that have strict sanctions on those who violate their codes. The greater degree of freedom in modern American society, compared to earlier ages or other cultures, may be the real reason why people of many religious backgrounds can basically do what they want without fear of tremendous social repercussions (as long as they do not violate civil law). There is certainly no reason to propose that films lack a moral vision, for while we may not always find the morality of films to be profound or deep, there are clear moral norms that are upheld in most popular films. This does not mean that characters never do a bad thing, or that they are always punished for it, but overall films tend to support a variety of moral positions that are often repeated: for example, violence is justified when used against tyrants or criminals, family and love are more important than money, and individuals who fight for their convictions should be applauded. These moral messages may go unrecognized by audiences, but they are there nonetheless in the narrative and in its appropriation by viewers.

Finally, Doty's view sees myth everywhere from the Bible to popular culture, and so avoids the elitist judgments that distinguish "our" myths from "theirs" or view one as better than the other. This does not mean that he suspends the role of judgment altogether, for he looks to find interpretations of myths that are socially progressive rather than regressive. In this way, he neither rejects popular culture altogether (as "ideology"), nor avoids judgment of it out of a supposed attempt at "tolerance." In chapter 5, we shall look more closely at the question of how to make informed judgments on religion that are based in an effort to understand rather than on mere prejudice, and I will suggest how this might apply to the study of religion and film.

This chapter has sought to critique various ideas of myth in order to suggest that the best of them might profitably be applied to film. The next chapter looks at the concept of ritual and how it might apply to film—and also includes some reflections on the third aspect of the definition of religion, a set of morals, which forms the connecting point between myths and rituals. Myths develop an imaginary view of "that which is," but this is always linked to a notion of "that which should be"—and this ideal is often enacted in ritual.

4

Rituals and Morals

Theories of myth are very often linked to theories of ritual. Rituals have been viewed as myths enacted or dramatized; they re-present the world depicted in the myth, and so provide a link between that world and the realm of the everyday. To be sure, while one is in ritual time and space, one is outside of ordinary (profane) time and space, but ritual makes the religious realm visible in the world in a way that myth cannot. This may be why ritual is often perceived as the place where an attempt is made to actualize the ideal world of myth, to bring its power to bear on ordinary life. If myths present a vision of the way the world is believed to "really" be (at the ultimate level), and as such a vision of the way it ought to be (in the empirical world) as well, then rituals act out that vision by seeking to make the ideal (what ought to be) into the real—and in this way, to connect morality to ordinary life.

Rituals have not always been appreciated as much as myths. Many of the proponents of myth theory have viewed ritual as subordinate and inferior to myth, a mere acting-out of the ideas already present in the myth. In this view, the fact that the myth is enacted ritually is of little religious significance, and one might just as well do without it. Ivan Strenski has argued that this belittling of ritual was linked to anti-Judaism just as the exaltation of myth was linked to Aryan racism.[1] Judaism, as a modern religion based more on performance of rituals than on systematic theology, challenged the mythophiles' thesis that ideas, as expressed in the mythic narrative, are more important than ritual enaction, and for this reason Judaism came under critique for its ritual focus. Of course, there is precedent for this antiritualism even in the origins of Christianity and the denunciations of Pharasaic religion found in the New Testament. As the Pharisees were represented as caring more about the details of ritual than moral practice, Judaism came to be seen by most Christians (as it still is) as a religion excessively focused on mechanical repetition of ritual rather than faith. Protestants in particular have utilized this stereotype, as they likewise criticize Roman Catholicism for its ritual focus. The fact that Protestants themselves have just as many rituals, albeit of different sorts, often goes unacknowledged by them.

Recently, however, rituals have begun to gain more credence as an essential part of religion. Modern groups often invent their own rituals, believing that they have some therapeutic or spiritual value that cannot be supplied simply by hearing or telling stories. In part, this may reflect a reaction against Protestant antiritualism, just as the New Age fascination with myth often reflects a reaction against Christianity—but even within Protestantism there are signs of the increased recognition of ritual, for example, in the practice of more frequent communion. In any case, scholars of religion as well as others are now more willing to admit that ritual, the "doing" of religion, is just as critical to religious life as the beliefs and ideas expressed in mythology or theology. Essentially, religion must be performed to become meaningful.

As with the concepts of religion and myth, there are many understandings of ritual that are possible, and the way in which we conceptualize ritual will affect what we view as ritual and how we view it. In dealing with myth, we were already dealing with ritual to some extent, but there are some specific ideas about ritual that bear discussion (especially in relation to the experiences of film viewing).

In *Ritual: Perspectives and Dimensions*, Catherine Bell has outlined six basic genres of ritual activities: (1) Rites of Passage, (2) Calendrical Rites, (3) Rites of Exchange and Communion, (4) Rites of Affliction, (5) Feasting, Fasting, and Festivals, and (6) Political Rites.[2] These are clearly meant by her not as inviolate or absolute categories, but as scholarly constructions that may be useful in helping us to understand the great variety of ritual activities (which do not easily conform to any typology). Each of these deserves some consideration, although certain of these categories are more relevant to film viewing than others.

First, there are rites of passage from one state in life to another, for example, rituals regarding admission into the community at birth, entering adulthood at puberty, the passage into marriage, and funerals that convey the person into the next world. These are very important rituals, but they seem to have little parallel to the practice of moviegoing itself—unless one considers it a rite of passage to see one's first R-rated movie. On the other hand, movies frequently depict rites of passage and their significance to characters, so that audiences at least vicariously engage in these rituals by identification with the characters. Story events may include formal cere-monies of passage such as weddings and funerals, but also depictions of informal transitions of life such as that into adulthood. Young characters frequently have to undergo some ordeal of maturation (e.g., shooting ra-bies-infected Old Yeller or saving E.T.) that aids in their own personal de-velopment to a new stage of life. Such informal events may not be consid-ered rituals, but when they are dramatized in film they acquire signifi-cance beyond the individual character so that that person's journey becomes one that can be symbolic of our own transitions in life as audi-ence members.

Bell's second category, calendrical rites, seems to have little to do with filmgoing insofar as films gain their power (and their profits) from re-peated viewings rather than once-a-year showings. One might point to the fact that some movies released at Christmastime do deal with the holiday, just as *Independence Day* (appropriately released on July 4, 1996) offered a patriotic devotion to the ideals of American civil religion celebrated at that time of year, but even in such cases the film's link to the day is tenu-ous as it is viewed at plenty of other times. In fact, before the invention of the VCR, it was probably easier to argue for the link between certain films and certain days, as they might only appear on television once each year. *The Wizard of Oz* (1939) obtained much of its power for a whole genera-tion that grew up seeing it in this ritualized fashion; but even in this case, the day on which it was shown had no particular significance for one's in-terpretation of the movie. Most of the ritual significance of films is clearly not related to the sort of "founding events" usually commemorated by re-ligions on an annual basis, such as harvest and solstice festivals, births of founders, or memorials of conquest over enemies.

Momentarily skipping to the last of Bell's categories—political rituals that promote, display, or construct power—we may see some connections between this type of ritual and the experience of film viewing. Films often promote political ideologies, and although they are not coronation cere-monies they may assist in constructing power relationships, as ideological critics have observed. It may be obvious that a film has a political message, as in 1968's *The Green Berets* (which offered John Wayne's rather unpopu-lar defense of the Vietnam War), or it may be less obvious, as in a film like *Forrest Gump* (1994), which most people took as a "feel-good" movie about a mentally challenged man who succeeds just by "being nice," but which is also a revisionist history of the 1960's that manages to belittle those who protested the Vietnam War even more effectively than *The*

Green Berets. This shows that a film may be more successful as political propaganda to the extent that it hides its objectives and appears to be just entertainment or a "personal" story.

There is a great deal of good ideological analysis of film that highlights its political messages, explicit or otherwise. I have criticized such forms of analysis for their limited focus in that they look only at this ideological dimension and so often miss other ritual functions of films. This is not to deny the importance of such analysis or the fact that many films clearly have such ideological dimensions to them, and I will not eschew ideological analysis in my own examination of particular films later in this book. I will not spend much time on this aspect here, however, partly because it has been so well covered by others and partly because I am pointing to other ritual functions of film besides the political or ideological.

Bell's remaining three categories have certain similarities among them that also may connect these types of rituals with filmgoing. Rites of exchange and communion, which include offerings and sacrifices; rites of affliction, purification, healing, and catharsis; and rituals of feasting, fasting, and festivals—all involve giving and receiving gifts that symbolize connection and mutual obligations between two parties. A communion or covenant is established by such giving and receiving, whether it be concrete sacrifices of food or blood or sacrifices enacted by self-affliction of cuts or whippings. Such rites of affliction are viewed by modern Western sensibilities as "masochistic," implying a psychological assessment of them as neurotic; but to understand such rituals it is more helpful to look to their religious functions, associated with purification and healing. In order to heal, whether of sin or disease (often viewed as the same thing in many religions), there must be something given up; and as pain gives up pleasure, this is one form of sacrifice. It is not so much payment for the healing, as it is an indication of the commitment (of the patient or the healer) to the task that requires this sacrifice. Similarly, fasting expresses a giving up, a penitent attitude on the part of one who voluntarily separates himself from the worldly pleasures of food.

Such rituals of sacrifice are perhaps more often accused of being sadistic rather than masochistic, as they may inflict pain and suffering on a surrogate victim. The centrality of such rituals to religion and the important role their assessment has played in religious studies makes them worth examining in greater detail, especially because they have parallel to many of the ritual functions associated with film viewing.

Sacrifice of the Scapegoat

One of the most influential interpretations of religious ritual can be traced to the work of James Frazer in his magnum opus *The Golden Bough* (1890–1915). Here he suggested that the central act of religion is the ritual performance of the murder of a king in order to pass his magical power to the next ruler, or to release his divine energy into nature and so guarantee agricultural fertility. Myths of the death and resurrection of a god or ruler are viewed by Frazer as linked to the need to bring new life to the crops each spring, as someone must be killed to supply the life force needed for new growth. Since kings do not usually relish being sacrificed on an annual basis, substitutions were often made; a slave or an animal might serve the purpose. Frazer also noted that cannibalism is linked to this form of ritual, as the victim is sometimes eaten in order to utilize his life force as a source of energy. Frazer held that even Christian beliefs about the salvation gained by Christ's death and resurrection, and the need to "eat his body" in order to gain this benefit, relate to this form of ritual.[3]

Although Frazer's analysis has been severely criticized for its tendency to ignore details of individual rituals and myths that do not fit with his theories, and for oversimplifying the history of religion and ritual, he has proven very influential. Sigmund Freud developed his understanding of the history of religion in part from Frazer's idea that tribes seek to replace their rulers via a ritual process that legitimates their murder and sanctions its necessity—this being, for Freud, an instance of the universal Oedipus complex that desires the death of the father.[4] Mircea Eliade's view, already discussed, also focused on myths of death and resurrection as linked to rituals meant to restore agricultural life and new growth. And most recently, René Girard has developed the view that the history of religion is based on violence directed against a sacrificial scapegoat.

Girard's theory, developed out of both Frazer and Freud's works, suggests that religion evolves out of a "mimetic desire" to replicate the being of the other. This desire of the self for the other is doomed to frustration insofar as it is a desire to violently take the other's life, and yet to do so is to destroy the source of the desire itself. For this reason, a surrogate victim is chosen to be the one on whom anger and violence are released. Once the victim is destroyed, the community can be restored, as the tensions aroused by desire have been dissolved—until they build up again, requiring a similar ritual. Girard believes this violence goes unchallenged in the whole history of religion until Christianity, which effectively criticizes the act of scapegoating by showing the injustice of Christ's murder and so proposes an end to the violence.[5]

Girard, like Frazer, risks oversimplification of the history of religion by proposing that mimetic desire is the source of all religious ritual, and that all religion is based in violence. But Girard, like Frazer before him, has hit upon a feature of religion that, even if it is not the key to all ritual, is a major factor in many rituals. Sacrifice and scapegoating are common religious practices and many rituals are structured around these functions. It is also clear that many films engage in scapegoating, and that audiences experience some sort of catharsis in seeing victims violently sacrificed in movies. This may explain the popularity of horror movies as well as action movies that feature ever-increasing doses of violence. Although special effects have made it easier to depict violence (through the use of computer-generated images), there is also an appetite for extreme images of violence that is fed by such films. It is common to blame the movie and television industry for promoting and making such images, but this criticism ignores the fact that they tend to give audiences what they want, that is, what sells. No one is making people see violent movies; they go to see them with eagerness, again and again, so that if movies are to become less violent it will have to be because people stop liking violent movies. At the present time, this prospect does not seem very likely.

There is a great temptation to moralize on this point, and it may in fact be necessary to make moral judgments on the violent nature of films (as well as of religion). But I have also argued from the beginning of this book that one cannot legitimately critique or dismiss films (or religions) without first seeking to understand what they are saying, and violent films are no exception to this rule. We should be wary, most of all, of setting ourselves up as judges over certain phenomena with the implication that we have achieved some superiority over them. When Girard, for example, argues that Christianity has transcended scapegoating, he puts himself in a good position to criticize everything else. While he acknowledges that Christianity has not in practice held to its ideals very well, and so has also participated in the evils of scapegoating, his idealized construction of Christianity still allows him to take the high moral ground. Perhaps Christianity is not as different from other religions as he would like to think, and perhaps the positive features he finds in the Christian critique of scapegoating are not altogether absent from other religious traditions. After all, there is a significant tradition of the critique of sacrifice in many religions, including Judaism and Islam (as God is not believed to require a violent sacrifice to forgive) as well as in Hinduism and Buddhism (in which nonviolence is a fundamental principle; theistic Hinduism has also argued that the grace of God is so great that sacrifice is unnecessary for atonement).[6]

There are also other ways to understand the power and benefit of sacrifice besides that proposed by Girard, and perhaps better ways of understanding why people regard it as valuable. His rejection of cults of sacrifice actually has a long history in Western culture, as both Judaism and Christianity have for almost two millennia eschewed sacrificial cult because "God desires mercy and not sacrifice." It is believed by both religions that we do not need to offer up victims to atone for our sins, as God's mercy and our repentance are sufficient. What is often ignored, however, is the fact that the destruction in the year 70 c.e. of the temple in Jerusalem was what ended the Jewish cult of sacrifice, and not philosophical or moral objections to its practice. Christians, also, developed the view that Christ is the final sacrifice largely after the destruction of the temple, and they thereafter understood his significance in the light of this end of the cult. All moralizing about sacrifice, then, should take into account that its rejection in Western culture was based not on a critique of the notion of sacrifice itself, but on the fact that it was no longer possible or necessary to perform sacrifices in the Judeo-Christian tradition. It can even be claimed that the idea of sacrifice remains critical to these religions in spite of its literal impossibility for Jews (due to the absence of a temple) and its metaphysical superfluity for Christians (due to the final nature of Christ's sacrifice). The Jewish thinker Michael Wyschogrod, for example, has argued that sacrifice is still a critical part of Judaism that is often illegitimately ignored. He claims that the modern rationalist rejection of sacrifice ignores the ritual need to confront God that is supplied by sacrifice. Furthermore, Wyschogrod points to the fact that Jewish commemoration of the cult of sacrifice (e.g., on Yom Kippur) itself constitutes a form of the cult, as the idea of sacrifice is not totally rejected; indeed, prayers for the return of the temple and thereby the cult of sacrifice are also part of contemporary Jewish religious observance.[7]

If we are to allow such a positive function to sacrifice, we might be willing to counter Girard's suggestion that it is based in a violent desire for the life of the other with the assertion that its purpose is to ritually expiate one's own guilt—which is, after all, the stated purpose of rituals of sacrifice. Neither is this expiation accomplished in a mechanical fashion without the repentance of the sinner, which remains a precondition for the efficacy of the sacrifice. Sacrifice should not be understood as an alternative to repentance, as if it excused one from taking responsibility for one's sins in its "projection" of sins onto another, but rather as the external act that gives physical expression to the internal act of repentance.[8] This is true for the ancient Jewish ritual of driving the scapegoat off a cliff just as it is for the ritual commemoration of Christ's death in the sacrament of communion. Perhaps we need to redefine the term "scapegoating," noting that it did not originally imply its contemporary meaning of "blaming someone else for your sins," but rather a ritual whereby one's own *repented* sins are carried away via a sacrificial act. In both Judaism and Christianity, the ritual could not be effective in removing one's sins unless the sinner had already repented and believed in this ritual as the completion of the process of repentance rather than its replacement.

One might argue, especially in the case of the Christian view, that God's act of sacrifice in Christ precedes and grounds our act of repentance, making it possible; but it is still true that the death of Christ will be ineffective for those who do not repent and allow God's act to be efficacious in bringing salvation. Even those theologians, like Augustine, who have insisted that it is God alone who saves us (as we lack the free will to repent) have had to admit that the sinner cannot be saved unless he repents; they simply viewed that act of repentance as ultimately made possible by God, as the one who makes the human will repentant. Whether it comes from God or ourselves, however, that repentance is necessary to make the salvation brought by the sacrifice effective.

Another apparent difference between the Christian view of sacrifice and other religious views of sacrifice is that, in Christianity, God offers up the sacrifice rather than humans. But even here, the sacrifice must be offered by one who is human as well as divine, or it will not be effective as a means of atonement and reconciliation with God. Christ is not viewed as a *replacement* or *substitute* for us so much as a *representative* who makes possible our reconnection to God; as such, the fact that he is human is crucial in allowing an identification with him and thereby our own repentance.[9]

Against Girard, then, I would argue that sacrificial "scapegoating" is based not in a violent desire to destroy the other that is projected onto an innocent third party, but in the need to be reconciled to the god(s), to present a gift to the divine as sign of one's contrition, to heal the gap that has opened between the divine and the human as a consequence of human wrongdoing. Girard views the Christian idea of sacrifice as unique in representing a critique of sacrifice as such, chiefly because the victim is *perceived* as being innocent and his murder as unjust. However, this idea, too, already had precedent in the Jewish notion that righteous martyrs who were killed for their faith in God can, by their death, atone not only for their own sins but for those of others as well. This concept is found in the "suffering servant" poem in Isaiah 52–53, and it was developed in later Jewish writings.[10] The idea that those unjustly murdered for their faith might serve as an atoning sacrifice for sin is continuous with the notion that one offers up something of great worth to God as a sign of one's devotion and repentance, and it does not necessarily discredit the idea of sacrifice as such. The difference is in the fact that the martyrs (and Jesus) willingly went to their deaths and were not unwilling scapegoats. In being a sacrifice for the sins of others, then, they can only be viewed by those others with feelings of gratitude and the desire to emulate their faith and sacrifice, as they are held up as a model "for the godly life." This encourages their followers likewise to be willing to sacrifice to God, whether it is their possessions or their lives. It might be argued that sacrifice has always represented such a giving of self rather than a projection of guilt onto another.

Surely, Girard is right to criticize those forms of sacrifice and scapegoating that sanction violence, especially against oppressed groups who are accused of either imaginary crimes or the crimes of the group in power. He is right to note a family resemblance between the lynch mob and the sacrificial cult, but he is wrong to ignore the differences. There may also be an important function to sacrifice that cannot be entirely discarded, which cannot be met in any other way. This does not mean that all forms of sacrifice are equally acceptable ethically, but that it may be impossible to avoid all notions of sacrifice in any religion, even though some may be more "ethical" than others, meaning, for example, that they do not rest on violence done involuntarily to other persons. Christianity, too, may not have left sacrifice behind so much as transformed it, just as each religion develops the concept of sacrifice in its own way. To suggest that the Christian approach to sacrifice is the only valid one is to fail to look at how the concept functions in diverse religious traditions, many of which may have equally "valid" concepts—if by "valid" we mean that it functions as a ritualized expression of penitence that does not sanction involuntary violence toward others or the avoidance of responsibility for one's own misdeeds.

Sacrifice in Theater and Film

I have spent some time on the concepts of sacrifice and scapegoating be-cause these ideas appear as part of the rituals of filmgoing as well. This is not so surprising when one notes the long history of these ideas in associ-ation with literature and theater. It is not always recognized that Frazer had a great effect not only on religious studies but also on literary studies, and that his own work is sometimes considered more part of literary criti-cism than religious criticism.[11] Also, Girard has a background in literature and has continued to write in this field.[12] This situation appears less coin-cidental when one looks deeper into the history of literary theory, as Aris-totle's *Poetics*—the text that has been regarded as the basis for almost all subsequent theory of theater, and for a good deal of literary theory—de-velops an understanding of tragedy, the highest form of drama (in Aristo-tle's estimation), based on an interpretation of Sophocles' *Oedipus Rex* that emphasizes its connection with scapegoating.

Aristotle defines a tragedy as follows: "Tragedy, then, is the imitation of an action that is serious and also, as having magnitude, complete in itself; in language with pleasurable accessories, each kind brought in separately in the parts of the work; in a dramatic, not in a narrative form; with inci-dents arousing pity and fear, wherewith to accomplish its catharsis of such emotions."[13]

Aristotle differed from Plato in his appreciation of theater chiefly be-cause he believed the "catharsis of emotions" it involved was not harmful but healthy. Theater satisfies the need people feel to express certain poten-tially negative emotions, such as pity or fear, but in a socially acceptable manner. In order for theater to be effective in arousing pity and fear, how-ever, certain plots are to be avoided. First, the plot should not involve a good person passing from happiness to misery, as this is "not fear-inspir-ing or piteous, but simply odious." Second, it should not involve a bad person passing from misery to happiness, as the injustice of this arouses no pity or fear. Third, it should not involve an extremely bad person falling from happiness to misery, as this will arouse neither pity nor fear, for "pity is occasioned by undeserved misfortune, and fear by that of one like ourselves," with neither condition being met in this situation. What remains, then, is "the intermediate kind of personage, a man not preemi-nently virtuous and just, whose misfortune, however, is brought upon him not by vice and depravity but by some error of judgment."[14] In this way, we see someone with whom we can identify, who is neither perfectly good nor perfectly evil, who suffers because of a "tragic flaw" that leads him to disaster. This situation results in catharsis because we are able to feel the suffering of another even while we recognize that it is not wholly undeserved. We identify with the tragic hero as a victim of fate even while we realize that he has made that fate through his own actions.

Sophocles' *Oedipus Rex* typifies Aristotle's view of tragedy and is used repeatedly by him as an example. In this play, Oedipus has already killed his father and married his mother long ago, but still does not know this as he was adopted by others shortly after his birth and never knew who his true parents were. As ruler of Thebes, he seeks to find out who has brought suffering on his city, only to find that it is he who has done this as a result of his transgressions. After learning the truth, he blinds himself. His own desire to know and his pride and overconfidence are his undoing. The pleasure of the tragedy, according to Aristotle, is that Oedipus is not a very bad man, and in fact he means to do good, so we can identify and sympathize with him; and yet he has committed evil deeds (albeit unknowingly) and so deserves punishment. This means that his suffering is not "odious" to us, although we regret it and suffer with him. Oedipus may be considered a "sacrifice for our own sins" insofar as we can identify with him (as one who is neither totally good nor totally bad) and can experience catharsis in witnessing and *participating* in his suffering. He is a "scapegoat" in the sense we have defined the term, not as one whose suffering *replaces* ours, but as one whose suffering *represents* our suffering.

Literary scholars have noted the connection between religious ritual and drama, and in particular the structure of tragedy as interpreted by Aristotle. In a seminal essay, Francis Fergusson argued that *Oedipus Rex* is best understood in relation to religious rituals of the sacrifice of the king or a surrogate (following Frazer's view) to restore life to the infertile city.[15] According to such a view, Sophocles saw drama as a means of conveying the ideas of sacrifice and redemption present in the old myths. The redemption of Oedipus himself is enacted by the end of Sophocles' oedipal trilogy, in *Oedipus in Colonus*. A similar structure can be found in Aeschylus's *Oresteia* trilogy, as Orestes is redeemed at the end of the last play, *The Furies*, when the titular entities are deprived of their vengeance on Orestes for the murder of his mother and he is restored and forgiven. As with Oedipus, we feel for Orestes and desire his restoration because we identify with him and can understand how he came to commit his crime, even if we cannot excuse it—in his case, he killed his mother, Clytemnestra, for killing his father, Agamemnon; and his mother's deed in turn was understandable, as Agamemnon had (albeit reluctantly) sacrificed their daughter to the gods in fulfillment of an oath to do so if he had victory in battle. We can identify and sympathize with all the characters in this story, and that is what makes it such a fine tragedy, in Aristotle's terms.

Some scholars have criticized Fergusson's thesis, suggesting that there are more differences between religious rituals and drama than similarities, as rituals involve a designated community that participates in certain actions in order to effect a certain result.[16] But the similarities still exist, and the effect of a drama on an audience can be just as significant as the effect of a religious ritual; there may even be no real distinction between the two, except that we call one "religion" and one "theater." There are also communities of theatergoers and filmgoers, after all, which at least exist during the performance and often outside of it as well, and the functions the drama performs may be basically the same as those performed by the rituals we more often designate "religious," namely, the transmission of catharsis, redemption, hope, and so forth.

If there is a connection between tragedies and religious rituals of sacrifice or scapegoating, perhaps it is in the fact that both help people to recognize the imperfections in themselves and in others, to admit the suffering associated with such imperfections, and to work to overcome such. The possibility of forgiveness and redemption is also invoked. To suggest these things is not to "Christianize" either tragedy or the related rituals, as Aristotle's view was developed long before the Christian era, and its continuing influence on theater is not strictly confined to the Christian background of Western civilization. Even as significant a non-Western myth as the Indian religious epic, the *Mahabharata*, seems to have much the same structure when dramatized, in that audiences can identify with the characters and feel their tragic plight because they have both good and bad qualities, and often do not fully deserve what happens to them.

In this story, one set of cousins must displace the other from the throne of the kingdom to restore justice and peace to the land, even though this forces them to do combat with beloved members of their own family. It is not an imposition of Christian or Greek categories on this story to note the tragic qualities of Karna, who unwittingly becomes the enemy of his own brothers when he pledges his allegiance to their enemies, or those of Bhisma and Drona, who fight for the king against those whom they have raised and taught as their own children. Everyone must do their duty (*dharma*) in this Hindu epic, and they are redeemed for doing so in spite of (or perhaps because of) the suffering this action brings on them. This is clearly the religious message of the *Bhagavad Gita*, the climax of the *Mahabharata*, in which Krishna tells Arjuna he must do his duty and fight even though it may seem wrong to do so. I do not mean to deny the uniqueness of Hindu tragedy in distinction from Greek or Christian tragedy, or to insist on a "universal form" of tragedy, but simply to suggest that there are cross-cultural similarities here in the notions of suffering that is only partially deserved, fates that must be accepted, and possible redemption that results from virtuous behavior.

Interestingly, however, most films do not utilize the classic structure of tragedy—because even though they have elements in them that parallel aspects of tragedy, including sacrifice and scapegoating, these elements are understood in a variety of ways that differ from their use in tragedy. The *Godfather* films represent a somewhat rare case of a set of films that do approach classic tragedy. We identify with Michael Corleone and understand how he is led to do evil to protect those he loves, even while we also see that he deserves the punishment that befalls him in the loss of his family—the very thing he sought to save. But even these films are not exactly like classic tragedies in that they also have characteristics of the gangster film genre; in particular, audiences admire and like the gangsters, identifying with them even in their acts of violence that are viewed as justified in the context of the film. This genre allows audiences a fantasy of rebellion and power, even though the gangsters suffer for their rebellion in the end. In this way, we might consider them to be the scapegoats who represent our own selfish desire for power and who are also punished for it in our place—but this "punishment" may not be viewed as entirely deserved by those who identify with the gangsters' resistance to the dominant culture.

There are also those films in which the hero sacrifices himself (or herself) for a greater cause, and in these too the hero may be flawed and so in need of atonement for his or her own sins. These are not exactly tragedies in that the hero is not required to suffer *because* of misdeeds, necessarily, but takes on suffering partly for the sake of others and partly because recognition of his or her own imperfections leads the character to choose a certain path. It may be that a past history of violence taints the hero, as in *Shane* (1953), so that even though he is the only one who can dispatch the villains he must leave at the end to keep "guns out of the valley." He knows that he will always be a gunslinger and cannot avoid the consequences, which include exclusion from society and family life. We are relieved that he saves the farmers, and so identify with them, but we also identify with Shane in his imperfections, which we share—for all of us have violent impulses we need to control, just as he does. The fact that this prevents him from being more fully integrated into society is his personal tragedy. He is the scapegoat for our violent feelings that are projected upon him, but this does not disown us of responsibility for them (as Girard might say). Rather, he represents our guilt and suffering related to our own ambiguous feelings about violence; we sometimes believe it is necessary, even though it cannot be accepted as part of normal societal behavior. The fact that we feel for him shows that we feel the pain of his difficult decision, and that even if he does the dirty work we share in it as the ones represented by him.

It is not only Westerns that have such "tainted heroes" whose sins lead them to sacrifice for others. *Sling Blade* (1996) dealt with a retarded man who had been in a criminal institution since childhood after he hacked to death his mother and her illicit lover. He now understands the consequences of his actions and so is released into the world. He meets a family who befriends him (just as Shane did) and who are in need of protection from the woman's abusive boyfriend. The hero takes it upon himself to kill the abuser as he feels it is necessary, even though he believes murderers go to hell, as he wants to save the family. He suffers for being the only one who could save them, like Shane, and in a similar way audiences felt his suffering as one who is excluded from society for doing the dirty work we would like to do ourselves. Our guilt is projected onto him, but we also feel that guilt and pain as our own.

Such films may be criticized for giving tacit approval to the violence of the heroes, and may be viewed as simply expressing the dominant ideology that legitimates violence in the service of "self-defense." They certainly express and contribute to the common morality that finds violence easy to sanction and excuse. But in seeking to understand the appeal of these films, we need to understand the need they fulfill of dealing with our conflicted thoughts and feelings regarding violence and its justification. Every religious tradition has wrestled with these issues, and the filmic religion does as well.

Horror movies also feature sacrificial victims, who tend to be (at least in recent movies) sexually active teenagers. In this sense, they are "guilty" of actions deemed sinful by parents though not really by the young audiences that see such films. It can be suggested that audiences identify with these victims because they feel they deserve punishment for their own sexual "sins," and they experience catharsis through witnessing their destruction. But it is also an important fact that horror movies are seldom taken seriously, so that the ritual performed by their viewers may be one of laughingly denying that there is any boogey-man waiting to kill them when they have sex. The whole idea of punishment for sexual transgressions is rejected in the comic tone these films assume, and in the humorous appropriation of them by their audiences.

It can also be observed that films frequently deal with suffering that seems totally undeserved, and the genre of "melodrama" is sometimes distinguished from tragedy in this aspect. Aristotle dismissed such stories as incapable of arousing fear or pity in us, but it is hard to see why. Granted that we do not feel fear or pity for an evil character, whether he suffers good fortune or bad, if an innocent character suffers that situation seems quite capable of arousing both our pity and our fear. Perhaps Aristotle's objection to the dramatization of totally undeserved suffering is more moral than aesthetic; it may be equally cathartic for the audience, but it depicts a less just situation. What audiences see in a melodrama is not punishment for wrongdoing, but a representation of how to deal with suffering that is not deserved, which is another important function of religion.

The success of a film (or novel) like *Gone With the Wind* (1939), for example, is surely due in large part to women's ability to identify with Scarlett O'Hara and her troubles, even though they are clearly not all her fault. Some feminist analysis of "women's films" (perhaps the most popular form of film melodrama) has suggested that the apparently undeserved suffering of the heroines is in fact implied to be deserved by the narrative, and that women are thereby told they deserve to suffer—especially when they seek to challenge the male hierarchy. But another analysis might conclude that women enjoy these films not because they have accepted the idea that they deserve to suffer, but because they identify with the women who are made to suffer so undeservingly. They find resources for how to deal with the unjust suffering they undergo through witnessing and participating in the heroic efforts of female characters to challenge and overcome their situations, even when they are ultimately not successful. When the heroine of *Waterloo Bridge* (1931/1940) is forced to turn to prostitution to survive after her true love goes off to war, we are not meant to think that she deserves this fate, but that circumstances have unjustly forced her to it. Such films are "tearjerkers" because they make audiences (especially women) cry with sympathy; they can identify with them, and they see how an unjust world often makes women suffer. There is an implied criticism of a male-dominated world that does not give the same options to women as it does to men, and that makes women pay dearly for this. Male viewers of *Anna Karenina* (1935/1948) may have thought the adulterous heroine gets what she deserves, but female viewers may have identified with her as one who could only find true love outside of a marriage that was like a prison. Just because women lose out at the end of such films, this does not mean that the films support the status quo; they are simply being realistic about the patriarchal nature of the world, even while they critique it. In a similar way, the female action movie *Thelma and Louise* (1991) was criticized for telling audiences that women who challenge patriarchy must die, but the film was rather clear in its message that they do not deserve to do so. Their choice to die rather than be captured implies a rejection of the male world, even though it means they can no longer live in this world at all. If they really had escaped to Mexico, the criticism of patriarchy might even have been muted as this would make it appear as if patriarchy was not such a serious threat to women's lives. The fact that women who have challenged patriarchal structures die at the end of a movie does not automatically make the audience think it is right that they die. Along these lines one could note that no one claimed *Boys Don't Cry* (1999) was a sexist film because it told the true story of a woman who was raped and murdered for assuming the role of a man; rather, it challenged the sexist forces that killed her by its clear depiction of their brutal and violent consequences.

We can see, then, that there are numerous ways in which films may offer rituals by means of which audiences can identify with characters and their sufferings, whether such sufferings are viewed as just or unjust. In either case, a catharsis of emotions is achieved, but also a message is received about how to deal with such sufferings and the conflicts associated with them. Films, and religious rituals, involve cognitive strategies to help us deal with life as well as affective release of emotions; to view them as only involving cognition or only emotion would be to miss the fact that such rituals address the whole person in its dimensions as a thinking, emotional, and moral being. As Geertz put it, suffering poses challenges to all three of these faculties (intellectual explanation, emotional endurance, and moral will) which require a response; and that response is often made by religious rituals.

Liminality and Carnivals: Challenging and/or Reinforcing the Status Quo

There are obviously many other functions of ritual activity that cannot be reduced to forms of sacrifice. Alongside rituals of fasting, which seem to express a penitential function, Bell places rituals of feasting that may express thanksgiving (especially as a feast after a fast) or a sense of the unity of the community. They may also express the power of the giver who creates a sense of obligation in those to whom he gives the feast, as in North American potlatch festivals for which the host spends a small fortune. There is nothing really analogous to this ritual function in moviegoing in spite of the large amount of candy and popcorn consumed in theaters.

There is another type of ritual Bell mentions that I have not yet touched upon, however, and that is the "carnival." Carnivals feature an atmosphere of jubilation and celebration; but more than that, they rejoice in lampooning the status quo and even apparently reversing or overthrowing it. The anthropologist Victor Turner made the study of this aspect of ritual a focal point of his own research, as he argued that societies need to periodically challenge the status quo in this ritualized fashion. Turner draws on the work of his predecessor Arnold van Gennep, who analyzed the structure of rites of passage as including a separation from the community, a "liminal" phase during which one exists outside the community, and a reintegration into the community at a new level.[17] Tribal male puberty rituals, for example, clearly utilize this schema. Turner develops this idea by suggesting that the liminal phase involves a suspension of societal structures that allows people to engage in activities that would normally be considered inappropriate or even obscene. Among the Ndembu, for example, a ritual of cross-sexual joking involves the chanting of songs that refer frankly to sexual organs and functions as men and women comically insult each other with accusations of adultery even while they exalt their sexual prowess over the opposite gender. But this ritual can only occur because a special formula has been previously chanted that legitimates such normally inappropriate behavior for the purposes of the ritual; in this way, the "singing is without shame" because it is done for healing purposes, in this case, to strengthen a woman who is about to bear (or has just born) twins.[18]

One might wonder why displays of obscenity would help a pregnant woman. Turner suggests that the connection can be found in the fact that twins were perceived as a danger in the African cultures he studied, and that danger required drastic (ritual) action to be neutralized. It was not only that twins involved a practical hardship for the mother (who must nurse two children, etc.), but that twins are unusual enough to be viewed as representing a potential threat. Twins are strange in being two yet one, and this strangeness must be domesticated as part of the social order through some appreciation of their unity-in-duality. Men and women represent a similar unity-in-duality as they are distinct and yet can operate in harmony, and indeed must in order for society to survive.[19] This is why a ritual that jokingly depicts the tensions between the sexes via normally inappropriate humor can serve as a way of calling attention to the differences, and yet also reassert the harmony of the two—not only through a joyous depiction of sexual union, but through the fact that after this liminal suspension of decorum, life returns to its normal structure. The need for the structure of society or proper gender relations is asserted precisely through its questioning, because that questioning occurs in a liminal period in which the normal rules are suspended. One can gain a new appreciation for structure through momentarily stepping outside of it, and that is what such rituals do for the communities that practice them.

Aside from simply depicting a contrast with the ordinary, however, the liminal phase of ritual can also depict the ideal of the unstructured community, what Turner calls "communitas." In communitas, in distinction from the hierarchically structured society, all are equal and there is no ranking to give one power over another (except perhaps the authority of the ritual elders).[20] This form of utopia cannot really exist, as no society can exist without structure—but this utopian ideal of communitas is just as critical to the functioning of society as the realism that requires structure, for it reminds a people of their essential unity and the need for all to exercise power justly and benevolently toward everyone.[21] Turner describes, from the notes of McKim Marriott, the Holi festival of Indian villages as a form of ritual that demonstrates the necessity of communitas. All normal rules of propriety are suspended at this time, so that low-caste people may without fear "beat up" and ridicule members of the upper classes. The comic tone assures that no one is really hurt, though the measures taken may be more than merely symbolic. The village landlord had diesel oil poured on his head, Brahmins are hit with sticks by female latrine cleaners, husbands are attacked by their wives, a moneylender was given a mock funeral, and the anthropologist (Marriott) was made to dance in the streets wearing a necklace of shoes. The "victims" in each case, however, are seen to be smiling and seemingly enjoying the disgrace, as they undoubtedly know the humiliation is temporary and represents a harmless challenge to their authority. But it is not only a reversal of status that takes place, in which the subordinate become insubordinate; there are also unlikely alliances formed in the streets between members of upper and lower classes, as Brahmins and washermen sing together, and priests and water carriers join together in throwing dirt on leading citizens. Turner views this as evidence of the fact that communitas is being ritually established as a place in which social distinctions are not reversed but abolished altogether. This reminds everyone of the ideal of unity, even as it reestablishes the hierarchy in purified form at the end of the ritual.[22]

This sort of ritual is not totally absent from Western societies. The favorite high school teacher or coach who is thrown into the swimming pool at the end of the year usually bears this well because the "disrespect" in this case represents an attempt by students to overcome the structured gap between the teacher and themselves in order to show affection—in Turner's terms, communitas. Turner also notes that the ritual of Hallowe'en represents an opportunity for children to challenge their low social status with the imaginary threat of a "trick" and their allegedly frightening costumes, and so to deal with their own fears of authority figures by acting the criminal (e.g., pirate or gunslinger).[23]

We also find the "inappropriate" or extreme enacted in popular films, and that is why this aspect of ritual is particularly apposite to our analysis. Frequently, moralistic or religious response to films condemns the outrageous behavior of movie characters as they make such poor role models. This argument misses the point that many people have no intention of actually doing the things they see done in movies; the benefit they receive from seeing the "extreme" enacted is not moral advice on how to behave. Rather, viewers see the film's characters flouting authority and structure, and this serves both to maintain that very structure (through the temporary challenge to it, which delineates its opposite) and to challenge it by expressing the hope for an alternative form of society. This alternative may not always look like utopia, but it tends to express some of the hopes of the target audience.

Movies targeted at adolescents express liminality particularly well. Most of the teenagers who liked *Risky Business* (1983) did not emulate the protagonist in setting up brothels in their parents' homes, but they vicariously enjoyed this extreme action as a form of protest against the strictures of their own lives. It also can be noted that the hero does not take this course as a sort of deliberate affront to his parents; rather, he is coerced into it after he hires a prostitute, and then finds himself initially unable to pay her high fee. Her boss robs his house, and in order to restore his parents' possessions he agrees to host the "risky business." Needless to say, all is returned to normal by the time his parents return so that they never know; in addition, his brothel inadvertently services an admissions counselor from Princeton, who in gratitude assures his admission to the college. No teenager would consider this a realistic way to get into a good school, so parents need not fear their children will take the narrative as a literal model for their own behavior; but it does allow young people to temporarily step outside of acceptable norms of behavior so that they might return to their prescribed roles refreshed and perhaps willing to accept them for the sake of structure. The hero is allowed to do this, as he ends up following the role his parents expect of him, being a good student at a good school—and no consequences for his rebellion are observed. The filmgoers, through identification with him, undergo the same process of stepping outside cultural norms in the viewing of the film, as well as the return to normalcy when they leave the theater. In their case, too, there is no punishment for the ritual participation in normally proscribed behavior. Their desire for freedom is affirmed and legitimated in the context of the film, even while they know that such an ideal is impossible in the "real" world.

The inappropriate behavior is not always sexual in nature. In *Ferris Bueller's Day Off* (1986) the hero is a high school student who skips class for the day with his friends, and manages to avoid both detection by his parents and capture by a school administrator. Their adventures seemingly have no ill consequences except for the friend's willful destruction of his father's prize sports car, but this is legitimated as a necessary if drastic measure for getting the attention of his neglectful father. Ferris, however, has loving parents who believe he has been sick in bed all day and think of him as sweet and kind—which he actually is, as he is a loving son and friend who has no desire to hurt anyone. He is thus able to step outside of structure for the day, but can also return to it without resentment and without consequence.

Movies directed toward even younger viewers also feature plots in which the child heroes challenge the structures of their lives, notably the subordination to parental authority that prevents them from taking any really significant action. Children desire control over their lives that societal structures do not allow them, and so they enjoy movies that indulge their fantasies of having the upper hand. Classic children's books (often made into films as well) also have this structure, in that parents may die or disappear toward the beginning of the narrative (e.g., *The Secret Garden*, *The Little Princess*, *James and the Giant Peach*, and even *The Cat in the Hat*) in order to allow the children to respond to and control the action more directly. In *E.T., The Extraterrestrial* (1982), the father has left and the mother remains, but she is so distracted that she does not even notice the alien in her house. This leaves the children to care for him, and ultimately to get him to his spaceship in defiance of the authorities. Viewers enjoy watching the children seize control, for in this way they show what children would like to believe about themselves, that they know better than the grownups what is right.

It is not only movies designed for adolescents and children that depict "liminal" behavior we are not really meant to emulate. Infidelity is frequently romanticized in films, and although there are usually consequences for such immoral behavior, audiences temporarily enjoy stepping outside accepted norms as much as children do. Even those who would never consider infidelity may be refreshed by their identification with unfaithful spouses. Women's romantic fiction operates on this premise, providing faithful wives with a fantasy escape from their marriages—not that their marriages are necessarily bad, but they enjoy the temporary suspension of structure that such narratives invoke. The immense popularity of the book and film *The Bridges of Madison County* (1995) was largely due to the tremendous sympathy the story creates for its heroine, who is married to a good man with good kids and yet longs for adventure and romance, found in the traveling photographer with whom she has a brief affair. She stays with her husband in the end out of duty and love of family, but she still felt the pull to escape. The story is told in retrospect, as her grown children have discovered her diary many years later after her death, and the legitimacy of her feelings is finally recognized by them when they accept her dying wish to have her ashes tossed off one of the bridges she associated with her illicit lover. Initially repelled by this, they come to allow this ritual closure to her life precisely because she remained a dutiful mother all her life (accepting structure) and so can be permitted this liminal violation in death. Again, the audience replicates such a desire to balance duty/structure with freedom/liminality, and the story's treatment of this duality was probably much of the reason for its popularity.

Adults also have nonsexual fantasies, such as abandoning an unfulfilling job (expressed well by at least the title of 1981's *Take This Job and Shove It*, a film inspired by the popular country music song) or making the workplace more hospitable to women (e.g., 1980's *Nine to Five*, in which three women kidnap their boss and create a nonsexist office). Violent movies also clearly offer such opportunities to those frustrated by their place in society, as working-class men enjoy seeing Bruce Willis defeating the capitalist villains of *Die Hard* (1988) and watching a corporate office being destroyed in the process. The immensely popular war film *The Dirty Dozen* (1967) also traffics in liminality, as the heroes are all criminals who have a great deal of trouble accepting military authority. While this valorization of criminals offended some viewers, the popularity of the film among nonconvicts attests to the fact that even law-abiding citizens can identify for a brief time with those outside of society and enjoy being nonconformists with no real cost. They can return to their daily lives having fantasized about violating the codes they must normally uphold.

Although we may see a psychological function in such fantasy, as it involves certain cathartic benefits for the viewer who indulges himself or herself in this way, we should not reduce the benefits to only those that accrue to the isolated individual viewer. Such an analysis might miss the communal function of this liminal representation by reducing its role to that of merely private fantasy/catharsis. The fact that a film is usually shared by an audience makes it a communal experience in which the group together experiences the benefits of temporarily discarding social norms. Teenagers enjoy seeing movies like *American Pie* (1999) together precisely so that they can share the pleasures of challenging the status quo, as their own ideal teenage "communitas" forms a challenge to the parental society of structure and rules.

Although I have been arguing that moral critique of this aspect of film may be misguided in that it misses the necessity of challenge to the social norms embodied in the "inappropriate" or risqué, I would not abandon the possibility of moral critique altogether in a celebration of relativism. Not all depictions of the inappropriate are necessarily harmless; it has been argued, for example, that violent movies may cause people to be more violent. The evidence for such claims is rather weak, and such arguments usually ignore the fact that most people do not become violent by watching violent movies as such films may for them be harmless or even healthy exercises in liminality and catharsis. But this does not mean that there can be no harmful effects to the depiction of liminal behavior. The Ndembu were able to engage in "obscene" behavior in a prescribed manner because they also knew they would return to normalcy afterwards, just as some people in our society can enjoy the depiction of inappropriate behavior before returning to social conformity. If people have already rejected authority and structure, however, films that depict liminality may simply confirm them in their rejection of societal values. Without a strong system of social sanctions against inappropriate behavior in place, the invocation of liminality may be dangerous. In a society without a homogeneous set of moral norms, like our own, this danger is more obvious.

One should also note in all the rituals of liminality described by Turner that no real harm is done to anyone. The flouting of societal and sexual norms leads to no actual infidelity, rape, or significant bodily harm. The "beatings" and insults suffered have no permanent effects and are accepted in the same comic spirit that pervades the play of children pretending to fight in our own society. It is as yet unclear whether the depiction of violent behavior in popular films is such a harmless form of play, or whether it actually incites some to violence. If the latter can be shown to be the case, then it is not a form of speech that is legally protected in the United States. In practice, however, it is very difficult to prove that a particular example of speech is either helpful or harmful. For our purposes, we need only affirm that films may be either, and that we have no a priori reason for assuming that a particular film has to be read one way or the other; what is harmful to one may be helpful to another, and vice versa, which is another reason that we need to consider audience reaction rather than assume that a film will necessarily lead to antisocial behavior just because it offends us.

Of course, not all films can be reduced to exercises in liminality any more than they can all be reduced to forms of vicarious sacrifice, but both these categories which arise from ritual studies can be profitably applied to the study of film. It may be suggested that filmgoers do not actually engage in the liminal behavior themselves, but only observe it, yet the participatory nature of film I have already discussed makes it possible for viewers to identify with the actions of characters and so vicariously gain some of the benefits of their actions. As a ritual space, film offers a separation from the everyday as viewers temporarily accept it as an alternative reality, even while they know they must eventually return to everyday reality.

I have noted how the liminal scenario not only suspends ordinary rules but also invokes a utopian ideal, and this returns us to the idea that rituals connect the world of "reality" (how things are) with "ideality" (how things ought to be). Myth describes what the fundamental nature of reality is really believed to be, but this does not always conform to empirical reality as we know it. Thus, the myth also describes how we would like ordinary reality to be, and so provides a model for how it should be. This moral vision is enacted via ritual.

The Relation of Real and Ideal in Ritual

We examined Jonathan Z. Smith's view of myth in the preceding chapter and noted how he believes both myth and ritual present the incongruity between the ideal and our actual experience as "an occasion for thought." I have also suggested that the incongruities may not be as absolute as he seems to think, as myths and rituals do seek to connect the ideal and the real and not simply set them incongruously side by side.

Smith looks at rituals of North American bear hunting as an example of the gap between actual hunts and the ritually prescribed "ideal" form of them. Many rules govern the approach to the animal and its actual killing in an "honorable" fashion, as the bear must be standing and facing the hunter and only struck in certain places to achieve a bloodless wound. The fact that the bear is viewed as a spiritual being requires this respectful treatment, as it can only be killed if it offers itself willingly to them and not if its life is taken by stealth or trickery. In fact, however, actual hunts in these tribes make use of traps, pitfalls, snares, and none of the respectful address and honorable methods prescribed by the ritual. Bears are ambushed in their dens and killed by whatever "unsporting" methods work—including shotguns, which usually have messy results. From this incongruity of actual behavior and prescribed behavior, Smith concludes not that these people are unaware of the difference, but that the ritual is actually designed to call attention to the difference. The ritual does not compel the ideal to come to pass, but rather expresses "a realistic assessment of the fact that the world cannot be compelled."[24]

What Smith does not explain is what benefit the presentation of such incongruity might have for the people who hunt bears in this fashion. Because he has not asked them, he can only speculate, and he suggests that the ideal is invoked only to present its difference from reality. Fieldwork might have disclosed other details and motives that might suggest more of a connection between the ideal and the real. Some tribes raise a bear from a cub and kill it in the prescribed ritualized manner, which may be viewed as atoning for the hunts in which such rules are not followed. The forgiveness of the bear is asked, which may cancel out the inappropriate means used to kill it—especially as the tribe effectively suggests by the ritual that they know how they ought to kill even though they fall short of the ideal. These are only speculations, but there is no reason to consider them less viable than Smith's conjectures, and in fact they may suggest a more reasonable understanding of how people connect the real and the ideal in practice.

Christians and members of other Western religions also engage in similarly incongruous ritual behaviors, which may suggest a means of understanding how the real and the ideal may be related. Biblical passages about turning the other cheek and loving your enemies don't seem to be literally followed by many Christians, not even those who claim to be biblical literalists, just as injunctions about sharing everything with the poor seem to get ignored in wealthy (and not so wealthy) congregations. One may take this as a sign of hypocrisy, or conclude that they have simply chosen to ignore the biblical passages in question. When one talks to Christians, however, they usually have a variety of responses to such aporia, for example: we give what we can to the poor, but we obviously can't give everything; we don't approve of unnecessary violence, but defending one's country is another matter. Such people accept the idea that the ideal cannot always be followed and that realistic considerations may require us to act differently, but that does not make the ideal totally irrelevant to our daily lives. The ideal may prompt us to make an effort to approach it even though we cannot fully realize it, to attempt to eliminate unnecessary violence and greed from society and our personal lives. Reinhold Niebuhr gave a theological defense of this approach in a small and difficult book with the unassuming title *An Introduction to Christian Ethics*. Here he argued that an ethical ideal, while impossible to realize, remains relevant to our lives as it can inspire us to do more than we would if we only acted on the basis of "realistic" considerations.

In such a case, the incongruity between real and ideal is not simply presented for viewing, but the ideal is presented as one that can affect how we behave in the real world. The ritual of filmgoing may have a similar function, in that we see "ideal" worlds in movies which we know are not "real" and yet these may inspire us to make the world a little bit more like the ideal. The people who loved the movie *Gandhi* may not have become pacifists, but perhaps the film had an effect on their subsequent behavior or political views. In Turner's terms, even though the ideal of "communitas" cannot be realized, a ritual representation of it can affect one's behavior in the postliminal reintegration into society by suggesting that the ideal of unity and equality can be balanced with the necessity of societal structure.

We are not meant simply to realize that the world is not ideal, but are called to find ways to bring that ideal into relation with the real, however partially or fragmentarily.

Ritual and the Secular

Some readers may still be skeptical about the thesis that filmgoing has a ritual quality to it, as we tend to associate the term "ritual" with certain kinds of religious activity but not necessarily with watching movies. "Secular" or supposedly nonreligious activities may have many of the characteristics we associate with religious ritual, however, as Catherine Bell has noted. In particular, she defines six general characteristics of ritual that are reproduced to some extent in secular activities: formalism, traditionalism, invariance, rule-governance, sacral symbolism, and performance.

The first four aspects she describes all seem to speak to the aspect of changelessness that we associate with ritual. Not all rituals have all of these characteristics, but each of them can be found in a variety of religious rituals as well as secular activities that are ritual-like in nature. First, rituals often have a prescribed form and so are "formal" rather than informal, as they cannot be performed in any old fashion. In the secular realm, manners related to eating and other social activities are often governed by such formal norms, which are seemingly arbitrary but invested with meaning insofar as the one who flouts them shows himself to be a boor. What is signified, then, is that those who know the conventions know how to behave "properly" as they have been educated about social interaction and have a respect for the distinctions in rank and class often suggested by such conventions. The second aspect, traditionalism, supports formalism by suggesting that "we have always done it this way" even when that is not properly speaking true (as with traditions that are relatively recent in origin, such as the American celebration of Thanksgiving Day). Along the same lines, invariance insists that the ritual be done the same way always, with as little change as possible; it may be viewed as a ritual precisely because it is repeated according to such a set pattern. Rule-governance, the fourth aspect, reinforces such invariance by requiring that pattern.[25]

The rituals of film viewing may not seem so invariant or rule governed, but that does not mean that such activities are not rituals. Invariance and formalism do not as such constitute either sufficient or necessary conditions for rituals: not necessary, as there are some relatively informal and flexible rituals in a number of religious traditions; and not sufficient, as we cannot conclude that an activity is ritualistic simply because it is repeated on a regular basis according to a set pattern. If I drive to work every morning at the same time with a cup of tea in my car, this is not a ritual so much as a habit, based mainly on the fact that I am required to be there at a certain time, and the fact that I like to drink tea in the morning. A habit or a custom is not a ritual unless it has some significance attributed to it beyond the fact that "I always do this."

Bell also speaks of "sacral symbolism" as a characteristic of ritual, in that rituals point to greater realities, which we see even in secular rituals such as the pledge of allegiance to the U.S. flag. The flag comes to have a greater significance than a piece of cloth through rituals that suggest it symbolizes the country "for which it stands," and that it should therefore be treated with the appropriate respect. An object has this sort of "sacrality," according to Bell, not because it refers to a divine figure but because it has

> a quality of specialness, not the same as other things, standing for something important and possessing an extra meaningfulness and the ability to evoke emotion-filled images and experiences. In other words . . . the object is more than the mere sum of its parts and points to something beyond itself, thereby evoking and expressing values and attitudes associated with larger, more abstract, and relatively transcendent ideas.[26]

Rituals, then, traffic in symbols—whether such symbols refer to traditional religious referents or not. It is widely admitted (e.g., by semiotic analysis) that films have this characteristic as well, for they are filled with figures and symbols that metonymically refer beyond themselves: the gangster, the cowboy, the cop, the fallen woman, the nerd—all refer as characters to ideal types that speak to identities within ourselves. Their props, too, refer symbolically to larger realities—the gun as representation of both law and violence, their clothes signifying conformity or nonconformity, the railroad as symbol of progress and the end of the frontier, huge modern offices as symbols of corporate power, and so forth.

Finally, Bell notes the performative aspect of ritual, which is also found in secular activities such as theater performances. I have already noted the connection between theater (and therefore film) and religious ritual, in that both dramatize narratives in order to make them seem "real" to audiences and thereby to convey a certain vision of reality. Much like Geertz,

Bell also notes that drama creates an "artificial world" which reflects a "coherently ordered totality" that attempts to project meaning onto "the chaos of human experience."[27]

Bell herself, however, is skeptical about attempts to erase any difference between religious rituals and secular rituals, in spite of the similarities, because when cultures make such distinctions we should respect them. At the same time, she notes that the distinction between theater and religion does not seem to exist in some cultures, as, for example, traditional Chinese theater (Peking Opera) involves ritual exorcism of demons and an initial performance of the opera that is done just for a god.[28] Rather than ask why such cultures "confuse" the two, we might ask why Westerners so radically distinguish religious rituals from other types of rituals, and what this separation signifies. As this book has been arguing for a recognition of the religious dimensions of a phenomenon normally viewed as nonreligious, this is a good point at which to ask whether the distinction between religion and secularity has any merit to it.

One reason for the distinction may be that the chief religions of Western culture have defined their identities in large part by their opposition to the surrounding culture (paradoxical as that might seem, given the fact that they also reflect the culture). In the first chapter, we examined some theological approaches to religion and culture that characteristically oppose them, approaches that reflect a long heritage within Western religion of defining the norms of religion against the norms of society. It may be because Judaism, Christianity, and Islam all began as minority religions that consciously distinguished themselves from the religious majority of the culture, which in each case was polytheistic. Today, these religions typically define themselves against secular culture instead. But we could also see this conflict, just as that between monotheism and polytheism, as a conflict between two religions rather than as a conflict between religion and nonreligion. It may be that the insistence on a distinction between religion and culture mainly signifies a battle between one kind of religion and another, although this is not always admitted as we do not wish to dignify secular culture with the name of "religion."

The study of "secularization" reveals some points about how we define the opposition of secularity and religion.[29] Advocates of the secularization thesis initially held that "religion" was losing its power in Western society, being replaced by the "secular" as the central determiner of cultural norms and values. But increasingly it has become apparent that traditional religion is not dying out, and it even gains strength in some situations through its perceived need to battle "secularity" (as with fundamentalism). The process that has been called secularization is not really the eclipse of traditional religion so much as the evolution of more religious alternatives. It represents the greater pluralism of some societies that have enough cultural heterogeneity to sustain a variety of religious options, none of which has hegemony. This heterogeneity frustrates traditionalists who would like to restore their own hegemony, such as the so-called "Christian right" in the United States.

If secularization represents religious pluralism, and the "secular" alternatives to traditional religion are simply new religions that compete with the old, then it may make sense to view secular culture as itself religious rather than nonreligious. This option has not been embraced by many in our society, perhaps because people fear the tolerance of secular culture that might be required if it were to be dignified with the name of religion. After all, we guarantee freedom of religion, and it is not politically correct to attack anyone's religion, so calling secular culture a religion might thus seem to put an end to all critique of secular culture by traditional religions. This fear is unfounded, however; the fact that groups have a legal right to practice religion as they see fit does not require everyone else to agree with their views. In practice, this is impossible, as we cannot agree with all religious (or cultural) views, and are entitled to critique those views even as others are entitled to hold them—and critique ours in turn. This holds as much for "secular" views as for traditional religious views. But in critiquing these views, we should at least try to assess them fairly and not automatically dismiss them as invalid simply because they differ from our own. Such uninformed judgments have too often been the norm in the history of religious interaction, as they now seem to be the norm in "religious" critique of "secular" culture. Perhaps what is needed, both for traditional and "secular" religions, is a fair assessment based on an attempt to understand the views in question and what they mean for their followers, as well as an honest admission that there may be truth found in unlikely places. If popular culture contains truth, it need not only be because it is disguised Christian (or Muslim, or Jewish, etc.) truth, but perhaps because it has some validity in its own right. The next chapter seeks to give some guidelines about how we might seek the truth in other belief systems based on analogies drawn between the history of religious interaction and the interaction between religion and secular culture.

5

The Religion-Film Dialogue
as Interreligious Dialogue

In the last few chapters, we have mapped out an understanding of religion that applies to film and film viewing as aspects of popular culture. We have seen that the line often drawn between religion and culture is an artificial one based on a theological agenda that favors some religious views, identified as "religion," over others. Those that are identified as merely "culture" may be viewed as having some characteristics in common with religious views, but they tend to be denigrated as lacking certain dimensions that "real" religions have. Both theological and ideological approaches to film and religion have relied on this distinction, and in so doing have failed to take seriously the religious elements in popular culture as representing a distinct religious tradition. Popular culture may not be as formal or as institutionally organized as "official" religions, but it functions like a religion, and may thus be viewed as a religion.

Many people will still be concerned with a definition of religion that is so broad that it appears to include all of human culture. If we cannot distinguish religion from nonreligion, has the term not lost all specific meaning, for it can apply equally well to anything? This criticism ignores the fact that we are using a specific definition of religion and can identify aspects of popular culture such as film viewing that relate to it; we are not identifying religion with culture as such, as if the words were synonymous, but rather identifying the religious dimension of culture, which may be more widespread than suspected. To find the religious dimension in all of culture, or to examine culture through the categories of religion, is not to reduce religion to culture (or vice versa) any more than an economic or political analysis of all aspects of culture reduces culture to economics or politics. Such analyses only become reductionistic if they insist that they are exhaustive and have explained all aspects of culture such that no other forms of analyses are possible or necessary. Studying film or popular culture as a religion is not the only way, but one can legitimately study it this way. And I believe this method may offer new insights into popular culture that have been largely missed by religion scholars as well as scholars of film and cultural studies.

If it is valid to interpret film viewing as a religion in the way we have defined it, then the dialogue between traditional religions and film can be understood as a dialogue between religions. Interreligious dialogue has evolved a great deal in recent years, and there are insights from this aspect of religious studies that can be applied to the dialogue between religion and film as well. In particular, we can learn from encounters between religions that there are natural stages through which such dialogue moves, usually from demonization (seeing only evil, as difference) to idealization (seeing only good, often through noting similarities), and finally to an attempt to actually hear what the other is saying. At this point one can see both similarities and differences between one's own view and that of the other religion, and one can make some judgments based on a more objective assessment of the other. This last stage is not always or adequately reached, but it is the goal of many of those involved in interreligious dialogue, and it might also be the goal of the dialogue between religion and popular culture.

Understanding the Other

The initial attitude that religions take toward one another is often one of incomprehension. This is not so odd when one realizes that to encounter another worldview is to encounter a separate subjectivity, a different way of thinking about reality, which by definition is not one's own. We have no categories with which to approach that which appears totally other but those of the exotic, the weird, the savage. The history of religious interaction is full of examples of gross intolerance and lack of understanding based on such assessments of the other as in principle unknowable. We believe we have nothing in common with this other and so reject it, often with undisguised hostility. Sometimes we cannot even recognize that a different religious view is a religion at all, because it differs so markedly from our own views.

As we have seen, the encounter of European Christians with the religions of Native Americans is a case in point. The religious practices of

Native Americans did not look like those of the Western monotheistic traditions, so they were not recognized as "religion" at all by many of the European explorers. Christopher Columbus observed that the natives he met seemed "to have no religion" as he could not discover "any idolatry or other religious belief among them." Immediately after having drawn this conclusion, however, Columbus goes on to describe in some detail practices and beliefs that we can only regard as religious in nature, for example, prayers and rituals directed toward wooden images, and beliefs about the afterlife.[1] Even if he was unable to find monotheism among them, it seems odd that he was unable to class this activity as a form of "idolatry"—the fact that he did not seems to indicate that their activities did not fit his definition of idolatry, which presumably came from the description of such in the Bible and might have been assumed by him to include animal sacrifice or other elements he did not see. Although they believed in spirits, a supernatural realm, prayer, and a world beyond death, these were not enough to qualify for his definition of religion, shaped by his own experience. What he did see he interpreted basically negatively, believing that the worship of the images was a sham perpetuated by the religious leaders in order to enforce their own authority (a sort of proto-Marxist view).

Others, such as Gonzalo Fernandez de Oviedo (1478–1577), engaged in outright hostility toward Native Americans and their religions by viewing them as forms of worship of the devil. Oviedo did not really have any evidence for this view, as he simply assumes that their word "tuyra" means "devil," which he says is "a name very sweet and agreeable to many of them" that they also apply to the Christians. He does not seem to consider that "tuyra" might be a benevolent deity, or even the same as the Christian God, because he has already classified them as evil in their actions as well as their beliefs. His views conveniently provided ideological ammunition for those who argued that the natives were naturally fit for enslavement by the European settlers, essentially depriving them of a common humanity with their enslavers.

On the other hand, Bartolome de las Casas (1474–1566) defended the natives against exploitation, arguing that they were "neither proud nor ambitious" but "quiet lambs" of true virtue, lacking only belief in God for eternal perfection. Las Casas denounced the genocide perpetrated on the natives by the Spaniards through remaking their image into that of docile and simple primitives. Although one can certainly not quarrel with his desire to criticize the terrible mistreatment of the natives and the attempts to demonize them that were used as justification for genocide, Las Casas's image of the natives is just as much a Western construction as that of his opposition is. Whereas Oviedo saw only evil, Las Casas saw only good; where Oviedo saw only difference, Las Casas saw only similarity. We are all human, and therefore all human cultures are alike, Las Casas assumes; he points out that they have art, government, and language, just like us; they are intelligent, and morally civilized. In short, the only real difference is that we are Christians, and they are not. Las Casas sought to remedy that by converting them, so that all difference would be erased.[2]

Neither of these approaches takes the other seriously in itself. Either difference is all that is seen, or similarity is all that is seen. As Jonathan Z. Smith has observed (quoting Wilhelm Dilthey), interpretation of other cultures is impossible if they are seen as completely strange, and unnecessary if they are seen as completely familiar; interpretation must lie between these extremes. Or as Smith puts it: "If they were like-us why should we want to know about them? If they were not-like-us how can they be comprehended?"[3] To understand the other, we must use analogies to our own experience, but we cannot ignore the uniqueness of the other in our attempt to homologize it to our own categories. If we reduce the other to a mere instance of a generalization, or to a form of ourselves, we have not understood it—as Smith has tried to show in many of his critiques of the history of religions.

The attempt to show that they are "just like us" also has an agenda, as can be seen in the case of Las Casas. While his opposition wished to demonize them in order to justify their subjugation, Las Casas wished to justify his attempts to convert them to Christianity by showing that they were already almost Christian anyway. Later approaches developed this view by identifying the "Great Spirit" of some tribes (such as the Sioux) with the God of the Bible, so that they were understood to be practicing a form of monotheism already, and simply needed to gain a bit of refinement in their religious views to be fully Christian.[4] They were viewed, then, either as demon worshipping idolaters or anonymous monotheists—it was even suggested that they were descended from the lost tribes of Israel—because these were the only categories available for Westerners who drew all their categories regarding religion from the Bible, and who needed to "place" the natives somewhere within its worldview.

It might be believed that many Westerners are closer today to understanding Native American religion, as we no longer tend to view it either as idolatry or disguised proto-Christianity. The current New Age construction of Native American religion, however, is just as much of a distortion, some would say more dangerous for its apparent benevolence. Today we romanticize the Native American as one who never despoiled his environment, who was peaceful and community oriented, not acquisitive or greedy, connected to nature, and "spiritual" rather than "religious." This latter distinction is usually taken to mean that they sought the divine within themselves and nature rather than in authoritarian institutions, as Western religion is believed to do. What is not often seen is that this construction is more a product of post-Christian disaffection from Western traditions than a genuine representation of Native American views. Those who see Native Americans in this way are still seeing themselves, although in this case they are seeing their own New Age religion, itself a Western construction based largely on a rejection of Christianity.

It is also rarely noted that this idealization of Native American religion and culture primarily serves as a critique of Western greed and environmental destruction rather than an accurate picture of Native American life, past or present. Like all peoples, Native Americans have not always been peaceful or environmentally conservative, but when we view them in this way we put them in a pristine paradise that is not of this world. This is why it is sometimes believed that all evil came to Native Americans as a result of the Western invasion, as if they were somehow free of vice prior to this. It is certainly true that the West brought terrible and unjustified destruction to Native Americans in the form of genocide, disease, alcoholism, and theft of their land, but this does not mean that Native Americans lived in perfection prior to the white man's coming. Sam Gill argues that such an idealization harms Native Americans by viewing them as "timeless and ahistorical, changeless and nonprogressive." This construction essentially deprives them of a future, as they are not allowed to develop as all peoples must to survive; they are expected to act and dress "like Indians," remaining in their own world (the reservation) and not participating in the larger society in any meaningful way. Their only function is to put on their costumes and remind us of what we have lost, a perfect and natural way of life that is long gone.[5]

In sum, Westerners have had a great deal of trouble understanding other religions and cultures, for whether they viewed them as demonic or noble, with horror or with romantic idealism, they have tended to construct images of them out of their own desires to make them totally other or totally the same as ourselves, and so have failed to understand them at all. One might wonder whether there is any hope here, for it might seem that we cannot transcend our own cultural categories and so are doomed to construct others in our own image (or its reverse). But the fact that these distortions have been detected seems to show that a relative degree of objectivity is possible in that we can try to get our facts straight about a religion, listen to what its adherents say, and generally progress toward a greater understanding of it. This change is in fact what is now happening in many fields of religious studies, partly because more voices from other religions are being included among the informants as well as the scholars. To note this new view is not to subscribe to some impossible ideal of full objectivity, but to recognize that even though our subjective views affect our assessment of others we should not abandon an attempt to understand them better. A recognition of our prejudices is not license to utilize all prejudice freely in our interpretation; while we cannot be entirely free of prejudice we need not succumb to it without question. Or, as Clifford Geertz has put it, the fact that we cannot create a totally aseptic environment does not mean we should "conduct surgery in a sewer."[6]

Theological Developments in Interreligious Dialogue

While Western scholars who study non-Western religions were wrestling with these issues of understanding, those involved with Christian theology were developing through similar stages regarding their assessment of non-Christian religion. The parallels are not exact, in particular because there is less consensus among theologians as to the correct approach to take. At the same time, as new options are developed, they replicate the tendency within the field of comparative religion to move to approaches that seek to understand the other as neither totally different nor totally the same as ourselves, and overall to come to a more accurate and fair understanding of the other.

The issue for the theologian differs from the issue for the comparativist insofar as it concerns not merely how best to understand the other, but how to view the other in relationship to one's own religious views. Because theology involves the self-expression of religion, it raises the question of the impact of other religions and their claims upon our own claims, for example, can or should we regard other religions as flawed in their views of reality or the path to human fulfillment? Can or should we regard them as "saved" or as "lost"? And must they do something further in order to be fulfilled or saved?

Such issues seem to be of special concern to Christians because Christianity has maintained for much of its history that it is the exclusive path to truth and salvation. It is not the only religion to do so, however, and even religions that are less exclusivistic tend to maintain that their own views may be the best understanding of reality, or even the only correct views. Tribal religions, for example, may not commit Christians to hell—and may not even believe in a place of eternal torment—but they may believe that their own religious views offer the only correct understanding of reality. This is the view often known as "exclusivism," because it holds that truth is the exclusive possession of one tradition, or that the possession of truth by one's own tradition excludes the possibility that other religious viewpoints may be true.[7]

Some theologians are troubled by the apparent narrowness of the exclusivist view, even though it has been the dominant paradigm for much of the history of religious interaction. In the twentieth century, Roman Catholic theologian Karl Rahner took it upon himself to develop an alternative view that is often now called "inclusivism." Following a tradition in Roman Catholic teaching regarding the possibility of an "implicit faith" in those who never had the chance to hear the gospel or be baptized, Rahner argues that this possibility should be extended to followers of other religions, and that we might even view other religions as vehicles of grace for those in other cultures. For if God truly wishes to offer salvation to all peoples, then "it is quite unthinkable that man, being what he is, could actually achieve this relationship to God . . . in an absolutely private interior reality" apart from the religions of his culture. Rather, the possibility of salvation must have been offered "in the concrete religion in which 'people' lived and had to live at that time."[8] One who accepts this salvation of Christ, even without knowing its name, Rahner calls an "anonymous Christian."[9]

There are a number of problems with Rahner's view that have been identified by his critics. One is that it is unclear exactly how the grace of Christ is made available "through" another religion if it has very different concepts of "salvation" or, indeed, no concept resembling any form of "salvation" at all. One could also ask why this ability is restricted by Rahner to those aspects of culture we call "religions," for (as we have seen) the definition of religion is itself a Western invention and a rather slippery one at that; what are we to allow to be a "religion" and what not? Can one be saved by communism, Nazism, secular humanism, or film, all of which have been called religions? Another issue is that this view seems primarily designed to salve the consciences of Christians about the fate of those born outside of the realm of Christian influence; it does not help us understand the other religion better, and in fact may prevent us from fully understanding it if we assume it to be more "Christian" in content than it really is. Members of other religious traditions may not feel complemented by being called "anonymous Christians," as this label does not take seriously their own religious beliefs and identities, and they may feel as if they are being forcibly baptized into a tradition that is not their own.

A number of theologians who are unsatisfied with either exclusivism or inclusivism have developed other alternatives, usually classified under the label "pluralism." Some of them have followed the approach of John Hick, who for many years has been calling for the equivalent of a "Copernican revolution" in theology. Just as people were once reluctant to accept the evidence presented by Copernicus and other astronomers that the Sun and not the Earth is at the center of our solar system, so we now resist the view that our own religious tradition is not at the center of religious truth. Rahner's view, according to Hick, is analogous to the attempts of medieval astronomers to keep the Earth at the center through the artificial concept of "epicycles," used to explain the apparently erratic orbits of the celestial bodies allegedly circling us. Ultimately, it had to be admitted that the simplest explanation of the data was a heliocentric system, and so also with theology Hick believes that Rahner's attempt to keep Christianity at the center must finally be abandoned for a more natural (and just) view that places no single religion at the center. Each religion encounters the same ultimate reality and expresses its understanding of it in a different way, according to Hick, so that no religion can claim to be closer to the truth than any other.[10]

Although Hick's view appears to be much broader in its ability to appreciate other religions, as it claims to avoid giving favor to one over another, many of his critics have observed that it does preference a particular view which, although not Christianity as such, seems to have the basic outlines of Western monotheism. There is one reality, in Hick's view, which all religions encounter, and which assists them in the process of moving from self-centeredness to "reality-centeredness."[11] But many religions could not recognize themselves in this construction, as they do not believe in a single absolute and transcendent reality. Buddhists reject the idea of any permanent and unchanging "reality" and regard the attempt to achieve permanence as itself an illusion to be dispelled before enlightenment can be reached. Hick reinterprets Buddhism so that it coheres with his theory, but it is far from clear that this is doing anything other than imposing an alien conception on Buddhism. Likewise, tribal religions that worship numerous gods may not believe in a single ultimate "reality" as the basis for their lives in the same sense that monotheists do. Even religions that bear a closer resemblance to Hick's metareligion may resent being characterized in this way, as their own claims are put aside as but phenomenal forms of the noumenon that transcends them all. What makes each religion distinct is ignored as unimportant to its essence as a "religion," so that it is the lowest common denominator of generic monotheism that defines Judaism, Christianity, and Islam, rather than their individual beliefs in Torah, Christ, or Shari'ah.

What Hick seems reluctant to admit is that his theory embodies a particular religious view just as much as any form of exclusivism or inclusivism. Certain religious views he finds unacceptable, for example, those that deny the reality of the ultimate (atheisms), those that deny the unity of the ultimate (polytheisms), those that deny a distinction between ourselves and the ultimate (mysticisms), and those that claim their view alone expresses a valid understanding of the ultimate (exclusivisms). Hick's view is in fact just a somewhat larger version of inclusivism, as it wishes to define all religions as forms of "anonymous reality-centeredness" if not anonymous Christianity. Like Rahner, Hick believes his own understanding of what the religions are about is to be preferred to the self-understanding of the religions themselves; he regards them as irrational and unfair if they insist on holding to their traditional views as the correct understanding of reality in distinction from his allegedly more "pluralistic" hypothesis.[12]

Some pluralists such as Hick claim that it is necessary to put aside our individual religious beliefs and seek such a homogenization, even if it entails some loss, as this is necessary for achieving world peace among competing religions. What this view ignores is that similarity of religious beliefs does not guarantee peace; in fact, many of the most violent religious conflicts are often between those with similar views (e.g., both Jews and Muslims in the Mideast are monotheists; both Protestants and Catholics in Northern Ireland are Christians). It is also not very realistic to expect religions to give up all their points of disagreement as the price of world peace. In addition, most of the conflicts involve political, economic, and cultural issues that would not be settled in any case by theological agreement—does anyone really think Northern Ireland's problems would have ended if both sides agreed to a common view (or the rejection of all views) on such things as the papacy, justification, and transubstantiation? Such agreement would not settle the issues of home rule or the right to bear arms. And although it might be nice if residents of Jerusalem did not care about the sacred sites of the various religions that continue to be a source of conflict, even if they did not, that would hardly end all the reasons for political conflict in the region. Even with theological agreement, groups have differing ethnic and cultural identities that seem to fuel the fires of civil war worldwide to a greater extent that mere religious differences.

Religions and cultures can also not be expected to all hold the same moral views, as pluralists have sometimes argued they should if there is to be peace between them. Although it seems that there is a core concern at the heart of most religions with moral behavior, and some form of the "golden rule" may be found in most of them, their interpretations vary widely. Religions have different views on killing in self-defense, violent revolution, individual rights versus group preservation, and so on. We have different views of how we would like to be treated, so that if we treat others according to our own norms we may not be treating them as *they* would like to be treated. There is no absolute standard for justice and morality that transcends culture; liberation theologians may seem to evoke such a standard, but it is in fact a construction based on Western forms of social analysis originating in the work of Marx, Durkheim, Weber, and others.[13] To assume that these norms can be applied to all cultures without offense is to ignore the individual cultural views on morality and justice that will affect how they do business with one another; one morality cannot be imposed on all, but we can discuss morality together in the hopes that some degree of consensus or compromise will be achieved.

Some theologians have rejected exclusivism, inclusivism, and the form of "pluralism" defended by Hick and those who are like-minded as all too narrow in that these approaches fail to let the other be the other. All three approaches seem bent on conversion to a single view as the goal of interreligious dialogue, so that the inability of exclusivists to take seriously the view of the other echoes through the other approaches as well. Although Rahner and Hick are apparently kinder than exclusivists in that they refuse to damn the non-Christian, they effectively baptize the non-Christian in the claim that she has already accepted the same "gospel" we have, whether she knows it or not. In Rahner's case, the others are really Christians already; in Hick's case, all of us are directed to the same reality, and it makes no difference what path is used to relate to that reality. But none of these views takes seriously the possibility that the other may have a different view that is important to recognize and that may be legitimately held by the other, that indeed the other may be enriched and fulfilled through her own beliefs precisely in their difference from our own. In this sense, they are following in the footsteps of Las Casas in his efforts to accept the Native Americans not in their difference from us, but as "just like us."

George Lindbeck has pointed out that, if we do not wish to damn those who follow other religions without a hearing, we are not constrained to adopt the view of Rahner that they can be saved because they are really already Christian. Lindbeck objects to Rahner's view because it reduces faith to a matter of inner experience that can be appropriated in multiple forms regardless of the cultural-linguistic form of expression; in contrast, Lindbeck holds that the particular concepts and language used to express religious beliefs are fundamentally determinative of that belief, so that there is no sense in calling someone "Christian" who does not yet hold to the beliefs we identify by that label. An alternative approach to the salvation of non-Christians, supported by Lindbeck, is to hope for their ultimate salvation in that they too will in the end become Christians. Many Christian universalists have taken this approach and so have not sacrificed the importance of Christian belief nor the importance of recognizing how other religious beliefs differ from it. Instead, they have simply expanded the realm in which persons can encounter Christ to states beyond the present life on Earth. In this way, a Christian can believe that all humans will find salvation in the end, for if they do not become Christians in this life they will do so in the future life or in the transition to it.[14]

Lindbeck does not accept the equal validity of other religions in that he still holds that Christian language "is the only one that has the words and concepts that can authentically speak of the ground of being, the goal of history, and true humanity" even though it may be "enriched" by its encounter with other religions.[15] The lesson he offers, however, is that one need not abandon the claim that there are significant differences between religions in order to avoid viewing them as "lost." Even if there are differences, and even if one religion is "right," this does not mean that all who do not follow it are eternally lost; they may yet be saved by coming to the view of that religion in the end.

Other Christian theologians involved in interreligious dialogue have gone farther in affirming the value of other religions as distinct ways of viewing the world. John Cobb has been critical of pluralists like Hick who assume that all religions refer to the same reality, as this ignores the particular contributions to religious understanding that each religion can give. In his own dialogue with Buddhism, Cobb has not sought to establish that Buddhists and Christians believe in the same "thing" and simply refer to it differently, for he does not find this conclusion supported by study of the religions; rather, he finds that they believe different things, but that each religion can learn from the other and be enriched and transformed in the process.[16] Contra Hick, Cobb claims that Buddhists do not mean the same thing by "Emptiness" that Christians mean by "God," for Buddhists do not believe in any "transcendent ground of existence" (which Hick identifies as the reality all religions "worship"). In addition, Christianity is also impoverished and misrepresented in the dialogue if it is identified only with belief in a transcendent reality, as this does not include the notion of an incarnate deity that is so critical to Christianity.[17] Each religion has its own unique contributions to make to the history of religions, which should not be sacrificed in order to establish a generic "core" of religion allegedly present in all.

In his insistence that Christians take seriously the claims of Buddhists and other religions in dialogue, Cobb is not suggesting any sacrifice of Christian beliefs, but rather that Christian belief may change and grow as a result of its encounter with other religions. Although Jesus remains the center of history for Cobb as a Christian theologian, he also states that the center is not the whole of history. There are other channels of Wisdom that have been found by other religions, for "the Wisdom we meet in Jesus is precisely the Wisdom that is already known by all." To suggest that this Wisdom is only present in Jesus is to deny the omnipresence of God, that God can be and is present in more than just one place. In this sense, Cobb believes that real faithfulness to Christianity demands the rejection of exclusivism and the affirmation that God/Wisdom is present in many places.[18]

To suggest that "Wisdom" is present in all the religions, however, is not to insist that every religion speaks of the same "reality" or that they are really just saying the same thing in different ways. Instead, Cobb claims that the differing claims of religions are in fact different, but that this does not require us to decide that one is "right" and the other "wrong." For example, it may seem that we face a flat contradiction when the Christian asserts

"God exists," and the Buddhist asserts "no God exists." But each of these claims is embedded in a religious context that gives the specific words their meaning, so that "God" and "exists" may not mean the same thing in both cases. When we look deeper at what each religion is saying in these statements, we may discover that the Buddhist is saying that "there is nothing in reality to which one should be attached," while the Christian is saying that "there is that in reality that is worthy of trust and worship." There is no reason why each could not learn to affirm what the other is saying without abandoning her own claims, and therefore come to a recognition of the "truth" of both claims as complementary rather than contradictory insights. As Cobb puts it:

> The Buddhist could in principle acknowledge the reality of something worthy of trust and worship without abandoning the central insight that attachment blocks the way to enlightenment. And the Christian could come to see that real trust is not attachment in the Buddhist sense. Both would thereby have learned what is most important to the other without abandoning their central concerns.[19]

Cobb does not see the goal to be that of "converting" all to Christ, if this is taken to mean that all should "join Christian churches." Rather, the goal is that all "appropriate" Jesus by discovering what he can contribute to their own religions. "If Jews appropriate Jesus while remaining Jews, and Buddhists, while remaining Buddhists, I, as a Christian, see nothing lacking in that."[20] Presumably, Cobb means more than simply a recognition that the historical Jesus had some good things to say (as is already admitted by the Dalai Lama and some rabbis, among others), as Cobb also states that he hopes other religions will find "a deeper faith in what we know as Christ."[21] But, as Christ can be present in many ways to many people, this would not necessarily involve acceptance of all the doctrines usually associated with Christian belief.[22] And in Cobb's view, the goal of interreligious dialogue is clearly not only that other religions should appropriate Christian insights, but also that Christians should appropriate insights from the others. He avoids the triumphalistic assertion that Christianity is "better" through his insistence on "mutual transformation" as the goal of interreligious dialogue.[23]

Raimundo Panikkar has also been critical of the attempts of pluralists like Hick to reduce all religions to a unity in which the claims of individual religions are ignored. There are conflicts between the views of religions on many subjects that cannot be glossed over through the creation of a universal synthesis. Real "pluralism," in Panikkar's view, requires us to admit that there is diversity, and that we cannot create a "niche" for each religion within a larger superstructure of our own construction. If we do create such a superstructure, we do not take the claims of each religion seriously but instead incorporate them into a system of our own devising, and we may not hear what the religions are actually saying.[24] Panikkar seems to have those in mind who, like Hick, reduce all religion to "belief in a transcendent reality" and so ignore the individual beliefs that distinguish religions—about, for example, incarnation, atonement, sin, law, enlightenment, dependent arising, emptiness, duty, and so forth.

We should always try to understand the other, Panikkar believes, but we should not always expect to agree with the other. Some views ought to be rejected, according to any view, as there is no system that could incorporate all viewpoints; in its attempt to unify all under a comprehensive view, any system will always exclude those that do not fit with it. In this sense, supersystems are never as comprehensive as they may seem (as we saw with Hick's view, which cannot allow atheism, polytheism, mysticism, or exclusivism). This is not necessarily bad; it is, in any case, unavoidable, for every viewpoint (even that of a system) involves a particular view. What we can do, however, is recognize that multiple perspectives on truth are possible, and that our view only represents one of the possible views. Truth is relative and relational in the sense that things can only be true in relation to a particular context, and we must understand the context to understand the truth-claims of that context. This does not mean that all must be tolerated, as if we were not allowed to make any judgments—but any judgments we make are inevitably based on our own standards and values, not on some universal perspective that stands outside all others.[25]

Pluralism, for Panikkar, involves the recognition that truth is neither one nor many. It cannot be said to be one, for we do not all agree, and to claim that we do is to ignore our differences and individual beliefs; and it cannot be said to be many, as there cannot be many true answers to a particular question. But if we admit that different things can be true in different contexts and from different perspectives, then we can allow for the differences without abandoning the notion of truth altogether to fall into total relativism.[26] From our own perspective, we take the "part for the whole" (*pars pro toto*), but this also means that we see "the whole through a part" (*totum per partem*). Other views see other parts that they take for the whole, and they are right, insofar as they see the whole through their own distinct perspective. The perspective does affect what they see and how they see it, but it is not less valid for being a particular perspective.[27]

The Christian, then, can see the whole of reality through Christ, but also can recognize that the Hindu may see it all through Krishna or Rama, the Buddhist through Shakyamuni Buddha or Shunyata, and so on. This does not mean that these are simply different names for the same thing. Panikkar would prefer to say that each is an aspect of the whole of reality through which the whole is understood; or, as he puts it, "It is not that this reality *has* many names as if there were a reality outside the name. This reality *is* the many names and each name is a new aspect."[28] Each religion is a separate language that can only say what it says in that language, and each language adds to the totality of the ways in which we speak. Words do not translate exactly from one language to another, and there is no universal language that could give a perspective outside of all of them. Each religious language contributes its understanding of the whole precisely in the unique way in which it describes its own experiences.[29]

Panikkar also reworks Hick's Copernican revolution to suggest a view of the religious universe that reflects the parallel way in which the physical universe has come to be understood, in the light of Einsteinian relativity theory:

> The center is neither the earth (our particular religion), nor the sun (God, transcendence, the Absolute . . .). Rather, each solar system has its own center, and every galaxy turns reciprocally around the other. There is no absolute center. Reality itself is concentric inasmuch as each being (each tradition) is the center of the universe—of its own universe to begin with. The theanthropocosmic insight (which sees the unity between the divine-human-cosmic) suggests a sort of Trinitarian dynamism in which all is implied in all (each person represents the community and each tradition reflects, corrects, compliments, and challenges the other).[30]

There is no center, but each religion contributes something to the others as they form part of the same world. Panikkar finds that the religions interconnect not in similar *content* but in similar *function*, and in this way his "definition" of religion, such as it is, echoes the functionalism of Clifford Geertz. Specifically, each religion purports to provide some solution to the problems of the human condition, however they are defined;[31] and each religion has a basic confidence or trust in reality that it is "ordered—in other words, good, beautiful, and true."[32] As Geertz put it, each religion offers models of and for the world by which it can be seen as orderly rather than meaningless. Religions do this in very different ways, however, so that this similarity of function is not tantamount to a universal theory of religion that would impose a particular understanding on any religious tradition. The ideal is not univocity but a harmony of different voices, in fact a discordant harmony that does not resolve all discord but leaves it in tension with the more concordant moments of agreement.[33] To understand a religion, we must learn its language and hear what it has to say, whether we agree with it or not, as no other religion speaks in exactly the same way about exactly the same things. There is enough similarity in the function of language, or of religion, that "translation," dialogue, and understanding are possible, but all translations are imperfect and perspectival. We must remember that we never have the whole picture, no matter where we stand, as we undertake the difficult task of gaining understanding of the other.

Recently, Mark Heim has followed on the work of Cobb and Panikkar to suggest what may be an even more thoroughgoing form of pluralism. He affirms both Cobb's ideal of mutual transformation of religions in dialogue, and Panikkar's Trinitarian perspectivalism, but goes beyond both in developing his own position of "inclusivist pluralism."[34] Like Cobb and Panikkar, Heim has criticized such "pluralists" as John Hick, Wilfred Cantwell Smith, and Paul Knitter for imposing unity on religions where none exists. He argues that they have not avoided a particular religious viewpoint so much as invented new ones through their metareligious theories that insist all "true" religion must cohere with their views. But there is not one transcendent reality, one faith, or one ideal of justice invoked by all religions; and to claim that such lurks behind the apparent differences in views is to ignore the details that actually comprise the individual religious traditions. If we find a lake filled with trout, bass, and other fish, we can logically conclude that the lake is filled with fish, but not that it is filled with a "fishy ultimate" that "manifests itself to some as trout and others as bass, but which is beyond characterization as one or the other."[35] Heim believes that this is basically Hick's position when he claims not that religions have various beliefs about transcendence but that they really all believe in the same transcendent, which they experience in different ways. To the fisherman, however, it matters whether one catches trout or bass—just as the differences in religious belief matter to those who hold them.

In order to take the differences that exist among religions with full seriousness, Heim argues that we should accept the thesis that they may be oriented toward genuinely different religious objects, goals, or "salvations"—that is, ways of finding meaning, fulfillment, wholeness, and so on. And this does not mean simply that they use different paths to the same goal of "fulfillment," for they find personal fulfillment by reaching different goals. The extinction of self, envisioned as Nirvana by Buddhists, is not the same goal as unity with the Triune God in Christianity. To deny this is again to ignore the obvious differences in goals and to create a metagoal that does not resemble the goal of any of the religions. If a travel agent was to tell a customer that it does not matter where he goes, as Jaffna, London, and Kyoto are really just forms of "the destination" that all travelers seek, he would doubtless find such an abstraction from actual travel to be absurd.[36] It does matter to us where we go and how we get there, and depending on the decisions we make we may choose various destinations as well as various paths. What we get out of the trip is directly tied to the decisions we make about such things; it is not the case that all travel results in the same thing for all people.

Heim, then, proposes not only that we acknowledge the differences among the religious states obtained by people in this life (e.g., enlightenment, salvation, etc.), but also the states they believe they will ultimately obtain. He finds no reason why we cannot allow for the possibility that many such states are possible and realizable beyond this life. In the noumenal realm, Nirvana as well as unity with Christ could be realities, and each may be really obtained by those who seek it. There is a genuine pluralism of religious ends that is accepted on this view, even in the eschatological dimension. To deny this, to insist that all those who obtain the fulfillment of their religious goals will experience the same thing in the afterlife, is to once again impose a view on them that fails to take their individual religious beliefs seriously. Heim does not find it necessary to assume that only one vision of our postmortem state could be actual; he finds no logical or theological reason why we should not accept the plurality of postmortem ends as a real possibility.[37]

Heim does not suggest that we are or can be without preference in regards to our religious ends, for each religion has specific ideas about what will or should happen to us, both in this life and hereafter. But he finds no a priori reason for assuming that the goals sought by other religious traditions are either false or wrong. We may believe, from the point of view of our own religious tradition, that all would be better off if they followed our path to our goal, and we may even believe that they ultimately will end up at our goal; in this, he admits that insofar as we all prefer our own views and believe them to be the best alternative, we are all inclusivists of a sort. But Heim's form of inclusivism differs from Rahner's in that he is "willing to entertain the possibility" that the goals achieved by other religions "could endure as the religious fulfillments of those who pursue various religious ends."[38] Nirvana could exist alongside of the Christian version of salvation, in this sense, perhaps without one dissolving into the other, even though Buddhists and Christians will obviously view their own goal as "higher" or "better" than the other. It may be the case that "one may ultimately be subordinate to the other," but it may also be the case that both may be subordinate to "some other absolute."[39] We do not know who is "right" about such things, and we may be right about some things but wrong about others.[40] As long as we are willing to acknowledge the possibility that our view is not the only one, and that none of us is likely to be exactly right about everything, we can hold our own views even as we have a dialogue with others and learn from them in the process.

In such dialogue, we do not need to accept everything the other says nor agree with everything the other says. Heim sketches at least four possibilities as to how we may make judgments about the claims of other religions. First, we may judge certain of their claims to be simply wrong— judgments of error. We will always have some judgments of this sort, but this does not make us exclusivists unless we dogmatically assert that all judgments about other religions must fall into this category, or that our own views are the only cogent possibility. Second, we may judge their religious goals as actual and valid, but different from our own—judgments of alternativeness. Cobb makes such judgments about Buddhism's complementary truths, and Heim makes such claims regarding the viability of other religious goals. He also allows that such alternatives are usually viewed as penultimate in regard to the goals of one's own religion, but they still may be viewed as valid. Third, judgments of convergence or identity may decide that another religion seeks or comes to the same goal in another way, as when Christians involved in Jewish-Christian dialogue claim that the two religions have dual covenants, each of which is a valid way to God. And fourth, classically inclusivist judgments may view other religions as in fact on the way to the goals of our religion rather than their own, though they do not yet know it.[41] All four of these types of judgments are possible and valid, Heim claims, and there is no reason to assume that only one such type is to be preferred in any given situation. We must allow particular dialogues to develop as they will without prejudicing them toward a particular preconceived result. Just as each religion is unique, so is each dialogue unique to the participants and the situation in which they find themselves, and they must discover the extent and form of their own commonalities and differences.

Even more than Cobb and Panikkar, Heim allows for a real pluralism of religious beliefs and ends that allows for the truth of both our own view and that of another. Neither does this view fall into the subjective relativism of claiming that a view is only "true" for its adherents because they have found it true for themselves; Heim still believes that there is an ontological state of affairs to which religious claims refer, and to which they may either be referring truly or falsely. One religion may have a more accurate description of reality than another, but we cannot know for sure at this time, so that fruitful dialogue will involve our admission that we can learn from another because none of us has absolute certainty for any of our beliefs.

Interreligious Dialogue and Film

If the practice of film viewing can be understood as a religion, as I have argued, then the dialogue between "religion" and "film" is really just another form of interreligious dialogue—and perhaps the insights gained by historians of religion and theologians in regard to how religions should understand one another may be applied fruitfully to this dialogue as well. Rather than assume that religion and culture are entirely different entities, or that religion can assume a hegemonic position in relation to culture, perhaps traditional religions might benefit from learning to listen to the religions of popular culture just as they are learning to listen to one another.

To adopt such a view is to follow the broader approaches of Heim, Cobb, and Panikkar rather than those of traditional exclusivism, Rahner's inclusivism, or Hick's pluralism. It is to suggest that we not assume that we are right and the other is wrong, or that there is only one possible valid view. It is to allow for genuine differences in approach and perspective so that our judgments do not condemn others simply for disagreeing with us but rather seek to hear and allow for different goals and purposes as potentially valid. It is not to accept all points of view as valid, but it is to consider the reasons why people view them as valid and to consider that they might be valid for them in their particular context and from their particular vantage point.

This might not seem so revolutionary an idea with respect to the dialogue between religion and culture, but as we have seen, most traditional religious approaches to the dialogue assume the subordinate status of culture and reject its views when they do not cohere with that of the religion. In fact, the history of interaction between traditional religion (mainly Christianity, in the United States) and film shows the same stages found in the history of the interaction between religions. At first, there was a period of hostility, rejection, and demonization of the movies by the church; and secondly, there was an inclusivist attempt to read the movies as expressing "Christian" values (at least in some instances). In neither case do we really hear what the other is saying, but only seek to establish a view of it as either "not-like-us" and therefore "bad," or "like-us" and therefore "good." The possibility that it might be "not-like-us" but nonetheless valid in its own unique way is not really admitted; difference is not understood to be good. Just as the classic forms of exclusivism, inclusivism, and pluralism all assumed that there must be one correct religious view and so disallowed the possibility of multiple valid religious perspectives, so also standard religious approaches to culture have assumed that culture is valid if it coheres with religion/theology. Examples are the approaches of Niebuhr and Tillich mapped out in the first chapter, and their related intellectual descendants among the writers on religion and film. It has not really been considered whether it is possible for culture to be "right" precisely in its difference from (other) religions, in the way that John Cobb has allowed that Buddhists may be "right" about emptiness even though this idea is not a Christian one.

The "exclusivist" phase began almost as soon as the movies themselves. In 1896, a one-minute film entitled *The Kiss* that re-created a scene from a current play, *The Widow Jones,* called forth the criticism that "the spectacle of the prolonged pasturing on each other's lips," which was bad enough in the play, only got worse once it was "magnified to Gargantuan proportions" on the screen. Critics had already recognized that film was literally and metaphorically "larger than life" and that it had the power to control and seduce audiences in ways that live theater could not. Sexual themes in the movies, in particular, gave rise to attempts at prohibition or censorship. Chicago police, for example, were given the authority to seize any films they deemed "immoral or obscene." In other cities, church leaders pressured city leaders, and in 1909, a National Board of Censorship of Motion Pictures was created, which the film industry agreed to heed as an alternative to government censorship. In practice, however, decisions were often made by local censors, and there was little consistency among them.[42]

One episode that galvanized the Roman Catholic Church in its opposition to the movies involved the World War I film *Fit to Fight* (1918), which purported to educate soldiers about the dangers of venereal disease while overseas. Although the film shows that abstinence is the best policy for avoiding VD, it also shows that medical treatment can achieve the same healthy end; therefore, the Church saw the film as essentially promoting sexual promiscuity as long as appropriate precautions were taken. Today's conservative arguments that sex education in the schools can only encourage sexual activity bear a remarkable resemblance on this point. What particularly enraged Church leaders, however, was the titillating nature of the images, which showed a brothel and indecent "caresses" between the soldiers and prostitutes. This was to be a familiar critique of movies; even though the message of the movie might be that one should not visit a brothel, the depiction of it would arouse the desire to go there, in spite of the "moral" of the story. The same issues arose with *End of the Road*, a film that told the stories of two young unmarried women, one who abstains from sex and one who does not. The latter contracts syphilis, showing the "wages of sin," but her subsequent treatment and cure seemed to some critics to indicate that "sexual intercourse is not bad if one knows how to avoid the consequences." The films were also very popular, indicating most probably that audiences rushed to see them not for the moral message but out of a desire for titillation. The moviemakers could not have been blind to this, either; they could market a film as "moral" even while its drawing power came largely from the attraction of the immorality depicted in it.[43]

The censors were not fools; films did make wrongdoing look attractive, even though a moral lesson was always added to it. This remains a fundamental structure of many films to this day. We sympathize with gangsters and villains and are encouraged to identify with them, and we enjoy doing so for a brief time, even though they suffer justice in the end. This approach relates to the rituals of liminality discussed in an earlier chapter; we step outside the bounds of acceptable morality for a time, so that we might return to it in the end. This return occurs both in the film's moral message and in our own exit from the theaters to our ordinary lives that subscribe to moral conventions. Few fans of gangster movies actually emulated the actions of James Cagney and Edward G. Robinson that they saw on the screen, but they did enjoy fantasizing being them for the duration of the films.

It was precisely this perceived "attraction to the immoral" by viewers that caused the churches—in particular, the Roman Catholic Church—to take stronger action against the movie industry. In 1929, a "Catholic Movie Code" was drafted that called for censorship of such factors as nudity and explicit sexuality, and it also effectively called for the positive reinforcement of religious, family, and societal values. The church had perceived the power of the movies to promote certain religious and moral values and intended to make sure that this power was used to reinforce the status quo values of "church and state" rather than the decadent values of the movie industry.[44] This code was to become the basis for the so-called "Hays Office Code," which ostensibly governed what was to be shown in movies for the next thirty years. Will Hays had previously been named as president of the Motion Picture Producers and Distributors of America (MPPDA), a watchdog agency employed by the film industry itself to police the content of movies. That the industry accepted Hays and the code shows the lengths to which they were willing to go to avoid government censorship.

The Hays Office had little power of enforcement, however, between the years of 1930 and 1934, when many films of "questionable" morality were produced.[45] This changed when Hays appointed Joseph Breen as head of the Studio Relations Department. Breen was an ardent Catholic and a virulent anti-Semite. He believed that Hollywood was being run by "the Jews," the "dirty lice" who were corrupting the American people with their debauched values. He was not above intimidating the Jewish Hollywood moguls for whom he had no respect, and Church leaders did not rebuke him for his anti-Semitism as it served their purposes of cleaning up the industry.[46] Here again we see the conflict between movies and the Church understood as a religious conflict, even though Breen's view of it was based on a distorted and prejudiced image of Jews. For although most religious Jews (certainly the Orthodox) were probably just as unhappy with the lax morality of the cinema as their Christian counterparts, and in that sense it was not actually a battle between the values of Judaism and those of Catholicism, it was still configured as a battle between religious values by many of the participants in the struggle—whether that battle was viewed as being between Christians and Jews, or between Christians and immoral libertines.

Like all censorship standards, the code proved difficult to apply and enforce largely because of the subjectivity involved with deciding what were acceptable values. It was not simply a question of whether a film showed too much skin, but whether the dialogue or plot suggested indecent content—and this was finally a matter of opinion, as so much is in film and all artistic critique. Adultery could be in a story, for example, as long as the undesirable consequences of it were shown, as in the film version of *Anna Karenina* (1935) in which the heroine commits suicide in the end as in the book. But the film also depicted Anna's husband as so cold and unloving, and Anna so sympathetically, that at least many female members of the audience would probably not judge her as much as feel for the injustice of her situation. Breen did not see this and approved the film, but the Chicago Legion of Decency condemned it.[47] Similar conflicts occurred over the merits of film adaptations of famous novels by Ernest Hemingway, William Faulkner, and Sinclair Lewis. Some thought they were brilliant and challenging, and others found them sordid and base. When he won the Nobel Prize for Literature in 1930, Lewis had criticized those conservatives who would reduce literature to the depiction of the pretty rather than the sordid that marks real life. The Catholic Church had tried to police literature in just this fashion, but seemed to have more success with the film adaptations of novels than the books themselves.[48]

The end of the era of censorship came in part from the changing attitudes of society, which tolerated more and often found the churches' condemnations outdated. But the censors themselves also came to see the difficulties involved in their task as they grew more tolerant and appreciative of the artistic use of "questionable" themes and images. As early as 1937, Breen himself was impressed by the tough quality of the film *Dead End*, which realistically depicted the desperate life of poverty and crime that was the fate of children in the slums. The film passed the censors with minimal changes, even though it did not present the happy picture of America they normally favored, because its social message was viewed as powerful and significant, albeit critical.[49] At the end of the censorship era, a similar case occurred with *The Pawnbroker* (1965), which was granted a special exemption to show nudity. The shot in question involved a prostitute bearing her breasts to the title character, who as a result undergoes a flashback of his wife's rape by Nazi soldiers in a concentration camp. The importance of this to the story, and the social and moral message associated with it, convinced the censors that this shot was not designed to titillate but to shock and challenge the audience. The Catholic Legion of Decency condemned the picture anyway, as they held to a legalistic rejection of all nudity in movies, but as a result they lost credibility and suffered something of an identity crisis.[50] Within three years, the code was replaced by a form of the current ratings system (G, M, R, and X) in an effort to police content for juvenile consumption while allowing movies to present any images or themes they wished.

The Catholic Church, and other religious groups, shifted gears to accommodate the new era fairly quickly. Even a film that initially received an X rating, *Midnight Cowboy* (1969), received critical acclaim from some within the churches for its gritty realism and its moral message of the possibility of self-sacrifice and friendship even among those whom society has rejected. The "inclusivist" phase of film interpretation had begun, as religious film critics began to appreciate "artistic" (often foreign) films for their "Christian" moral themes. The work of these writers, analyzed in the first chapter of this book, forms the real beginning of the appreciation of film by the representatives of traditional religion. This view, however, relied extensively on stark distinctions between "good" and "bad" films that might allow explicit sexuality and violence if it seemed to serve a "moral" message of a "challenging" film, but not if it was deemed to be "exploitative" or purely for purposes of "entertainment." Although they were willing to allow value to some films, this determination was based on a highly subjective assessment of the meaning of the terms I have placed in quotation marks and the ways in which particular films connect with these. Essentially, they were looking for a way to avoid being completely judgmental of culture, as this poise was becoming impractical and increasingly absurd for those who do not wish to reject culture entirely, but they also wanted to find a way to uphold "Christian" values as normative. Films were viewed as good if they subscribed to such values, and bad if they didn't. This theological method of analysis is still being used today, as we have seen.

Those scholars of religion who follow a more ideological than theological form of analysis of film are often still in the exclusivist phase, as seen by the desire for censorship sometimes found as much among left-wing ideological critics as among right-wing critics of film. The difference between right-wing exclusivists (exemplified today more by conservative evangelical Protestants than mainline Protestants or Roman Catholics) and left-wing exclusivists is that the latter have as their orthodoxy not Christian doctrine but their own forms of ideological analysis that take on the contours of a religious tradition for them. All films (or at least all "popular" films) may be judged to be found wanting from this perspective if they are seen as supporting hegemonies of gender, race, and class, even prior to the actual analysis of the films. Such films may be viewed as incapable of having a positive function for women or other oppressed groups, if they are made by and therefore assumed to represent the interests of the dominant group. As we have discussed, this viewpoint makes a priori assumptions about the meaning of films without any real study of audience appropriation, and so may miss the fact that films may have a more positive role in the lives of women and other oppressed groups than many ideological critics are willing to allow.

There must be an alternative to the exclusivism of left-wing and right-wing ideological critics as well as to the inclusivism of theological interpretations that read film only through Christian categories or those of other traditional religions.[51] I have suggested that this alternative can be found in viewing film as itself a religion. Interestingly, however, traditional religion has always reacted to film as if it were a religion, even when this was not explicitly admitted. By relating to it either as a demonic threat to their own religion, or a mirror image of it, religious film critics were essentially already viewing film through the categories of religion. If film did not supply an alternative value system and way of viewing the world, expressed through the ritual of filmgoing, it would not have been perceived as such a threat to traditional religion. The fact that it was perceived in this way indicates that it was perceived as addressing the same set of issues, albeit in a very different way. If it was denied the status of "religion," this may reflect an attempt to discredit the alternative it presented, in the same way that early Christian explorers of the Americas were reluctant to call the practices of the "Indians" by the name of religion. Not only was it so different that it did not seem to fit the category of religion as they knew it, but it was also successfully demonized and marginalized by refusing to grant it this title. Today it is much more the case than it was then that we feel we should tolerate that which we call "religion," and therefore we are reluctant to bestow this title on phenomena we would rather reject as "ideologies," "cults," and "sects"—thereby dismissing them from being serious dialogue partners. If it cannot be made to resemble our own religion, with an inclusivist interpretation, we reject it as other and therefore as bad.

Jonathan Z. Smith has reflected on the ways in which we marginalize others with whom we would rather not have dialogue, and nowhere more pointedly than in "The Devil in Mr. Jones," a short article written two years after the 1978 mass suicide of the followers of Jim Jones in Guyana. Here he suggested that scholars of religion cannot simply dismiss such a phenomenon as "demonic," as Billy Graham had done in that case, for it is our commission to seek to understand even that which we would rather not. If we choose to demonize that which is too shocking or offensive to us, falling into the sort of emotional judgments that characterized the media treatment of the situation, we are surrendering the scholarly value that seeks to understand all human behavior through the light of reason rather than through cultural prejudice. We are also essentially choosing to view such people as nonhuman if we decide that they are beyond reason or understanding, and in the process we make them totally other to ourselves and to our way of thinking. While Smith agrees that mass suicide is repellent to us and requires moral judgment, he holds that such judgment cannot occur without first seeking to gain some understanding of the motives of the participants. If instead we choose to dehumanize them, we give up the value of a common humanity, and relinquish the very value we hope to uphold.[52]

Since Smith wrote the article over two decades ago, research on "cults" like Jonestown has progressed beyond demonization toward the sort of understanding of motives and worldview that Smith was encouraging. He came up with two theories about Jonestown himself in the original article. One idea is to understand what happened as a sort of "Dionysiac praxis" that sought to overcome social and racial distinctions by a retreat to a created utopia. When this utopia was threatened by outsiders, the community saw no choice other than to leave this world for a better one. There are parallels here to the events at the Branch Dravidian compound in Waco, Texas, in 1993, which saw the followers of David Koresh seeking escape from this world before capture. Second, Smith believes that the mass suicide could be understood as an act of revolutionary protest against those who sought to destroy their utopia, and the audiotapes the community left behind seem to confirm that they understood their action in this way.[53]

Smith suggests that if we seek to understand their motives, we may have more sympathy for them and not simply view them as misguided or brainwashed followers of a psychotic leader. People do have reasons for their behaviors, and it behooves us to uncover those reasons even when we do not agree with them. Smith recognizes that we can no longer appeal naively to our own cultural version of "reason" as if this were identical with some universal reason, but he insists that our awareness of this cultural relativity should not lead us to the total relativism that says there is no basis for judging any culture but our own. We must continue to attempt to formulate "rules of reason" by which we can make judgments, even though we know we cannot come to a definitive formulation of them.[54]

Smith's approach also seems helpful in regard to judgments about popular culture. To admit that we ought to take popular culture seriously is to admit that we should seek to understand its worldview and values, and its appeal, rather than simply dismiss it as a mindless and nihilistic glorification of sex and violence. But to attempt to understand why people are drawn to movies, and what they get out of them, is not to celebrate all the values they present or to be totally uncritical of them. Ideological critics feel that they must guard against the uncritical acceptance of popular culture as "harmless fun," and indeed we should not preemptively decide it is harmless any more than we should preemptively decide that it is harmful. Any judgments that are made must be made on the basis of study and an attempt to understand how film functions for people as a worldview, a system of values, and a ritual practice for joining the two—in other words, as a "religion" in the sense in which I have defined the term.

Ideological criticism of popular culture, by religion scholars and those in other fields, will and should continue as a necessary method for uncovering the ways in which films function ideologically in support of hegemonic systems. But ideological critique cannot be the only method used for the analysis of popular culture, or we will find ourselves seeing culture only through the small aperture afforded by such a critique. Film should not be reduced to its ideological function any more than religion should be. If we analyze films utilizing such a method, we must remember that ideology is only one aspect of film and its appropriation by viewers. Within the field of film criticism proper, there has already begun the critique of ideological interpretations that decide what films "mean" for their audiences based not on what audiences say but rather on what the theorists believe; as a result, studies of audience reception of films have increased in number and quality.[55] Scholars of religion who interpret films would also do well to learn to listen to film viewers and seek to understand why they go to the movies and what they get out of them. Only then can we hope to understand the "religious" power of films, just as we can only understand Jonestown by studying what its members said and believed rather than imposing on them our own view of what they believed.

In the chapters that follow, we will begin to apply this method to the study of various films and genres. This is only intended to be a beginning, and the interpretations I suggest are necessarily tentative. I have based some of my ideas on audience response data when it is available, either from my own personal observations and conversations or from published studies of others, but the lack of extensive work in this area has made some speculation about audience reaction unavoidable. Of course, even with extensive data, the scholar necessarily imposes some categories on the data in the process of interpreting it. In trying to hear how films are understood by their audiences and what effect films have on them, one will never understand the viewers as they understand themselves—just as the best anthropologist never comes to understand her subjects as they do themselves, even if she "goes native." The unavoidability of the scholar's personal subjectivity, however, is not (as Geertz observed) license to do "surgery in a sewer." We can attempt to avoid the "contamination" of our own views, even though they will be present even in the "cleanest" of interpretations, first by being aware of them, and second by realizing that there are other ways of viewing things that we can seek to understand. This attitude will make us more open to seeing the films as their viewers may, instead of seeing them as scholars are wont to do.

There is another rather obvious point to be made here; scholars are viewers, too, and as such may participate in the filmic religion as well. Once we give up narrower definitions of "religion" that only identify it with formal institutions that go by that label, we can recognize that multiple religious influences affect each one of us. It is not the case that there are some who follow the religion of film and others who follow Christianity or Judaism; unless we completely distance ourselves from the power and pleasure of the movies (as some ideological critics have sought to do), we are already implicated in our subject matter. This does not mean that one is worshiping false gods every time one goes to the cinema, any more than a Christian who studies Buddhism has deserted his or her religion. We can learn from a number of religious influences, and if "religion" is not the monolithic entity it was once thought to be, then we may find ourselves drawing from a variety of sources in the construction of our religious beliefs. All the major religions of history have done the same thing, as, for example, Christianity developed out of Judaism and its encounter with Hellenistic religion, incorporating ideas from other religious communities and transforming them in the process. No religion appears in the world without a heritage of religious influences, and no religion remains alive unless it deals with the continuing encounters it has with other religions. When one realizes this, one sees another reason why the attempt to guard against all cultural influences is doomed unless one can completely isolate one's religious community.

In what follows, I focus on seven genres and some films that represent them. In some cases, I have amalgamated genres that are interrelated. These are westerns and "action" films; gangster movies; melodrama and "tearjerkers"; romantic comedies; children's films, with a focus on fantasy; science fiction; and thrillers and horror movies. For each, I will define the primary audience of the genre and what they may receive religiously from the film in the form of worldview, values, and ritual participation/catharsis, and I will also provide analyses of particular films as examples of this religious experience.

PART II

Genre and Film Analyses

In the remaining chapters we will see in greater detail how the method I have outlined so far may be applied to actual analysis of films. We will examine a variety of films from a variety of genres to show how the method can be utilized with divergent materials, while I give more extended analyses of one or two films from each genre. These analyses will attend to the myths or worldviews conveyed in the films, their ethical values, and the ritual processes by means of which these are appropriated for the viewer.

I have made some reference to the need for audience reception studies, especially insofar as these can lead us to understand better how ordinary film viewers (rather than film theorists or critics) understand the films. There are only a limited number of ethnographic studies surveying audience reaction to films, so one might think that the absence of extensive data would argue against drawing definitive conclusions about "what audiences really think." In fact, however, we can never draw definitive conclusions about this sort of thing, even if we should be flooded by audience studies, as ethnography by its very nature really only allows one to draw conclusions about the population surveyed (although the conclusions may have wider applicability, if one grants that the survey group is typical). Given that no amount of data guarantees certainty regarding generalized conclusions, I have not allowed the absence of extensive data to prevent me from drawing some tentative conclusions about the ways some audiences may appropriate some films. And, after all, using a little bit of audience study is better than using none at all, which has often in practice been the method of film studies. I have found a variety of tools to aid in the task of discerning the minds of audiences. I have utilized some studies of audiences done by others; I have utilized my own interpretive observations drawn from conversations with students and other viewers of films who are not professional film theorists; I have taken note of box office success as an indicator of the fact that a movie has something in it that

137

people like; and I have utilized a form of the concept of the "implied reader" developed by Martin Barker.

Barker's own approach to film analysis has been formed largely in reaction against psychoanalytic interpretations that he sees as unconnected with the ways any actual audience appropriates films. Such interpretations suggest bizarre ideas, such as that George Bailey of *It's a Wonderful Life* (1946) secretly wanted his brother and father to die, that he didn't really want to leave home, and that what he actually wants is to become more like a woman. Barker correctly, I would say, objects to such attribution of hidden motives to fictional characters that fly in the face of the entire narrative and its more "normal" reception by viewers.[1] His own approach is to suggest the ways in which audiences might make interpretive moves by reacting to certain elements of the film, based on their own prefilmic assumptions as well as how they connect the diverse elements of the film in their own understanding.[2] He does not see this approach as endorsing an "anything-goes pluralism" according to which we cannot view any interpretation as better than another, for we can still "test" interpretations against the text of the film, looking for the possible interpretations it invites. There may be a number of valid interpretations of a film rather than only one, but that does not mean that all interpretations are equally valid. He also suggests that we do not need to choose either textual analysis or audience reception studies, as if these were opposed, for it is precisely in interpretation that the text and its reception are connected; to neglect one or the other is to lose the possibility of any real understanding of how the response invited by a film is related to what is actually received by viewers.[3] With Barker, I would argue that we need to analyze what is actually in the film, but also we need to consider how audiences may be receiving it— and even with limited data, we are able to draw some conclusions that I believe may have wider applicability. At the very least, I believe that my own speculations about audience reception have greater credibility than many of the fanciful interpretations of ideological critics.

Another point I should note is that I have organized our discussion around certain genres, with examples of films from each. Although I have certainly missed certain genres (such as the musical), those that I have chosen to discuss are intended to give a sample of the range of film types seen today as well as in earlier points in cinema history, which continue to be popular. The fact that I have organized my remarks around genres should not be taken to imply that I would endorse many of the theses of so-called "genre criticism" that have sometimes assumed that genre conventions squelch creativity and artistry (and hence are bad). Early genre theorists held that all westerns or gangster pictures were basically the same, with just enough variation in plot or theme to keep audience interest. Closer study of these genres has shown that such conclusions were based on a limited number of films, and that the critics chose to ignore those films which did not "fit"—suggesting, for example, that a film is not "really" a western because it does not conform to the critic's model for westerns, even if it has all the usual elements of cowboys and ranchers and gunslingers.[4] I recognize that all genre labels are artificial, as they are based on generalizations about certain types of films that may or may not hold up with respect to a particular film. At the same time, generalizations are helpful tools for understanding, as long as one recognizes that they are our constructions rather than statements about the nature of reality in itself.

Furthermore, genre labels are used by audiences to help them decide what films to see, as different groups have differing preferences, and they use such labels to guide their viewing and their expectations. The film industry has also used this information about audience tastes to attempt to give audiences what they want. For example, when it seemed audiences were tired of westerns and biblical epics, the industry stopped making them, moving recently to more violent thrillers, action movies, and "grossout" adolescent comedies, as these are popular. This shows that genres are "real" as part of audience reception of a film, even though they are constructed by audiences and the industry that seeks to please them. In addition, films sometimes utilize elements from a variety of genres, showing the fluid nature of such labels but also showing how the industry taps into multiple markets by designing films that appeal to various groups with differing genre tastes. Such "hybridization" can be seen, for example, in a film like *Titanic*, which managed to be both a romantic tearjerker and an action/disaster movie (thus appealing to both female and male audiences).[5]

As we consider the following genres and films, it will become clear that some very different purposes are achieved by different types of films, but also that there are some similarities. The range of types of popular films also demonstrates that there is not a single set of religious structures utilized by films, but a diversity of beliefs and values appropriated in divergent ritual fashions. Although some ideological critics have suggested that all films express the same set of values, close study of the differences between films and film types would suggest otherwise. As with other religious materials, it does not pay to generalize in assuming that everyone believes or values the same things or expresses this in the same way.

6

Westerns and Action Movies

The first genres to be identified as genres by film theorists were the western and the gangster picture, largely because it was noticed that there were elements of plot, theme, and iconography that gave a distinctive look and feel to such films. In the case of the western, we have a genre that already existed in popular literature and was translated to the screen beginning during the silent era. Hundreds of silent westerns were made in the first two decades of the twentieth century, many of them focusing on "the Indian problem" more extensively than later westerns.[1] This is not so strange when one recalls that the period the western dramatizes, the post–Civil War expansion of white populations and the consequent displacement of the Native Americans, was still within recent memory. The massacre at Wounded Knee that followed the Ghost Dance movement had only taken place in 1890, and many film viewers would no doubt remember the times when Indians had been perceived as more of a threat than they were later. Some films romanticized the Indian, but most tended to sanction the dominant ideology of manifest destiny and the necessary extinction of the Indian. (In later westerns, once the threat was clearly in the distant past, more regret is expressed about this occurrence, even though it still tends to be viewed as "necessary.")[2]

The sound films that have come to determine the way most of us think of westerns, however, did not focus so much on "cowboys vs. Indians" as the trials of the frontier. In the myth of the western, law was almost nonexistent on the frontier, and justice and order only ruled through a few good men who were swift on the draw, whether they wore sheriff badges or not. There were bad men too, of course, and walk-down gun battles in deserted streets conducted according to some ancient code of honor that apparently dictated no one should be shot in the back (although this principle was often not observed in the final reel). Visually, the western was set in wide-open spaces punctuated by frontier towns filled with saloons and brothels, and there was usually a railroad on the way, bringing civilization and all its good and bad features. The western depicted a romantic time and space that probably never existed but that was effective for denoting a setting in which good and evil could fight to the death without the impediments of social convention, and we could be clear about which was which, as the moral ambiguity of modern times had not yet set in. In this way, the western evokes the same nostalgia one finds in fairy tales of chivalrous knights and virtuous damsels set in medieval times. This is not to say that there were no moral questions for the western; often, whole films were based around a moral question regarding when (or whether) it was justified to attack the bad guys. But the western hero always does attack, in the end, and we know that he has done what is right for he had no alternative: "A man's gotta do what a man's gotta do." In this way, westerns served to reassure audiences that good and evil do exist in clear form, even though the complexity of our own lives sometimes prevents us from seeing this. By creating an imagined world in which good and evil were clearly defined, the western lets us know that our own inability to distinguish them at times is not an indication that no distinction exists. Rather, it is an indication that we live in more complex times, and this fact is depicted with regret, as there is almost always sadness associated in the western with the demise of the frontier and the coming of east-coast civilization.

This regret associated with the "death of the West" is sometimes expressed in the fate of the western hero who cannot become part of the emerging civilization that displaces the frontier, perhaps because of his violent nature that, somewhat paradoxically, makes the taming of the frontier (and hence its transformation into civilization) possible. This theme takes on almost tragic proportions in many classic later westerns such as *Shane* (1953) or *The Searchers* (1956), in which we are made to feel the exclusion of the hero as sad but necessary. In both of these films also, the hero who saves the family cannot remain within it without disrupting it further. We saw in an earlier chapter that such films may relate to ideas of sacrifice insofar as the hero engages in the act of restorative violence necessary to the community, but must leave in order to free it of his taint; he becomes the scapegoat to which we transfer our own violent sins. As I suggested there, this feeling need not imply a relinquishment of responsibility on the part of the audience, for we "participate" in his violence via identification with his character. The plot may in fact offer an opportunity for people to work through their own ambiguous feelings about violence and its necessity in the service of various causes.

It is also not always the case that the western hero is "punished" for his lawless behavior, although he may have to leave "civilization" because of it. In director John Ford's *Stagecoach* (1939), Ringo (John Wayne) is allowed his revenge on the three men who killed his father and brother, and he is also permitted by the law to escape with his true love (who happens to be a prostitute with a heart of gold). At this point, there is still a frontier into which he can happily escape. By the time Ford made *The Man Who Shot Liberty Valence* (1962), however, Tom Doniphon (again John Wayne) not only loses the girl to eastern lawyer Ransom Stoddard (Jimmy Stewart), but also the credit for ridding the town of bad guy Valence. Stoddard, who eschews violence, finds himself in a gun battle with Valence, and thinks he kills him when in fact Doniphon shotguns him from the shadows. Stoddard has a successful political career because of this outcome, and Doniphon becomes an embittered drunk. The West and its heroes are depicted as dead at this point, and yet the myth lives on that it was tamed by men willing to kill for it. Ironically, the movie suggests that the myth or "legend" is that Stoddard, symbol of law and order, tamed the West (as that is what his adoring public thinks) when in fact it was men like Doniphon. But the real myth of the western which the audience sees, in this film as in many others, is that law and order will not suffice unless aided by those who are willing to use violence and occasionally step outside the law in the service of justice. No one who likes westerns believes that the frontier was tamed by lawyers like Ransom Stoddard.

Whether the hero is punished or not, therefore, has more to do with how far civilization has encroached and less with his guilt or innocence or our need for a sacrificial lamb to suffer for our own societal or individual violence. What is noble about most western heroes is their willingness to use violence, even though this act requires sacrifice from them, if such violence is in the service of a good cause, such as the destruction of evildoers. Western heroes are not above the quest for revenge, either, nor is this desire viewed as a dishonorable motive in most cases. Bad guys deserve to die, in westerns, both to prevent them from doing more bad and in punishment for past wrongs.

Since the 1970s, there have been far fewer westerns than earlier, though the reasons are unclear. One might suggest that the moral simplicity of westerns seems less credible, but actually contemporary films are sometimes more simplistic in their dualistic depiction of good and evil. Clint Eastwood has kept the western genre alive by reworking many of its classic themes in a nihilistic and excessively violent direction, creating antiheroes whose apocalyptic quests for revenge seem to transcend the grave, as in *High Plains Drifter* (1973) and *Pale Rider* (1985). These characters show none of the hesitation about violence that marked earlier westerns, having unleashed the anger of the westerner so that few restraints affect him. Perhaps the hesitation about violence that characterized earlier westerns seems unnecessary to modern audiences, who are more ready to accept excessive violence in the first reel. This does not necessarily mean that modern audiences are less moral; it may simply reflect the demise of the Hays Code and the consequently unleashed audience appetite for greater thrills, violence, and excitement. Audiences may lack the patience to wait until the end of the film for a gun battle, as was the case in many classic westerns.

But a decrease in the number of westerns does not signal the end of the themes of the western. In many ways, the modern action film has taken up those themes and transformed them into a form more acceptable to modern audiences. There have always been action films, of course; swashbucklers, for example, featured charming rogues played by the likes of Douglas Fairbanks or Errol Flynn who fought against tyranny by working outside the law, whether as Zorro or Robin Hood. In such films it is not that violence is needed to preserve society, but rather it is needed to overthrow it. The possibly revolutionary edge to such films is blunted by the fact that the hero is usually a displaced aristocrat who needs to oust the usurper (e.g., Prince John) in order to restore the "true king" to the throne. Politics aside, viewers probably enjoyed the liminal fantasy of "legitimate" revolt against the authorities, just as they enjoyed the westerner who could step outside the law to restore justice. Forms of both of these genres can be found in the modern action film.

The forerunner of the modern action film might be seen most obviously in the ever popular and extremely formulaic James Bond films, now forty years old and still going strong, which also invented the modern subgenre of the spy film. Although the Bond films would seem to be the height of antifeminist cinema in their reduction of women to sexual objects and in their absurd and almost pornographic portrayal of Bond's endless sexual appetite and ability, they have been popular with women as well as men. This may be because Bond remains more ordinary and vulnerable than some of the overly muscled macho men of recent action films, excelling in neither strength nor intellect but appealing because of his luck and sense of humor in facing mad scientists and giant villains. Bond also makes plenty of mistakes, but he learns from them; he also thinks on his feet in an emergency, remaining charming and dashing throughout.

Today, action movies are often associated with big-name stars who bring muscular bodies and martial arts ability to the task. The most successful ones, however, usually feature a central character with whom at least the male members of the audience can identify, so that he has a personality and not only a well-oiled torso. They seek to have some of the wit of Sean Connery or Errol Flynn, to show that they can laugh in the face of danger and provide some humor to the audience in the midst of the thrills. Two successful series of the 1980s and 1990s were the *Die Hard* and *Lethal Weapon* films, each featuring a sympathetic and imperfect leading character dealing with personal or family problems as well as the bad guys. *Lethal Weapon* (1987) featured Mel Gibson as Martin Riggs, a cop who is good at his job because he is near-suicidal due to the death of his wife. His willingness to risk his life makes him a "lethal weapon," as he has no fear of death but actually courts it. Early in the film, we see him ready to shoot himself in the head, only to back down at the last second, seemingly from cowardice. So the man who is afraid to kill himself is afraid of nothing else, and his reckless behavior drives his family-man partner Roger Murtaugh (played by Danny Glover) up the wall, as he would like *not* to be killed. Much of the humor of the film comes from the contrast between them, as in many "buddy" action movies. The resolution comes when Riggs saves Murtaugh's daughter in a daring rescue and finds the desire to live again. The sequels were unable to re-create this dynamic (as Riggs has already decided not to kill himself), but audience fondness for the characters continued and helped insure the success of the later films. To suggest that it is simply scenes of violence that keep audiences coming to such films is to miss the fact that characters matter to audiences; they need to be able to identify with them, to feel their plight as their own, in order to become involved in the story. Otherwise, all action films would achieve the same profits, and there would be no point in filmmakers bothering with story at all.

The action movie hero often invites audience identification in his willingness to challenge the rules of the establishment, as Gibson's character does in his reckless and not fully approved techniques for criminal apprehension. At the same time, he works to eliminate threats to the established order and so preserve peace. This is a reworking of the paradox of the western hero who stands just outside (or at the edge) of the law in order to establish law and order. And just as the western gunslinger was not always appreciated but was instead ostracized for his violent ways, even by those whom he had saved, so also the action movie hero sometimes goes unappreciated for his efforts. The hero of *Die Hard* (1988), John McClane (played by Bruce Willis), is such a hero. I will give a more extended analysis of this movie as an example of a modern action film that has consciously built upon the classic western and updated it in the process.

Die Hard (1988)

The film opens as John McClane, New York City policeman, is landing on a plane in Los Angeles to visit his estranged wife and their two children for the Christmas holidays. The limousine from her company picks him up, and the young driver (a likable African American named Argyle) manages to determine that John was unwilling to move to the West Coast when a career opportunity emerged for John's wife, as he had too many "bad guys" in New York still left to catch. Argyle agrees to wait in the garage of the building until John calls to let him know whether he can stay with his wife or not. Inside the Nakatomi Building, John finds his wife is listed under her maiden name—Holly Gennero—much to his distress. He takes the elevator to the corporate Christmas party on the thirtieth floor, where he is clearly out of place. He meets Holly's boss, a friendly Japanese American named Joe Takagi, before finding Holly. Another executive, Ellis, urges her to show John the Rolex watch she has been given by the company as a sign of thanks for her successful efforts on its behalf. Once they are alone, John begins a fight with her about the fact that she is using her maiden name; she claims that she needs to show her independence in the business world by this gesture, and the argument develops into one about whether it was necessary for her to move to Los Angeles so quickly. After she leaves the room, John immediately berates himself for starting the argument. He clearly wants to be reunited with her but his male pride is interfering with the process.

This domestic drama is interrupted by the arrival of the terrorists who seize control of the party, and John escapes undetected into the stairwell, albeit in his undershirt and bare feet. He manages to eavesdrop on the murder of Joe Takagi, who will not give the terrorists the code to the company vault. Their leader, Hans Gruber, is a suave and educated German who makes references to Alexander the Great and expensive suits, showing that he is of the same class as Takagi and the other corporate executives;

this is no low-class hoodlum. In fact, he and his men only appear to be political terrorists, for they are really only after the $640 million in negotiable bearer bonds kept in the vault. The idea that they are simply a more brutal form of capitalist than those they are stealing from is made clear by Ellis, who in a foolish attempt to negotiate with them suggests that "business is business. You use a gun, I use a fountain pen; what's the difference?" The difference is their willingness to use violence, a factor Ellis badly underestimates and which gets him killed, but in motives they are the same. Because of this, John's fight with them is a working-man's fight against the rich and powerful, sanctioned by the fact that these men (unlike the Nakatomi corporation) operate outside the law and so can legitimately be dealt with by the violent methods of his own profession. Whereas he had no socially acceptable way to show his anger at the company that has taken his wife from him, he can fight back against the darker form of capitalist incarnated in Gruber and his coworkers.

It is not only his exclusion from the power elites of capitalism that makes John an outsider and a representative of the disenfranchised. His methods go unappreciated throughout the film by a host of bureaucrats who insist on following rules rather than using their brains. When he manages to gain possession of one of the walkie-talkies of the terrorists and calls the police with it, he is answered by a policewoman who informs him that he is not authorized to use that channel as it is only for emergencies. As he has been describing the terrorist takeover, he answers with exasperation (and punctuated with appropriate obscenities), "Do I sound like I'm ordering a pizza?" She does not believe the threat is real, so only one policeman is sent to investigate—Sergeant Al Powell, who becomes John's only contact on the outside that he can trust. When the police arrive in force, however, Deputy Chief of Police Dwayne Robinson takes charge, and he orders a disastrous attempt by a SWAT team and an all-terrain vehicle to gain entry to the building, which results in the destruction of the ATV by the terrorists' missiles. John intervenes again by rigging up a bomb that kills the two terrorists firing missiles at the police, but Robinson does not appreciate this; when he talks to John on the walkie-talkie, he informs him, "You just destroyed a building, mister." John's response to this lack of appreciation is to insist he will only talk to Al, who reassures John, "I love you. So do a lot of the other guys," that is, the ordinary policemen who understand how to deal with bad guys. Robinson thinks that one can negotiate with terrorists, which the audience knows is false because we know their plan is to kill all the hostages and escape with the money. The FBI, in contrast, has no desire to negotiate but has a plan to gun down the terrorists from a helicopter once they are with the hostages on the roof. They calculate they will lose "25 percent tops" of the hostages in this gambit and are willing to sacrifice them—indicating their inhumane methods, which contrast with John's everyday policeman ethic that will not allow innocent deaths.

John also shows his outsider status and his links to the western hero through a joke that develops early in the film when Hans Gruber asks him (on the walkie-talkie) if he is just "another American who saw too many movies as a child" who "thinks he's John Wayne, Rambo, Marshall Dillon." John sardonically responds to this attempt to belittle his efforts by suggesting, "Actually, I was always kind of partial to Roy Rogers. I really liked those sequin shirts." He makes fun of the western myth of the hero by invoking the memory of a musical cowboy, who was neither macho nor menacing, and who does not at all fit the image of the cowboy hero. But John does take on the persona of a western hero, and the film consciously plays with this. Hans calls him "cowboy" and Al calls him "Roy" before his name is known, and the final confrontation between John and Hans is set up like a western showdown. John finds Hans with Holly, whom Hans has by now realized is John's wife, and John drops his machine gun and puts his hands on his head, apparently surrendering, as Hans is holding a gun to Holly's head. "You got me," he says, and Hans believes that John expects him now to release Holly, as if he was expected to abide by the same "cowboy" code of honor he believes John follows. "Always the cowboy," Hans remarks, "Well, this time John Wayne does not walk off into the sunset with Grace Kelly." John follows: "It was Gary Cooper, you asshole." This is a clear reference to *High Noon* (1952), which featured Cooper and Kelly; in that film, of course, Cooper's character, like John McClane, is completely alone in his showdown with the villains as no one in the town will help him, except (in the end) his wife. Continuing the joke, Hans quotes John's remark to him earlier which obscenely parodied Roy Rogers: "Yippee kayay, Motherfucker." John laughs insanely, and then manages to pull a gun taped to his back, shoots Hans and the other terrorist (he only had two bullets left, so aim was crucial), and blows across the point of the pistol in another clear reference to the western quick-draw gunslinger. Hans, who does not understand the ethic of the western hero, missed the fact that the hero will use trickery when necessary as he is not the servant of a code of honor when it comes to criminals; even John Wayne or Grace

Kelly will shoot someone in the back when necessary. "Happy trails, Hans," are John's parting words to him, as Hans falls out the window.

John's domestic troubles and their resolution also figure into this conclusion. Earlier, when he thinks he is going to die in the final confrontation, John tells Al that after all is over he should find Holly and tell her "I should've been more supportive, been behind her more" because "she's the best thing that ever happened to a bum like me." He admits he has never said he's sorry to her, and tells Al to "tell her John said he was sorry." Holly never gets to hear this speech, but the audience does, so they know that he regrets his unwillingness to support her career. Interestingly, however, the symbol of her corporate success—the Rolex watch—must be removed from Holly's wrist after Hans grabs onto it as he falls out the window. In addition, when John introduces Holly to Al at the end, he calls her "Holly Gennero," but she counters "Holly McClane." Feminist analysis might suggest that Holly is being reembedded in her husband's identity with this symbolic loss of her corporate status and her acceptance of his rescue and his name. However, Holly does not give up her career (as the sequels made clear), nor does John seem to have retracted his confession or his new willingness to allow her independence. The film holds in tension these elements of sexism and nonsexism, and there is no reason to believe the sexist elements will dominate in all audience appropriation of the film. When my own students discussed this film, they were split on whether the film was ultimately sexist or not, and the division did not occur along gender lines—that is, there were both women and men arguing both points of view.

My own speculations about the message the film conveys to its audiences would suggest that John effectively suffers for the male sins of sexism, his own as well as those of male audience members, as when we see him painfully picking glass out of his bloody feet during his "confession" to Al, so that he resembles the suffering savior of Christian iconography; the profanity throughout the film also routinely invokes the name of "Christ" or "Jesus," as Holly does when she first sees John's bloodied and damaged body when he comes to rescue her. I do not want to fall into the sort of theologically overdetermined analysis that I have elsewhere criticized by reducing him to a Christ-figure, but rather to suggest that the film uses this iconography to reinforce the idea of John's suffering and repentance for male sexism. He does not suffer in order to save Holly from her capitalist success and female independence, which he finally accepts, but in order to atone for his own sins and to save her from the ravages of capitalism run amok (Hans). Like the western hero, he paradoxically fights to preserve the very civilization that will ultimately displace him by eliminating the threats to peace and order within that civilization, and so preserves his honor and virtue. He is able to use his talents for violence in the service of order and so keeps his place in society, albeit at its fringes. In keeping with the western tradition, his sacrifice goes unappreciated by all but the audience and the woman he loves, but in this case that is enough. In many cases, the westerner had to give up all chance for love or family in order to be a hero, like Shane or Tom Doniphon, but John McClane is not asked to make this sacrifice. He redeems himself in his wife's eyes so that they can be reunited in the end.

The film does not suggest that women can only achieve freedom in divorce, or only achieve the status of servitude in marriage. Rather, it offers the fantasy of a man who can become sensitive to his wife's needs, admit he was wrong, and still be able to save her and his marriage from outside forces. He is allowed to be good at what he is good at, and to be strong as well as vulnerable, just as she is. As for the Rolex watch, letting it fall out the window along with greedy Hans and the money that fills the air at the end of the movie may represent the sacrifice of things financial for things personal, a common enough theme in many movies that tend to be designed for those near the bottom of the economic ladder. John McClane will never be wealthy or part of high society, but he knows that this does not particularly matter if one has family.

Holly is also shown to be tough enough to stand up to Hans, and to slug the obnoxious reporter at the end of the movie, and so does not exactly conform to the sexist model of a passive female. Her willingness to take his last name again does not indicate she is going to let John determine all aspects of her life so much as it indicates her willingness to be married to him, which will presumably include the negotiations that are part of every marriage for reciprocal recognition of rights and freedoms. This analysis may be unconvincing to those who believe the sexist components of the film outweigh the nonsexist, but one should at least see that the narrative does not suggest any capitulation by Holly (e.g., in a willingness to stay home with the kids or move back to New York), and audiences can see this as well; their interpretation of the film will not be determined entirely by any single feature, not even the loss of the Rolex or the Gennero surname. This is not to suggest that the film has no sexist aspects, and there are some action movies with considerably more; but we cannot a priori conclude that the sexist aspects will always predominate in the appropriation of this film or any other, for a given viewer.

A minidrama concerning Al's unwillingness to use a gun is also worth mentioning, as its resolution basically closes the film. He has told John that he cannot draw his gun on anyone, as he mistakenly shot a thirteen-year-old who had a toy pistol. As he says, "They can teach you everything about being a cop except how to live with a mistake." He is redeemed from his inability when Karl, the one terrorist bent on personal revenge against John (for killing his brother), emerges from the building with a gun with which he is about to shoot John and Holly. We see Karl gunned down, and then we see a close-up shot of a gun from the pistol point, which then reveals Al's face behind it. Close-ups of Al and John suggest their linkage and their awareness that Al has realized he can kill when necessary; triumphant music backs this up. This scene authenticates the power and use of the gun to do "good," to stop evildoers from committing their crimes. The whole film is in one sense about the legitimation of violence used for such purposes, a theme we find in most action movies and westerns. Freudians will also read a sexual content into the phallic presentation of the gun, as both John and Al have overcome their "impotence" through it, John even winning back his wife and the ability to be a hero to her.

The fact that Al is black and John is white is also significant, for they manage to bond in a way that makes this racial difference irrelevant—as when they first meet face to face and need no introduction to recognize each other before embracing with laughter and warmth. None of the conflicts are directed along racial lines, as there are both blacks and whites among the terrorists, the FBI, and the police. The African American who works for the terrorists, Theo, is a young and greedy computer wizard rather than a macho man, and he is appropriately captured at the end by Argyle, an equally nonmacho young black who resourcefully runs into Theo's van and punches him out. There are good and bad blacks and good and bad whites sprinkled throughout the film, as if to point out that the conflicts are more about class than race.

It would seem that this film is directed especially toward men who feel the need to experience more power in their lives, both in the personal and the professional arena. It offers them a ritual catharsis of their frustrations through identification with the hero who can be tough as well as sensitive, and who can, even if reluctantly, accept the coming of "civilization," expressed not in the building of farms, railroads, and churches (as in westerns) but through the coming of female equality and corporate power. As in the mythic worldview of the western, however, male power is not lost but still has a role in preserving justice and order, even if sometimes invisibly; and the ethics of the film support the justification of violence to achieve these ends. This does not mean that all those who liked the film will be unquestioning supporters of such violence, for not every fan of action movies is an NRA member devoted to the belief that all law-abiding citizens should own a gun. Rather, audience members may admire the hero of the action film due to his courage and personal strength in being willing to fight and sacrifice for others, and they may attempt to appropriate these values into their own lives in nonviolent forms.

Critics of violent films usually ignore the fact that most fans of such movies do not literally emulate the behavior they see in these films; seeing them is an exercise in liminality that allows them to step outside their normal social roles, to identify with behavior they would never attempt themselves, and to return to their daily lives with a sense that justice and order can triumph and that they can be part of the fight to preserve these, albeit in small ways. Admittedly, these films do not encourage pacifism or attempts to resolve conflict in nonviolent ways, and the American belief in justified violence is reinforced by them. But this is not the only value these films express, nor is the violence in them completely essential to the possible range of values and worldviews found in them by audiences.

7

Gangster Films

The generic conventions of the gangster film were identified by film theorists as early as those of the western, in part because of the attention attracted by three rather sensational films made at the beginning of the sound era: *Little Caesar* (1930), *Public Enemy* (1931), and *Scarface* (1932). In all three, the main character is a ruthless criminal who rises to the top of an organization through his unstoppable desire for success at any price. The fact that he is destroyed by the end of each film seems to indicate a moral critique, in that audiences are warned of the high cost of such lawless and violent behavior—and yet the gangster exercised a strange fascination on audiences, so that they sympathized with him more than they judged him. Whereas the western hero tended to be a good guy who worked a bit outside the law in order "to do right," the gangster operated outside the law to do wrong; his purposes were entirely selfish, and not at all noble. The censors correctly identified the attraction these seedy characters held for many audiences, and moral outrage at such films was one of the main motivations for the Hays Office to develop the enforcement of its code.[1] As an early draft of the code put it, "The sympathy of the audience should never be thrown to the side of crime, wrong-doing, evil, or sin" by making evil "attractive or alluring."[2] Ironically, however, even if evil was depicted rather brutally (as in *Scarface*), this might actually *increase* audience interest and fascination, so that the Hays Office not only had to assure that the criminal was punished in the end, but that the violence not be depicted too explicitly.

Robert Warshow has greatly influenced study of gangster films in his thesis that these movies embody the contradictions present in the American dream, which encourages all to succeed in the capitalistic system even though this is impossible. The gangster becomes a tragic hero in that he is doomed to be destroyed by the very system that has created him as a creature of greed and consumption; the fact that he employs criminal methods is incidental.[3] Ideological criticism has also usually assumed that gangster films serve a fundamentally conservative purpose in that they only question the system in order to reinforce it, showing lower-class audiences the necessity of capitalism as well as their inability to succeed in it.

Jonathan Munby, however, has questioned this common view by arguing that gangster films were seen as subversive by their audiences and by those who sought to censor them. Rather than expressing the epitome of the American ideology of capitalist success, the gangster was un-American in his refusal to play by the rules of the system.[4] The character of the gangster appealed to many audiences, Munby argues, precisely because he expressed their frustrations with America and their inability to find a place of acceptance in it. The development of sound cinema was crucial in this regard, as one was able to hear the ethnic accents of the gangsters who were explicitly identified as "hyphenated" Americans: usually "Italian-Americans" or "Irish-Americans" (although the actors were sometimes Jewish Americans).[5] These groups knew they had not been accepted by society, and the films often expressed the efforts of ethnic Americans to achieve acceptance that was doomed to fail. Although they can parody the dress and mannerisms of high society, they lack the language and cultivated tastes that signal the status of the upper classes. Even with money and fancy suits, their parties still devolve into food fights, and "Little Caesar" can only appreciate the gaudy frames on the paintings he buys.[6] Lower-class audiences would recognize such obvious ironies, even if the characters did not, and this served to demonstrate their own class exclusion, but it did not celebrate or legitimate it.

That ethnic groups were not imagining their disenfranchisement from American society is also reflected in the activity of the censors in regard to such films. *Scarface* proved so shocking to them that it was only to be approved with certain cuts, but also with the addition of a scene that was to make the moral critique of the gangster lifestyle explicit. The scene is actually two scenes, the first in a police office, the second at a newspaper. In the first, the chief detective likens the gangster to a "crawling louse" who should not be romanticized or glorified. In the second, the newspaper publisher argues that the government needs to institute martial law, crack down on crime, and deport the gangsters, for "half of them aren't even citizens." Although the scene includes a "good" Italian who supports what the newspaperman says regarding the need to deport his countrymen ("Thatsa true. They bring nothin' buta disgrace to my people"), it is clear enough that the progovernment judgment is xenophobic and intolerant of unassimilated ethnic groups.[7] The lower-class ethnic audiences who liked gangster films were unlikely to be affected by such moralizing, as it was directed against them; if anything, they would feel more identified with the gangsters because of such a scene, noting that they were among those rejected by the representatives of white America in the film.

Even films that did not seem to romanticize the gangster, but instead made him into a psychotic "mama's boy" like Cody Jarrett (James Cagney) of *White Heat* (1949), still held an attraction for viewers precisely because they crossed the line of normal, accepted behavior.[8] Anyone who has seen the film remembers the spectacular and shocking finale, as Jarrett yells, "Made it, ma! Top of the world!" before blowing himself up atop a huge gas tank. The G-man who was the ostensible "hero" of the film was not the reason that people went to see it; it was to see James Cagney's portrayal of criminal deviance. Any film with a criminal in it might hold this kind of appeal, even if it was not primarily the story of the rise-and-fall of a gangster; cops-and-robbers pictures, or even detective films, developed vicious criminal characters that exerted a great hold on the imagination of audiences (although the cop or detective might be a sympathetic character as well).

The ethnic resistance to the dominant culture embodied in gangster films is still present today, in "gangsta rap" and other popular cultural expressions of African American resistance, such as films about black criminals. Some watchdog groups have been concerned that films like *Boyz 'n the Hood* (1991) would add to black anger and crime, much as the Hays Office believed gangster films might add to crime in the 1930s.[9] There is little evidence that either set of films created any violence, but it is possible that they do express the very real frustrations of those who feel they have been excluded from the power structures of society and are feeling the need to find an alternative. In a similar way, many women found their frustrations with patriarchy well expressed by *Thelma and Louise* (1991) and its story of two women driven to crime by their own anger against rape and misogyny, although some anxious (usually male) critics seemed to fear that the film made their criminal behavior too attractive. Society's fears are most easily aroused when the group empowered in the film is one that has legitimate gripes about its powerlessness, and so is one that might actually be a threat to society's power structures.

Identification with such antiheroes, however, may not create any more real violence directed against society than identification with the heroes of action movies creates people willing to use violence in defense of society.

Gangster films express the frustrations of the disenfranchised, but this does not mean these frustrations will lead to revolutionary consequences. On the other hand, the fact that such films do not inspire revolutions need not lead us to the usual conclusion of ideological critics that they are inherently conservative, enabling people to return placidly to their subordinate status after having a liminal fantasy of escape. Although they step outside their usual roles when they view such films, this does not mean that they are totally unaffected by the message of resistance implicit in them. Too much analysis of films assumes simplistically that a film will either inspire social change or not, and that it should be condemned or applauded on that basis—leftists assuming change is good, conservatives assuming it is bad. But like religions, films operate in a more complex fashion. By presenting an alternative view of the world, they suggest things might be different than they are, but their followers do not always literally emulate the behavior of the characters in the myths or assume that they are to model themselves on them in every way. Rather, the ideal world of the myth is set up in contrast to the real world we live in, not as a literal model to follow in every respect but as a challenge to our ordinary ways of seeing and doing things. It can then be appropriated in a range of ways: to give hope that things will change, to exhort to action, to reassure that the ideal of purpose and meaning can be partially realized even in an imperfect world, and so forth. The values one finds in the film will depend on what one brings to it and how one appropriates it, as the meanings found in a myth can be interpreted in many ways even though the myth sets forth a basic pattern for finding those meanings.

The Godfather (1972) and The Godfather, Part II (1974)

The Godfather (1972) and *The Godfather, Part II* (1974) are among the most popular and the most critically acclaimed movies of all time. These two films were released close enough together to be considered almost as a single unit in terms of audience appropriation; a third film, which I will not discuss, was made much later (1990). What was unusual about these films, as gangster films, was the extent to which the audience was made to identify with the gangsters. Although this was always the aim of gangster movies, it was achieved with such brilliance in these films as to make it all but impossible not to applaud the gangsters, at least initially. As the extent of their violence and corruption becomes increasingly clear, however, the audience is given the chance to be horrified at its own complicity in the actions of the mob. We are so effectively brought into their world that we hardly notice when we/they cross the line into behavior that, while it seems justified in the context of the life they live, can hardly be countenanced by anyone with a "normal" sense of morality. This is probably why the films received acclaim from critics and audiences alike, as being both challenging and entertaining. Like the films of Alfred Hitchcock, which I will consider later, the *Godfather* films allow audiences to participate in forbidden actions and enjoy it, but they also have a troubling edge to them in that they push the boundary of "fun" beyond what we can normally accept as legitimate in this regard, thus challenging the entertainment value we find in them. In analyzing these films, then, I will try to walk the delicate line between viewing them simply moralistically as "art" films that challenge our violent nature, and viewing them merely as mindless entertainment that indulges our violent nature. We have to recognize the extent to which these films do both.

One reason for the popularity and success of the *Godfather* films beyond what is normal for gangster movies may be that these films were more than a saga of ethnic resistance to a subordinate status. Although they clearly work within the framework of Italian American identity, they also transcend this through a universal appeal to the notion of family. What motivates the Corleones is not primarily greed or a reckless desire to be admitted to the corridors of society traditionally reserved for those of northern European ancestry, although these elements are present. Rather, it is the preservation of family that undergirds almost all the actions of the characters of which we are meant to approve, and it is when the central position of family is shaken that disaster comes to them. If this is a tragedy, it lies in the fact that Michael Corleone's efforts to safeguard the family become so desperate that his methods represent the undoing of that same family, as his desire for success and assimilation cause him to sacrifice the values of his ethnic past.

We are initiated into the narrative of the first film through a scene with low-key lighting (utilized to great effect throughout the films) that highlights the face of a man describing how his daughter was beaten and her face permanently disfigured by her non-Italian boyfriend, and how the courts failed to punish him. He is telling this story to the Godfather, Don Vito Corleone (Marlon Brando), although we do not see his face for some time. Finally, Don Vito asks what he wants, and the man whispers in the Godfather's ear. We now see the face of the Godfather for the first time, and he speaks with authority: "That I cannot do." The man, Bonasera, has asked that the boyfriend be killed, but the Don answers, "We are not murderers." The audience has initially identified with the one who wants revenge, as we hear his story and feel for him; but as we meet the Don, the first impression we receive is of a man too moral to kill out of mere revenge—that is, he is already more moral than the audience feels at this point. Had the girl been killed, it would be "justice" to kill her murderer in response, but as it is the Don can only offer to do to the boy as he has done unto the girl: the biblical *lex talionis* of "an eye for an eye." The Don is also offended by Bonasera's offer of money, claiming that he would rather offer this as justice to a friend who respects him and his position of Godfather. In the end, Bonasera asks him to "be my friend, Godfather" and the Don accepts his gesture of respect as he kisses his ring. In this first scene, it has been established that the Don has a certain code of morality, that he values friendship and feels a sense of obligation to friends, and that his organization is more like a family than a corporation. We cannot help but like him.

The subsequent scenes show the wedding party for Vito's daughter, which involves convivial and healthy interaction of the family members; as traditional Italian music is played, the Don dances with his wife, and old men and children dance with each other. The only event to mar this harmony is when Sonny, the eldest son, illicitly sneaks off to have sex with a woman. Later, his father asks him if he "spends time with his family" as only this will make him "a real man," implying his disapproval of Sonny's promiscuity and neglect of his wife. In the course of the party, we also see the Don meet with a man who asks (properly) for his help in keeping his daughter's fiancé in the country; with Luca Brasi, one of the hit men, who drunkenly but fondly (and comically, for the audience) thanks the Don for being invited to the wedding; and with his godson Johnny Fontane, a popular singer who wants to be in a Hollywood movie but is being prevented from doing so by the producer. We are also introduced to Michael Corleone, the youngest son, who is in his military uniform (this is 1945, and he is a decorated war hero) and is accompanied by his non-Italian girlfriend, Kay Adams. He clearly disapproves of his family's criminal business, as he informs Kay of the tactics of intimidation and violence used by the family to achieve its ends. The party ends with a family photo, which the Don refused to have taken until Michael arrived; Michael also pulls Kay into the photo, indicating she will become part of this family as well.

This extended opening sequence has succeeded in introducing us to the family in a noncriminal context and so establishing our identification with them. The next sequence follows Tom Hagen, Vito's adopted son and the family lawyer, as he goes to Hollywood to politely offer Vito's friendship to the producer Jack Woltz if he will allow Johnny Fontane to star in his movie. Woltz's refusal is personal, as he holds a grudge against Fontane for stealing away a young starlet with whom Woltz had an affair. Woltz hurls racist epithets at the "wop" family and at German Irish Hagen, whom he calls a "kraut-mick." Hagen behaves like a gentleman and leaves. The next scene shows Woltz waking up the next morning with the bloody head of his expensive prize horse in his bed. He screams repeatedly, and the scene dissolves into a shot of Vito sitting calmly at home, as if to indicate his connection to the violent deed.

This scene is the first piece of violence we see in the film, and it is not even done to a human. Director Francis Ford Coppola has said that he found it ironic that this scene was viewed to be more objectionable and disturbing than many of the later killings (of people) in the film. Perhaps this was because it was done to an innocent animal, but it may be because the audience was shocked to see a violent act indirectly ordered by the seemingly humane Vito, with whom we have been led to identify. Before we can reflect too much on the violence of the Corleones, however, the story takes a turn that involves violence being done to them and which invites our righteous indignation on their behalf. The drug lord Virgil Sollozzo, backed by another criminal family, the Tattagglias, wants the Corleones to join them in the drug business, which Vito will not do as he disapproves of this as "dirty" and "dangerous"—the Corleones have made their money primarily through gambling and union protection, which he views as more acceptable. To get him to change his mind, Sollozzo has Luca Brasi brutally strangled (as he was sent to the Tattaglias as a spy) and orders Don Corleone shot. The scene in which Vito is "hit" in the street outside his office makes him seem weak and vulnerable, as his son Fredo cries helplessly at his side. Sollozzo tells Tom Hagen that his plan is "good business" and he assumes Sonny, the new head of the family, will see this. Vito survives, however, and Sonny will make no deals but only wants a war of revenge. Michael's involvement with the family abruptly increases when he goes to visit his father in the hospital and finds the bodyguards gone; he calls Tom for help, and until his men arrive Mike and Enzo the Baker (who has brought flowers) need to pretend to be the guards. "I'll take care of you, Pop," Michael tells his father. The police arrive, but they are working for Sollozzo, and the crooked Captain McCluskey punches Michael in the face and stomach while the other police hold him. This shocking reversal of the expected role of the police as the protector of the weak (which in this case happens to be Vito) puts the audience once again on the side of the Corleones and against the representatives of a legal authority that will not protect them.

Angry and defiant, Michael now comes to the defense of his father by offering to be the one to assassinate McCluskey and Sollozzo in an arranged meeting. As he describes this plan, the camera dollies in to create greater viewer identification with him and so invite complicity in his act. Though Sonny laughs at the suggestion, Michael insists that he is serious and that he views this as justified: "It's business, it's not personal," just as his killings in World War II were not personal attacks on the enemy. Michael actually understands better than Sonny at this point the need for pragmatic military defensive action on behalf of the family rather than a policy of revenge. Before he does the actual killing, Michael seems so nervous and delays so long that the audience begins to worry he won't do it; again, the audience is made complicit in the murders, so that we are practically applauding his act by the time he pulls the trigger.

Michael goes to Italy to hide out, and this time also allows him to reconnect with his Sicilian identity and perfect his Italian. He marries a young Italian beauty after bartering for her with her father as if she were an animal, trading on the power and fear behind his family name. Women tend to be relegated to secondary positions throughout these films, treated with respect for the most part but excluded from the operations of the family business or its discussion. In fact, Michael and his bride Appolonia can barely speak at all at first, due to their language differences, so that their relationship is clearly based only on physical attraction and his paternalism. This is the most traditional form of patriarchy, of course, in which women are protected by strong men who see to their every need, and the women dutifully accept this protective scheme and their subordinate place in it. In spite of the obvious sexism of this setup, my own female students (even the most liberal) admitted to finding the portrayal of this patriarchy very attractive in its ability to insure protection.

But Michael is actually unable to protect Appolonia, as she is murdered by a car bomb meant for him before his return to the United States. A year after his return he approaches Kay with a proposal of marriage, which she accepts. He is by this time the acting head of the family, as Sonny was murdered before his return in a brutal hit that causes Vito to surrender the war and leaves him a broken old man. After Vito's death, Michael has a number of his enemies killed in the famous sequence involving cross-cutting between the murders and his nephew's baptism. The irony of his vows to "renounce Satan and all his works," even as we see the violence he has ordered, brings us to the point where we are asked if we can go all the way with Michael in his protection of the family. In the final scene of the film, Kay asks Michael whether he ordered the murder of his own brother-in-law, Carlo (who had helped set up the murder of Sonny); Michael at first refuses to answer questions "about my business" but finally lets her ask "just this once." He lies and tells her he did not, and she seems to believe him. She walks out of his office and in a long shot appears in profile while Michael remains in the office, in focus and at the center of the frame. His men come in to kiss his ring and call him "Don Corleone," and as Michael's bodyguard closes the door on her, we see her look of incomprehension as she is excluded from his world and his "business." That this shot is from Michael's point of view is significant, in that the audience is still (albeit uncomfortably) identified with him.

This extraordinary film was followed two years later by a sequel that was in every way its equal, if not its superior. Some critics prefer it, and it also did very well at the box office, no doubt in part due to the success of its predecessor. It is a more disturbing and complicated film, however, so that it does not provide the audience with such an easy opportunity to identify with the Corleones in their murderous business. Although the first film clearly raised questions about the extent to which the family is able to commit violence to defend itself, the second film shows how Michael's efforts to safeguard his family backfire due to his own greed and desire for revenge. He makes a deal with the Jewish gangster Hyman Roth that proves disastrous when Roth betrays him, and Michael realizes that his own brother Fredo acted against him in giving assistance to Roth's attempt on Michael's life. Although Fredo claims he "didn't know it would be a hit," Michael cannot forgive him and finally has him killed, so that Michael's ethic of defense of family has tragically turned into its opposite. Michael's desire to be accepted outside the Italian American community also in many ways leads to his downfall, as his deal with Roth signals a willingness to be loyal to a Jewish American rather than his own Italian American family. His wife Kay leaves him when she realizes he will never end his business of crime and violence, as he had promised her when they were married, and she even tells him she has aborted his third child because "this must all end." Although Michael survives, his family has disintegrated around him, so that this film does not offer the viewer any satisfactory resolution. In contrast, even though the first film ended in lies and violence, it ended with an intact family and not nearly as many moral ambiguities for the viewer.

The second film also utilizes the brilliant device of intercutting extended scenes from the early life of Vito with the later career of Michael. These two stories are in stark contrast as Vito's turn to crime is made to appear completely justified, based in a need to survive poverty and to protect the innocent. Vito murders the local gangster, Don Fanucci, who preys on the weak Italian Americans in his area of New York; Vito then replaces him as Don, but in this role he becomes the benefactor of the powerless rather than one who exploits them. We are made to understand the source of Vito's peculiar morality of loyalty and protection to those of his culture, as well as its disintegration in Michael's life.

The film ends with a flashback to 1941, just after the bombing of Pearl Harbor, at a birthday celebration for Vito. Michael tells the family that he has enlisted, and Sonny is furious at his choice of country over family. As this scene dissolves into a shot of Vito with young Michael, and then Michael in the present, the audience is struck by the contrasts and ironies in the story of this family that has self-destructed through assimilation in America. Whereas the traditional gangster film featured the gangster punished for his desire to be accepted which cannot be fulfilled, this film features the gangster who gains wealth and American identity, but at the cost of his ethnic and family identity. We admire the devotion to family we see in the young Michael and in Vito, as well as the ethic of freedom and protection of the weak that began the family, but we also see its devolution through Michael's insatiable desire for success. But this is not simply a story of the ravages of capitalism on those who pursue it, nor is it a judgment on the desires of those who want to be accepted. Rather, it expresses the complexities involved in negotiating one's identity as family member, member of an ethnic community, and citizen of the United States. The audience feels an identification with those who are forced to use violence and coercion to survive, but we are also repelled by the forms this takes. Our own ambiguous relationship to violence is expressed in that we are both drawn to it and horrified by it. In addition, we are presented with the ambiguities inherent in assimilation, as it represents both a loss and a gain that every ethnic group has faced in America. Should one assimilate and sacrifice tradition and culture in order to succeed and be accepted? To what extent can or should one insist on maintaining an ethnic identity in a panethnic society? Every group in America has faced these questions at some point in its history, so that even those that have long been assimilated feel an attraction to the raw ethnicity of the Corleones and their outsider status, and viewers can enjoy a liminal identification with these outsiders while the film lasts.

There is not an obvious "moral" to the story, and to moralize its point is to simplify a complex text to which audiences will return precisely because it is both evocative and provocative of a range of values and concerns. This is the role of all great myths: to provide a resource for an ongoing wrestling with our own cultural questions. We suffer with Michael and the Corleones as they suffer for our own "sinful" desires for success and acceptance, but there is no atonement, only the recognition that we can share their story and their sufferings, as they represent our own.

8

Melodrama, Tearjerkers, and "Women's Films"

Although melodrama literally means simply a drama with action punctuated by music, it came to mean a drama with a certain emotional effect on the viewer; originally, what we now call suspense-thrillers were referred to as "melodrama." Over time, however, its meaning narrowed to be focused primarily on sentimental films directed toward female viewers that featured narratives about women and their sufferings, especially sound films made prior to the 1960s (though this type of film has not entirely disappeared even today). Sometimes the women achieved happiness after suffering, sometimes not, but they always demonstrated strength in their ability to survive sadness, especially in matters of love and family.[1]

Analysis of these films has been dogged by the inability of film theorists to understand why these narratives are popular with women in particular. As they rarely have unambiguously happy endings and are instead "tearjerkers," this may seem to suggest that women are masochistic in wanting to see movies in which women suffer. One could suggest that a male-dominated industry has constructed these films as cautionary tales, designed to show women the punishments in store for them should they decide to step outside their traditionally assigned roles, but this does not explain why women continue to go to such films. And much as the male-dominated industry might like to encourage women to be subordinate, it is more interested in making money, so that we could presume these films would not even be made were there not a market for them. What, then, are women getting out of these films?

Jeanine Basinger has theorized that the appeal of such films lies in women's ability to fantasize about socially forbidden behavior through identification with the "bad" women of such movies, allowing a vicarious thrill of being a woman who values career more than family, or sex more than a loveless marriage. As for the fact that the women who make these forbidden decisions are "punished" in the end, Basinger takes this as the necessary coda imposed by the Hays Office to blunt the subversive edge to the narrative, much as the fall of the gangster was similarly mandated for gangster narratives. Essentially, the films present women with the seductive possibility of release from their societally prescribed roles, but also tell them that "they shouldn't want such things; they won't work; they're all wrong."[2] When most women are faced with this dual message, Basinger suggests, they will listen to the conservative message, but they will be attracted to the subversive suggestion of freedom—and this is what keeps them coming back.

Basinger demonstrates her thesis in relation to three films that she believes tell "the same old story" that women should conform to their societally prescribed roles, with a few variations. In *Kitty Foyle* (1940), the heroine chooses to marry the "good" man, "a noble doctor who works among the poor and who loves her deeply" but is "almost an asexual male," rather than the "weak" man who represents "the wrong kind of life, sex without marriage." In this way, she makes the "right" choice for a woman of marriage over sex. In *Smash-up, the Story of a Woman* (1947), the heroine accepts her role as a loving wife and mother when she overcomes her self-destructive alcoholism that developed out of her anger over the loss of a career. In *The Guilt of Janet Ames* (1947), a woman overcomes her guilt about neglecting a husband she did not love when she finds another man to love her. All three films, according to Basinger, "demonstrate that women have a dual choice, or dual selves, and that they need to listen to reason and the rules of society in order to allow the good one—that is, the one that conforms—to dominate."[3] She suggests that these women are punished when they neglect their domestic duties, and this effectively embeds them in the subordinate status of wife and mother. At the same time, she would suggest that the attraction of the films for women lies in the moments when the women do *not* conform to these roles, thus suggesting a liberating alternative.

When one looks more closely at the plots of each of these films, however, we may find different messages that would have a more obvious appeal to women than a mere cautionary tale with a subversive subtext. When Kitty Foyle chooses marriage with the doctor over an extramarital affair with the "weak" man, this is not a choice to give up sex, but a choice of the man who really loves her over one who does not. She had first married the weak man, but this marriage failed when his upper-class family refused to accept Kitty, a lowly secretary not from their part of society. He then marries someone in his own class, but still wants to have sex with Kitty on the side. Her rejection of him is the rejection of someone who could not accept her as she was, and who put his own position and family above her; his offer to keep her as a mistress simply keeps her as his sexual toy. What woman would not cheer when she gets rid of this jerk? Furthermore, there is no reason to conclude that the man Kitty marries in the end is "sexless" just because he is also "good."

Janet Ames, too, realizes that she should only marry for love, and she needs to overcome guilt, not about the fact that she did not please her now dead husband, but about the fact that she did not marry the right person. There were probably lots of women after the war who realized they had rushed into marriage precipitously, whether their husbands came home or not, and they might have felt similar guilt about not loving their husbands. The film tells them they need to overcome their guilt and get on with their lives, and offers the hope that they can find real love. A woman locked in a loveless marriage might not have this chance, but the film would still offer a fantasy that might help her survive reality—and, in time, she might even have the courage and willpower to divorce her husband, as women began to assert themselves in this way in the decade following the war. They are not told by the film that they should be punished for such desires, but that they must overcome their guilt about such feelings and get on with their lives.

As for *Smash-up*, the film never indicates the woman should have given up her singing career, and it even seems to suggest that this was a mistake. Her problem lies not in an inability to sacrifice career to marriage and motherhood, but in the self-pity that threatens to destroy her as she neglects her career. The film seems to suggest that she can have both career and marriage/motherhood, if only she stops drinking. In fact, women's films do not always tell women they must sacrifice career to marriage and family. The extremely popular tearjerker *A Star Is Born* (1937/1954) actually tells the story of how a man finally sacrifices himself for his wife's career. Women obviously enjoyed this story of a successful woman and the man willing to die to insure her success. And in spite of the fact that the film ends with her identification of herself by his last name, this fails to subordinate her to him as he is no longer there to interfere with her life.

All three of these films offer hope for women to overcome suffering and oppression, to marry the right person, even to have a career. It is ridiculous to assume that everytime a woman gets married in a film, this implies she is simply conforming to a social role and would rather, all things considered, just have affairs with married men—as Basinger seems to think Kitty Foyle should have. There was nothing liberating about simply being someone's mistress ("a kept woman"), and women knew this better than anyone. Even in a musical like *Gigi* (1958), in which the heroine holds out for marriage rather than being merely a "kept" mistress, we do not get only the promotion of social conformity through marriage. It is also an endorsement of the ability of women to assert themselves in choices affecting their own lives—as Gigi states so well, in words adapted from a story originally written by protofeminist author Colette. While her grandmother and aunt try to arrange her fate as Gaston's mistress, Gigi is independent enough to refuse the status of a woman who is just one in a line of women to be used and cast aside by spoiled rich men.

Basinger's thesis works well with certain "bad girl" films that depict forbidden behavior as a subversive possibility, but it does not deal with those films that do not conform to this model. For example, she does not mention *Waterloo Bridge* (1931/1940), a film I discussed in chapter 4, which concerns a young woman's fall into prostitution after her beloved goes to war. Her life as a prostitute hardly presents a forbidden attraction, nor is it a punishment for her behavior; it is simply an undeserved disaster that befalls her. Women were moved by this wartime story as it depicts the sufferings of women left behind by their men. Although most women did not suffer as she did, they could identify with the sadness associated with her totally unwarranted fate as they sought to survive as well. Basinger also does not mention the ever-popular *An Affair to Remember* (1957), in which the plan of the two lovers to meet at the top of the Empire State Building is derailed when, on the way there, the woman is hit by a car, unbeknownst to the man; she becomes crippled, and he assumes that she does not love him, as she never showed up. She gives him up because of her injury, and it is only in the final scene when he visits her that he realizes she is crippled, after her attempts to conceal her condition fail. They are reunited, and she vows to walk again. It should be obvious why women love this film, as the man loves her no matter what condition her body is in. There is pain and suffering, but it is overcome with love. Her injury was not punishment for their affair, nor is she denied love in the end. Admittedly, she was willing to be a self-sacrificial female in her desire to conceal her injury, but the man does not permit her this self-sacrifice. The film would not have been very popular with women if Cary Grant had left her apartment without realizing she was crippled, or (worse) if he had abandoned her after learning of her injury.

Basinger also barely discusses *To Each His Own* (1946), which featured Olivia De Havilland's first Oscar-winning performance, except to ridicule it for its lack of realism. This film concerned a woman's quest to regain possession of the illegitimate child she gave up, a quest she pursues through becoming a ruthlessly successful businesswoman. The film does not suggest that women should keep their kids and not work, because it is only by working that she can gain her child. Recall that in the 1940s, when men were away at war, women often did have to work to support or keep their children (as they do once again in our own era of neglectful fathers). The character was not allowed to raise her child, but in the final scene her now grown son realizes who his mother is, and they are reunited. Although she missed his childhood, it was not her fault, and now she has a relationship with him as well as a successful business. This is hardly a narrative that tells women to stay in their traditional place; it even seems to suggest that they *can* have it all, albeit belatedly.

It is also odd that Basinger largely neglects *Gone With the Wind* (1939), which could be considered the most popular "woman's picture" of all time. In this film, Scarlett O'Hara shows herself an extremely strong and able woman whose main flaw is not realizing early enough that she loves Rhett Butler. She desired the respectability of Ashley Wilkes, but finally realizes Rhett loves her more, even if he is a scoundrel. In fact, it is his forbidden scoundrel status that makes him so attractive to women who want to escape from humdrum lives to a more "romantic" one. If it seems that women's desire to be dominated by men like Rhett only embeds them further into a patriarchal world, one must remember that such fantasies subvert the traditional role of women as servants of their husbands and children, introducing the idea that women can have passionate sexual relationships that are pleasing to themselves as well as their men; Rhett doesn't want a maid, he wants a lover whose passion matches his own. Even the infamous scene in which Rhett carries her up the stairs to the bedroom, which implies he forces Scarlett to have sex, seems to be a favorite with women who enjoy the same sort of scenes in romantic fiction. Some feminist analysis has suggested that such scenes appeal to women not because they want to be raped, but because in such a fantasy they are permitted their sexual passion. The traditional understanding of women does not permit them to be the aggressor or to overtly demonstrate sexual desire, but when they are "swept off their feet" they are allowed to be sexual without worrying about whether their own desires have been too conspicuous or inappropriate to their gender role.[4] We should also realize that women who enjoy this fantasy of the aggressive male might not enjoy it in reality, as it serves a primarily liminal function of temporarily invoking a forbidden pleasure in order to achieve a certain catharsis and liberation from social roles; as a fantasy, it is for the woman alone, whereas in reality in such a scenario she might feel reduced to an object of male pleasure. People can also enjoy other fantasies they would never consider realizing, such as violent revenge fantasies. As this book seeks to demonstrate, films evoke a variety of such liminal possibilities that most of us would never seek to actualize but which have an important function as fantasies.

Another extremely popular women's film that does not really fit Basinger's typology is *Now Voyager* (1942). In this film, the heroine desires to escape a repressive mother who wants her to marry a man she does not love because he is from "a good family." On a cruise, the heroine meets a married man and has a brief but fulfilling affair, so that having known real love (and presumably, sex) she can refuse the loveless marriage her mother has arranged. Her mother conveniently dies so that she can be free of her controlling influence. Although she cannot marry the man who truly loves her, she is able to be a mother to his child and achieves fulfillment in this way. The heroine demonstrates a tremendous degree of independence and self-reliance, as Basinger herself notes, and she is not really punished for these traits as she is allowed to make her own decisions about her life in the end. In spite of the fact that the lovers cannot be united and that she makes the "conventional" choice of motherhood over extramarital sex, the film offers a fantasy of female power and confidence that clearly attracted many female viewers.[5]

Tearjerkers in general demonstrate the suffering of women not as a way of inculcating the belief that they deserve to suffer, but in order to suggest ways in which women can deal with suffering and overcome it through their own inner strength. Especially in the decades in which women had relatively little freedom regarding career and marriage, these narratives offered them the chance to express their frustration and sadness at the limitations imposed on them as well as the hope that these can be borne and sometimes overcome. The most popular women's films do not tend to focus on punishment for bad behavior, but instead present situations in which women face unavoidable suffering that is not their fault but which creates the opportunity to demonstrate inner strength and conviction.

The fact that there are fewer films of this type made today may primarily be an indication of the fact that women are not nearly as constricted as they once were. It is now much more acceptable for women to have careers, to have children out of wedlock, to remain unmarried, to have sex outside of marriage. While the older films expressed the frustrations of women who were not permitted these things by society, our more liberal era does not offer the same strictures. This is not to say that women are free from oppression today, but that there are different problems focused upon. For example, there is greater awareness and more discussion of physical and sexual abuse of women today, so that women are sometimes given a catharsis for their rage against abusive men in films—although this applies mainly to thrillers and horror films, which often present a woman who is able to fight back against a violent male, thereby expressing a model of defiance.

Films that conform more clearly to the model of tearjerkers today often involve female friendships cut short by death, especially by cancer, as this slow death allows the characters time to deal with their suffering and express their feelings for each other, as for example, *Terms of Endearment* (1983), *Steel Magnolias* (1989), and *Boys on the Side* (1995). The first of these concerns a mother-daughter relationship, the second a group of women, the third a trio that includes a lesbian who loves a seemingly straight woman dying of AIDS. These films do not suggest that the characters deserve to die, but that we need to deal with suffering and death by expressing love in the midst of it.

The biggest box-office success of all time can also be considered as a women's film and a tearjerker, for although it has some of the form of an action and disaster movie, the plot is most similar to those targeted especially at women. *Titanic* (1997) has a plot in some ways like *Now Voyager* in that it features a young woman trying to escape her oppressive mother and the man she is supposed to marry, and it also features a shipboard romance as the form of her liberation. Its appeal to young women in particular should not have been a surprise, as its heroine defies her mother to do what she wants, which includes becoming an assertive woman with the will to live outside her socially prescribed role. The romance, in fact, is merely the means to her liberation of self, as her lover sacrifices himself (as in *A Star is Born*) in order that she might have a future unconstrained by any males. Perhaps these similarities to classic women's films may in part explain the reactions of many critics who found the plot contrived and the characters stereotypical, for they have made similar judgments on older films of this sort. A film does not need to be "realistic," however, to connect with viewers who find in it not a representation of their own experience but an alternative reality that is an exaggerated and idealized form of their experience. Female viewers in particular connected with its story, which more than any special effects guaranteed the film's success. Special effects can help tell a story, but they are not a substitute for it; as evidence, one can note that many movies with impressive visual effects do not do nearly as well as *Titanic*, for they may lack its ability to connect with basic concerns of the audience and address them in an effective way. James Cameron, who both wrote and directed the film, seems to have understood this fact when he created this incredibly expensive yet profitable film.

Titanic (1997)

The film opens in the present (1996) as a salvage ship looks for a precious diamond supposedly to be found in the wreckage of the *Titanic* on the ocean floor. Those seeking it obviously have no feeling for the personal sufferings associated with the disaster, but are only interested in the profits to be made from it. They find the safe in which the diamond should be, and it does not contain it, but they do find a drawing (marked with the date of the sinking) of a nude woman wearing the jewel. After this drawing is shown on television, they receive a phone call from one Rose Calvert. She claims to be Rose de Witt Bukater, supposedly killed on the *Titanic*, and she also claims to be the woman in the picture. They agree to let her come to their salvage vessel to hear what she knows about the diamond. This "frame story" surrounds the main story of the film, told in flashback by Rose, of the ship's voyage and sinking.

She recalls that the *Titanic* was the "ship of dreams, to everyone else . . . to me, it was a slaveship taking me to America in chains." She feels this way because she is engaged to Cal Hockley, whom she does not love and who tries to control Rose's every move. It is revealed that she has been pressured into the engagement by her mother, as their family has a "good name" but they have lost all the wealth they once had. The marriage with Hockley will "ensure our survival," as her mother puts it. Feeling no way out of this predicament, she rushes one evening to the stern of the ship and climbs over the railing, ready to commit suicide. Jack Dawson, who is clearly not from her class, sees her and talks her into coming back onto the deck. Although she is offended by this presumptuous young man, she agrees to climb back, but slips and has to be pulled over by Jack, which attracts some attention. Two crewmen arrive and call for Jack's arrest, as it appears he was attacking Rose; she clarifies to them and to Cal that Jack saved her from a fall, though she does not mention her suicide attempt. Cal "rewards" Jack with a twenty-dollar bill, and when Rose comments that this seems a cheap price for saving her life, Cal invites Jack to dinner with them the next evening. Before they retire for the night, we see Cal giving Rose the diamond, implying his desire to buy her affections and sexual favors: "There's nothing I would not deny you, if you will not deny me."

The next day Rose finds Jack, ostensibly to thank him for saving her and for not revealing her suicide attempt. She reveals that she feels trapped by her engagement to Cal ("I'm plunging ahead, powerless to stop it. . . . I'm screaming and no one notices"), and so Jack asks her if she loves Cal. She is offended by his question and will not answer, and in her best aristocratic manner belittles him, accusing him of rudeness and presumption, putting up the walls between their two classes again. He does not return her anger, however, and the fact that she continues to talk to him seems to indicate she is strangely drawn to him. As they talk, she admires his drawings, as well as his freedom. "Why can't I be like you, just head out to the horizon when I feel like it?" He encourages this tendency in her, suggesting that they should someday go on a roller-coaster and ride horses together, not side-saddle but "like a man" even as she should learn to spit "like a man." As he is comically teaching her this valuable skill, her mother sees them and (as elderly Rose recounts it) she looks at Jack as if he was "a dangerous insect" to be destroyed, as she is clearly threatened by the appeal Jack holds for Rose.

Jack goes to dinner with them, dressed "like a gentleman" courtesy of Molly Brown, who loans him some of her son's clothes. Molly Brown is of course a historical person who actually was on the *Titanic* and who had become wealthy through the luck of discovering a mine on her property. As the film portrays her, she has none of the affected mannerisms of the wealthy, being in reality just a low-class person who accidentally gained money—thus she is derided for her vulgarity by the aristocracy, but has empathy for the poor not shared by the other wealthy. She likes Jack and helps him, just as later in the film (after the sinking) she tries to help the poor who are not allowed on the lifeboats by trying (unsuccessfully) to convince those in her own boat to pick more survivors out of the freezing water.

At dinner, aided by the "disguise" provided by Molly Brown, Jack is accepted as one of the wealthy until Rose's mother reveals the fact that he is staying in steerage. Jack is unashamed to say that he won his ticket in a poker game and that he has no home and no money. He loves his freedom for the surprises and opportunities it grants him. "Life's a gift, and I don't intend on wasting it," he says, as he has learned to "make each day count." Before he leaves, he passes Rose a note that says: "Make it count. Meet me at the clock." She does, and they go below decks to a raucous lower-class party complete with wild Irish music, dancing, and drinking. Cal's bodyguard observes her there and reports back to Cal. The next morning at breakfast, Cal implies she should have come to his quarters to have sex the previous night, but she says she was tired. He reveals that he knows where she was, and commands her to "never behave like that again." When she suggests that she cannot be commanded like "a foreman in one of your mills," he flies into a rage, smashing the dishes and ordering "you will honor me the way a wife is required to honor a husband," viz., sexual favors on demand. In the very next scene her mother adds her enforcement to Cal's as she symbolically tightens Rose's corset, implying her constriction of Rose's freedom. When Rose balks at marrying Cal, her mother tearfully and manipulatively asks, "Do you want to see me working as a seamstress? To see our precious things sold at auction?" When Rose says that it's unfair, her mother replies: "Of course it is. We're women. Our choices are never easy." In fact, she is not giving Rose any choice at all, or is suggesting that there really is no other choice to be made; but ultimately, Rose will make a different choice.

Jack manages to get Rose alone once more, to tell her he knows he can offer her nothing, but that because he cares for her he can't turn away unless he knows she is all right. She lies, rather unconvincingly, and tells him all is fine and that she loves Cal. When he suggests that she will die inside if she doesn't break away, Rose says, "It's not up to you to save me." Jack replies, "You're right; only you can do that." Although Rose will later refer to Jack as her "savior," what he says is true; she must choose to be free, as no one can do that for her. And by the end of that day, she has made that choice, as she appears at the bow where Jack is alone. The scene has a dreamlike quality to it, due to the sunset-simulating lighting, the odd fact that no one else is there, and his invitation to her to stand at the very front of the ship with her arms outstretched so as to feel the freedom of "flight" at sea. They kiss passionately, and the scene dissolves back to the wreckage of the ship and Rose telling the story. We are temporarily lifted out of her narrative as if to remind us of the inevitability of the fate of the *Titanic*, that this ship is doomed to sink that very night.

In the next few hours, he paints her nude with the jewel, so that she can leave the drawing and the diamond in Cal's safe with an insulting note of rejection. In it, she suggests that Cal can keep her picture locked up, like the diamond, but not her; she is not his possession. When he finds the items, he is furious and plans to frame Jack for the theft of the diamond in order to win her back. Meanwhile, Jack and Rose have sex in a car below deck, and afterwards on deck she tells him she is going with him once they reach New York. At this point, the iceberg hits. After the collision, the ship appears to be in fine condition to its passengers, but its builder, Mr. Andrews, knows it will sink. Rose and Jack observe Andrews and the captain in conference and fear the worst. They therefore go to warn Cal and Rose's mother, but Jack is caught in Cal's trap and taken away. Soon afterwards, Rose learns from Andrews that the boat will definitely sink and also that there are not enough lifeboats, as she had observed earlier. We see the lower classes trapped below deck by locked doors, the call for "women and children first," and Jack handcuffed to a pipe in a room below deck, alone once the bodyguard leaves him. Rose is about to board a lifeboat when her mother suggests that she hopes they'll be "seating by class" in the lifeboats. Rose is horrified and tells her mother that half of the people will not be able to get in the boats at all, but Cal says that "the better half" (i.e., the rich) will survive. Faced with her mother and Cal's class prejudice and the impending fate of the rejected poor onboard, she refuses to board the boat and instead goes to save Jack, who she has realized is innocent.

After considerable suspense associated with Rose's rescue of Jack, they emerge on deck and again Rose is asked to board a lifeboat, this time by Cal and Jack together, and she does so. But at the last possible second, she gets off, unable to leave Jack. Furious with jealousy, Cal fires at them with a pistol and chases them below deck. After losing them, he realizes that Rose has the diamond in the pocket of the coat he gave her. Jack and Rose have more hair-breadth escapes below deck until they emerge once more on top. Cal manages to get onto a lifeboat with a child he borrows so he can look like a father. Lower-class Irishmen charge at one of the crew, who shoots two of them and then himself. Andrews and several of the wealthy men are prepared to go down "like gentlemen," showing that not all of the wealthy are as selfish as Cal—although Ismay, representative of the White Star Line that owns the ship, sneaks onto a lifeboat.

Here we have some historical details about real people who either did or did not get on a lifeboat mixed in with the fictitious story of Jack and Rose, adding verisimilitude to the story like the realistic depiction of the sinking. A few scenes of pathos involve those who know they are doomed to die: the musicians playing a hymn, an old couple holding each other in bed, an Irish mother below deck telling a story to her two small children to lull them to sleep. We see the ship self-destruct, and many people fall to their deaths as the ship turns until its stern is vertical. Jack brings Rose to the stern and they go down with the ship, temporarily losing each other in the water. As they wait for the lifeboats to return, Jack realizes he will freeze to death in the water but allows Rose to rest on a piece of wood floating in the water that is only big enough for one. He knows he is sacrificing himself for her, but has no regrets. He insists that she promise to survive, and "that you won't give up no matter what happens, no matter how hopeless" it seems. She agrees that she'll "never let go." When the lifeboat finally arrives, Jack is dead, and as Rose realizes this she makes a decision not to die with him but to swim to the body of a dead steward in order to use his whistle to call for help. She had assumed that her promise to "never let go" was tied to Jack, but she actually has to pry his frozen fingers from hers to allow him to sink and herself to live—she has effectively promised to "never let go" of life, not of Jack or any other man. After being rescued, she hides among the lower classes from steerage in order to avoid being found by Cal or her mother. She leaves them behind forever by taking a new name and a new identity, "Rose Dawson." This might seem to embed her in his identity, except for the fact that he is dead (compare *A Star Is Born*). With the Statue of Liberty towering above her, she gains her freedom.

Back in the present, the pathos of her tale has moved her listeners to the point that they have forgotten about the fate of the jewel, which now seems unimportant. The head of the salvage operation, Lovett, repents that with all the time he has thought about *Titanic*, "I never let it in. I never got it." Now he gets it, as does the audience that has visually experienced the disaster and is similarly moved. It is revealed (only to the audience) that Rose still has the diamond, and as she now drops it overboard it is suggested to us that wealth is unimportant to a fulfilling life such as Rose has had. We see the photos in her cabin as she sleeps, depicting scenes from her life as an actress, flying a plane, riding a horse next to a roller-coaster. She has done all the things that Jack told her to do, though oddly enough there are no photos of children or grandchildren (even though Jack told her to have "lots of babies"). She has achieved fulfillment not through marriage and children, though she had these as well, but from doing what she wanted to do and living a life of adventure such as Jack had. In the final scene, she dreams of a reunion with Jack onboard the *Titanic*, with all the dead present to applaud as they kiss in front of the clock where they met to "make it count." He is wearing his simple clothes, and she is dressed in formal evening wear, suggesting that their class divisions are no impediment to their union. It is also suggested that Rose dies at this point, so the union is not only in her dreams but in a transcendental reality.

It should not have been a surprise that this story was a tremendous hit with young female viewers. Teenage girls often feel constricted by their parents, perhaps especially their mothers, and the spoken or unspoken assumptions about how they should live their lives. They feel pressured to conform to a societally prescribed gender role by parents as well as peers and media images, as they are told to focus on their appearance so as to be thin and attractive and thereby win a boyfriend. Even in our supposedly enlightened era in which girls can ostensibly enter any profession, they often still assume that life is incomplete without a man to love and care for them. Teenage girls often have very low self-esteem due to their feelings of dependence on men and male acceptance, and this sometimes leads to suicide attempts. For example, if a girl is rejected by a boyfriend, she feels she has no worth, and no reason to live.[6] In the face of such pressures, *Titanic* offered the message to young women that they should go on, that life is worth living no matter how bad it sometimes seems, that one can survive without a man and be independent. Although Rose married and had children and grandchildren, this does not seem to have been her raison d'être, as we see and hear almost nothing about her family. Her photos tell her own story—of a woman who had adventures without a man at her side. Of course, if Jack had survived, we are led to think they would have stayed together—but he didn't, and that is a crucial part of the narrative. Furthermore, even if he had survived, he is depicted as a man who could give Rose her freedom and not restrict it like Cal. The choice between Cal and Jack is so starkly drawn as one between bondage and freedom that the characters are flat and stereotypical, which prompted much of the derision of the film by the critics. These are not meant as realistic characterizations, however, but as ideal images for Rose to consider as she makes her choice about her life. In myth, characters can be stereotypes, as they signify abstract attributes for us to consider as we select the values and beliefs by which we will live.

She also makes a choice to live without money and not be dependent on it, as she recognizes its fundamental unimportance for personal happiness. The audience for elderly Rose (the salvage crew) also realizes the unimportance of the jewel, as do those of us who hear and see the tale. The class warfare on the ship between the poor (usually Irish) and the rich (English and Americans) also expresses the tensions between them and the fact that the poor usually lose, trapped below deck, except when they fight back. As most audience members are not rich, they will identify with the frustrated and excluded poor, and will connect these circumstances with Rose's choice to go back for Jack rather than escape with the rich. She is a heroine because of her humane consideration for the less fortunate, to the point that she assumes their condition when she assumes a new identity as Rose Dawson.

The scenes of the disaster itself also serve as part of Rose's story. Young people tend to like disaster movies, perhaps because they enjoy the catharsis of emotions related to fears about death and undeserved suffering. The film shows that both rich and poor may die, that no one can count on life at any point. But this depiction of suffering is also linked to Rose's decision to go on, no matter what. You can survive, disaster movies tell their audiences, even if life seems hopeless and filled with catastrophe. We can leave the theater to resume our lives, and Rose can start a new life altogether. Perhaps some of her freedom can even become part of the viewers' lives, if they incorporate some of her guts and joie de vivre into their own lives.

Rose's choice is also attractive to young people as it subverts parental power over their lives. The adult world is shown to be filled with those like Ismay who boast of their power and what they can create, such as the ship itself, a symbol of male power. When Ismay notes that the name of the ship is meant to convey "sheer size" and power, Rose asks if he has read of Freud's ideas on the male preoccupation with size. He doesn't get it, but we do: men wish to demonstrate the power of the phallus through their technological creations and their efforts to control nature, concealing a fundamental insecurity about their ability to do so. They cannot admit their weaknesses, and this is why they speed up, even in iceberg-infested waters. The collision and the sinking show in graphic detail the fallibility of human technology and the tragic plight of those who wrongly trust in their own omnipotence. Cameron has dealt with this theme before, notably in the *Terminator* movies (analyzed below), which update the Frankenstein story of how man destroys himself by seeking to be like God, in that man's creature finally gains the power to undo its creator. Cameron's critique of this hubris suggests that those who are not tempted by power or wealth, like Rose, have chosen the better course.

When one sees some of these dynamics present in the film, it should be more clear why this film broke all box-office records. It tapped into the best tradition of women's films and their appeal, especially in regard to young women and their situation today. Critics who were puzzled by its success, or who attributed it merely to the special effects, have clearly not seen the "religious" power of the film to convey catharsis, hope, empathy, and the value of independence to its audiences.

9

Romantic Comedies

The romantic comedy is a relatively neglected genre, perhaps because its seemingly simple form does not encourage elaborate analyses; it is exactly what it seems to be. As Martin Barker puts it, the romantic comedy is "all surface" and so does not invite an analysis of its depth, as it does not seem to have any.[1] But we still should seek to understand the appeal of this genre, which remains a very popular one, especially with women.

The romantic comedy might be considered the sunnier cousin of the tearjerker, as it also focuses on the plight of women, especially in regards to romance, but it ends happily. This is an oversimplification, however, for (as we have seen) tearjerkers do not always end completely unhappily, tending to have "bittersweet" endings that feature some loss but also very often some form of triumph for the woman, even romance. Romantic comedies differ from tearjerkers not simply because they are "happier" stories or because the couple always ends up together—in fact, if one considers the extremely popular *Annie Hall* (1977) a romantic comedy, it does not even seem necessary for the couple to be united at the end. Rather, romantic comedies engage the viewer by treating romance itself as a source of humor, whether through parody, satire, or farce. We can laugh at and identify with the problems that keep the couple apart, and also enjoy the fact that they are usually united in the end.

I have rejected the standard view of tearjerkers as mere promoters of sexist ideology (with some suggestion of subversion thrown in) largely because I have found that such films usually portray strong women with which female viewers can identify, and because even though these women suffer they tend to overcome their suffering in the end without necessarily being reembedded in patriarchy. If I am right, this view may help explain the popularity of tearjerkers with women, who find in them not a call to subservience but one to freedom. Perhaps romantic comedies are just as

179

popular with women because most of them prefer seeing a couple end up together rather than apart. But whereas tearjerkers feature independent women, romantic comedies tend to represent women as ultimately dependent on men—in love and in much else—a fact that is not lamented but rather celebrated in such films. The women in romantic comedies want and need to have a man to care for them, making these films appear to be the *most* sexist of films. Yet, this is the genre that continues to be among the most popular with women, and one often neglected by male viewers.

As with tearjerkers and other films, we should question an ideological explanation of the success of romantic comedies that claims a male industry has simply created these films to indoctrinate women about their necessary subjugation to men. If that were their message, they should be more popular with men than with women. As we have seen, men like fantasies such as action movies in which men have the power to rescue women (and other men), but these films do not necessarily entail the complete passivity of women or the loss of all female power. On the other hand, in romantic comedies, women often have to wait for the man to come around, and the only power they really have is to withhold sex until an offer of marriage is made. But these films continue to attract women: if they had no appeal, women would not go to see them. We need to analyze why these films appeal to women in order to understand what they are getting out of them, which presumably is more than just an inculcation of social indoctrination. Furthermore, some romantic comedies are made by women, so one cannot conclude that only sexist men are making these movies in order to reenforce their own social position. The reasons behind the success of these films are complex.

The romantic comedy may be said to have been invented in its classic form in Frank Capra's box-office hit, *It Happened One Night* (1934). In this film, spoiled heiress Ellen Andrews (Claudette Colbert) is thrown together with brash newspaperman Peter Warren (Clark Gable) as she is escaping her father to be with "King" Westley, a man she married without her father's permission. Peter agrees to help her get to Westley in exchange for her story, but on their travels, the two fall in love. Through a misunderstanding (common in such films), she comes to believe he hates her and she returns to Westley for a formal wedding, now accepted by her father. Before the end, however, she runs back to Peter (leaving Westley at the altar)—at her father's urging. Though Ellen and Peter come from different classes and levels of society, they are able to overcome this obstacle through their love. She seems attracted to him as he is a "real man," unlike

Westley, with Peter being more aggressive and dominating as well as sure of himself. At the same time, he does not know everything, something she notices; for example, he claims to be an expert hitchhiker, yet is unable to get a car to stop for them. Ellen manages to best him at this game by revealing her thigh as a vehicle drives by, succeeding in getting a ride. Even though Peter tells her she is spoiled, and it seems she is, he finds her attractive as a woman who had the courage to run away and seek her freedom from social convention. Although she depends on him and at times acts like a woman who cannot survive without a man, she also stands up to him, and their spunky interchanges signal that she can be his equal, at least in some sense.

This film contains many of the tensions present in any number of romantic comedies. On the one hand, the film suggests that a woman wants and needs a dominating man around to run her life; on the other hand, the woman flouts social convention by doing what she wants, defying first her father and then Westley. The film also manages to be romantic by keeping the sexual tension between them in check; when they have to share a room, he puts up a blanket between them—"the walls of Jericho," as he calls its—so that it will be clear he will take no liberties. She is the first to cross the "wall," to confess her love to him, a gesture that demonstrates no small amount of female sexual power for 1934; she is a "modern woman" who is at least partially liberated from traditional norms. He is too honorable to take advantage, however, and feels he must have some money in his pocket before he can propose and properly remove the sexual "wall." Though he criticizes her, he also respects her, and in spite of his rebel status he follows a code of honor that includes refusing the reward for her rescue that her father offers (a gesture that wins the father's respect for Peter as well). Clark Gable as Peter was immensely attractive to women for his ability to be both a rebel and a man of honor, a domineering scoundrel and a man who truly feels love—the character he reinvented as Rhett Butler in *Gone With the Wind*. The man must be powerful to be attractive, as no woman wants a wimp; but he also needs to be sensitive and kind—the ideal union of opposing traits, of strength and weakness.

Romantic comedies, especially those of the "screwball" variety that were popular in the 1930s and 1940s, often similarly featured a somewhat contradictory mixture of traits in the characters, or even a reversal of traditional gender roles. In *Ball of Fire* (1940), Barbara Stanwyck plays a gangster's girlfriend who uses a house full of bachelor encyclopedia-writing professors as a hideout. Gary Cooper is the linguist who is ostensibly studying her speech patterns but ends up drawn to the considerable sexual energy she projects. In the end, she is also drawn to him, due to his gentle and kind nature, which contrasts with her own gangster boyfriend. In this case, the characters defy traditional gender roles to some extent, as he finds her attractive because she is aggressive, and she finds him attractive because he is gentle.

Both women and men can enjoy such films as they also want to escape from the gender roles that constrict them romantically, as men are usually expected to be aggressive and women are usually expected to be passive. Seeing characters who can break out of such roles, even in an "unrealistic" comedy, may offer viewers the hope that their own relationships need not conform to stereotypes, that women and men can be attractive even when their roles are reversed. Each character also manages to unite weakness and strength by the end of the film, as Stanwyck needs to be rescued and Cooper and his professorial buddies oblige; social convention in general is lampooned, and suspended, when we see shy scholars firing machine guns in the air in order to intimidate criminals. Some might argue that this film becomes conventional at the end, as the man rescues the woman by beating up the bad guy. But it remains true that Cooper is attractive in both his kindness and in his strength, and that Stanwyck is attractive both in her powerful sexuality and in her heartfelt confession of love. The ending of the film does not subvert these tensions in the characters, which remain as part of the audience's experience of them.

More recent romantic comedies, oddly enough, may actually be more conventional in their depiction of gender roles than some earlier examples of the genre. This would seem curious in light of the fact that women supposedly have more sexual freedom now than in earlier times, for they are not generally coerced into marriage, nor do they have to wait until marriage to have sex. But if we examine the contemporary situation of women, we see that they do not always understand this to be liberating. There are more unmarried women than ever before, including divorced women who may find it difficult to encounter an acceptable man, especially as they age. They also frequently desire to have children before they become too old to do so, which at least traditionally has entailed more commitment from a man than merely the desire to have sex. Women may have sex with men more easily, but they may also perceive this weakening of traditional sexual morality as a prison in that they are expected to have sex in order to keep a man satisfied, even fairly early in a relationship. There are no longer any "Walls of Jericho" to protect them, no societal taboos against premarital or extramarital sex. It may be for this reason that there has been some backlash against feminist ideals among women who feel that traditional roles would offer them some protection from a sexual freedom that has not always proved liberating for them. Whether or not they are right to feel this way, it is undeniable that this development is an aspect of women's contemporary experience, reflected in contemporary romantic comedies that often express a longing for a traditional, lifelong marriage. *When Harry Met Sally . . .* (1989) was an extremely popular romantic comedy that exemplified this circumstance.

When Harry Met Sally . . . (1989)

The film begins with an elderly couple sitting on a sofa talking about how they met and married fifty years ago. Actually, only the man talks, as he describes seeing her and instantly deciding to marry her. These faux interviews punctuate the narrative of the film, as it is periodically interrupted by the diverse stories of older couples about their courtships. Some speak of love at first sight, some speak of many years that had to pass until they found each other again, but all of them indicate the idea that they were "fated" to meet and marry, and that true and lasting love wins out in the end.

The story of Harry (Billy Crystal) and Sally (Meg Ryan) begins as they graduate from college and share a car ride from Chicago to New York, where both intend to settle. Harry passionately kisses his girlfriend Amanda good-bye, says he loves her, and tells her he will call her as soon as he can. Of course, the audience knows that this relationship will not last, as we know that it is Harry and Sally who are fated to end up together, not Harry and Amanda. His expressions of commitment to Amanda also ring false as he propositions Sally while on the ride; she turns him down, supposedly out of respect for Amanda, who is also her friend, but she clearly has no interest in Harry in any case. They are complete opposites, for he is sloppy (spitting grape seeds out the window—in fact, *at* the window) and she is neat, he is a pessimist and she is an optimist, he is casual and she is extremely structured (having already mapped out the places where they will switch drivers). She is also "practical," claiming that she would rather have gone with Viktor Laszlo (Paul Henreid) than Rick Blaine (Humphrey Bogart) at the end of *Casablanca* (1943), as she would rather be "the first lady of Czechoslovakia" than married to a man who owns a bar. Harry suggests that she simply hasn't had great sex yet, and this is why she is able to make such a "practical" and nonsexual choice. He also tells her that men and women can't really be "just friends" because men want to have sex with all women. He is blunt to the point of being obnoxious and she finds him repellent.

After they reach New York, they part and do not see each other until five years later, when they accidentally meet at an airport and end up sitting next to each other on the airplane. Sally is now with Joe, whom Harry knows, and at first Harry does not even remember Sally. He tells her that he is getting married, which she finds "very optimistic" for him. He says that he's tired of the life of a single man, dealing with questions like how long he should hold a woman after they have had sex. He still seems to be someone who is more focused on sex than marital commitment, in spite of the fact that he is engaged. Five years later, they meet again, just after Sally has broken up with Joe, and Harry has gotten divorced. We hear the story of Harry's separation first, as he tells it to his friend Jess (Bruno Kirby) at a football game. Harry has been made a shlimazl by his wife, so that his story sounds like a stand-up comedy routine; she had actually phoned the movers to take away her things before telling Harry, and she is already living with another man. We hear Sally's story when she tells it to Harry, who is surprisingly sympathetic due to his own breakup; she left Joe because she realized that she wanted to have children, and Joe did not. Even though her friends have told her that having children virtually destroys a couple's sex life, she is ready to make this sacrifice, as children are more important to her. Sally asks Harry to dinner; Harry asks her if they are becoming friends; and Sally says somewhat grudgingly, "Well, yeah." Harry is amazed to have a woman friend, and tells her "you may be the first attractive woman I have not wanted to sleep with." She wryly thanks him for this backhanded compliment. It seems that Sally would have been open to a relationship with Harry that is more than friendship, but she has also told her friends that she is not interested in getting serious with anyone so soon after her breakup with Joe. At the same time, she knows that they have urged her not to wait too long; even if you married someone who then died, she has been told, "at least you could say you were married," this being crucial to a woman.

We see a montage of scenes describing the friendship of Harry and Sally, as they do everything together; going to restaurants, museums, and so on. She claims not to be depressed about her breakup, but he says he is having a much harder time. Still, he has resumed a sexual life of one-night stands, even with women for whom he feels nothing—and he tells Sally about it. She tells him he is "an affront to all women" because he casts them aside so casually; he insists that they are having just as much sexual pleasure as he is, and that is all it means to any of them. While they are having lunch in a diner, she demonstrates to him (in the most celebrated scene in the film) how a woman can easily fake an orgasm. Her point is that women may be faking sexual pleasure with him in order to please him, which implies they are after more than sex—that is, commitment, which he is unable to give.

On a blind double date, Harry fixes up Sally with his friend Jess, and she fixes him up with her friend Marie. This arrangement falls flat, however, and instead Jess and Marie immediately hit it off and quite literally run away together. Once again, Harry and Sally are thrown together, as if this was unavoidable. Four months later, while buying a wedding present for Jess and Marie, they run into Harry's ex-wife, Helen, and her new lover, Ira. Harry expresses his frustrations about this meeting in front of Jess and Marie while they debate about furniture for their apartment, and tells them that they too will end up divorced in the end. When Sally berates him for being too emotional in front of them, he in turn accuses her of suppressing all her feelings about her own breakup, and tells her she should be sleeping with someone by now if she has truly gotten over it. She says she will have sex when it is "making love," that she will not seek to sleep with as many people as possible as Harry does, "like you're out for revenge or something." He apologizes and they make up. By the next scene, however, both of them are in relationships, as if they have heard the other's advice that they should be getting on with their lives and making a greater commitment to someone. At the same time, it is clear that neither of these relationships will last.

The event that brings Harry and Sally together sexually is a phone call from Joe in which he tells Sally he is getting married. She calls Harry and asks him to come over. Sally is upset not because she loved Joe, but because she now knows he really did want to get married, but not to her. She feels rejected and believes that she will never meet anyone; she knows she is difficult, too structured. She fears becoming too old to have children. As Harry comforts her, she kisses him sexually and he responds. The scene changes to indicate that they have now had sex; she is happy, he looks miserable. They barely talk before turning off the light, and in the morning he dresses and leaves quickly. He seems to be treating her just as he has treated all the other women he has slept with. Both realize it was a mistake and confess this to each other; but now they have nothing more to say.

Three weeks pass until Jess and Marie's wedding. Harry wants to "get past this" but Sally believes he is acting as if nothing has changed between them. She does not believe that they can "just be friends" at this point. When he asks her out for New Year's Eve, she replies that she can't be his "consolation prize" anymore.

On New Year's Eve, she attends a party with a blind date she dislikes and he stays home alone. As he walks the streets of New York, he recalls all the times they spent together and suddenly realizes that he loves Sally and rushes to find her. When he tells her he loves her, however, she does not at first believe him. He convinces her by reciting a litany of her idiosyncrasies, to show that he loves her precisely as she is. The final scene of the film shows them sitting on the same sofa as the older couples we have seen interviewed about their courtships, and Harry and Sally summarize (somewhat inaccurately) how they finally got together as well.

This movie was a great success, no doubt in large part due to the talent of the actors as well as the director, Rob Reiner. But it was Nora Ephron's screenplay that attracted much attention and assured her of future opportunities to both write and direct her own films. The dialogue was full of funny one-liners, but the story also seemed to exert a tremendous appeal due to its old-fashioned romanticism. The interviews of the elderly couples and the use of old show tunes on the soundtrack (as well as references to classic films) signal a bygone era of romance, and the plot was structured so as to suggest that even in our own era of casual sex it is possible to find true romance and lasting love.

In romantic comedies, something usually has to keep the couples apart for the duration of the film, whether it is the class differences between them, the fact that one is married, or other plot contrivances, and in this film it is the fact that they are friends. On the soundtrack, Harry Connick sings the old Rodgers and Hart tune, "I Could Write a Book," which includes the line, "The world discovers as my book ends how to make two lovers of friends." The movie also shows how friends can become lovers, though it may not be easy. More revealing is the fact that they become friends rather than lovers largely because Harry is interested only in sex without commitment (in spite of the fact that he was married, for we never actually see him as married), and Sally is interested in marriage and children and not very interested in sex. The one sexual fantasy she relates to Harry is comically unimaginative ("he rips my clothes off" and that's all), and she also suggests that she has faked orgasms to keep men happy. She also finds herself unable to go back to a mere friendship after having sex with Harry, which for her signals the necessity of greater commitment.

The movie casts each of them as a stereotype of their gender: men only want sex and resist commitment, and women are desperate to marry and have children. What makes this a "romantic" movie is the fact that he does not consent to marry her just to have sex; he has plenty of that elsewhere, but it is meaningless. There is something more to relationships than just sex, as both of them realize; in fact, it is perhaps the least important part of their relationship. It is because they are friends, because they like each other, that they belong together—not because they found each other attractive at first sight (for they did not). The movie thus questions the romantic notion of "love at first sight," even though the elderly couples' interviews tend to support this ideal, in that true love will be deeper than mere sexual attraction. In our own sex-saturated culture, this sentiment also makes the film a throwback to an era when sex was not foregrounded as the most important part of a relationship (even if it was in the background). Audiences no doubt found this romanticism refreshing, as it shows love to be more important than sex, and sex following love rather than the reverse.

To tell audiences that there is more to a relationship than sexual attraction, that they ought to be friends first, may not seem like a very subversive message—but it is one that they do not often hear. The notion of "love at first sight," which has been found in romantic films from the beginning of cinema to the present, may have done more harm than good in society because people tend to rush into relationships, and even marriage, with illusions of perfection culled from the movies. In discussions of romantic films with students, I have found that even today's otherwise cynical young men and women entertain amazingly naïve notions about love—believing, for example, that if two people love each other (now), they will master all difficulties "till death do us part." We seldom see couples in films work through the difficulties of a relationship; if they simply get together by the end, we assume no problems will remain. Unfortunately, real relationships are not nearly as easy to maintain. *When Harry Met Sally* does perpetuate the illusion of marital perfection after the union, but it also suggests getting together involves more than just achieving sexual excitement. By suggesting that marriages need to be based on more than physical attraction, it describes love as based in mutual acceptance and friendship.

At the same time, this film perpetuates current sexual stereotypes that suggest it is only women who want to get married and have children, and that they have few sexual desires. It also suggests that men are afraid of commitment, perhaps due to their allegedly voracious sexual appetites. One hears these stereotypes invoked so often that people begin to believe them, even though there are plenty of men who want commitment and children, and plenty of women who are afraid of commitment. There are also women who have lots of sexual desire, and men who have less. We are prevented from seeing facts like these by films that reinforce our cultural assumptions about men and women. Much has been made of the fact that movies neglect the reality of homosexual romance, which is true; but it is not always recognized that the standard depiction of heterosexual romance fails to represent the real experience of many heterosexuals as well.

Why do women enjoy seeing such stereotypes perpetuated, then? One can speculate that many women relate to the female characters who are desperate for marriage, as it is harder today to get and keep a "good man." Women wait longer to get married and thus may panic about whether they will marry in time to have children. Men and women are more able today to get sex without marriage and may therefore resist committing themselves; also, the ease of obtaining a divorce makes it less likely that a marriage will last. People romanticize the "good old days" when couples stayed married, not realizing that many of these people were miserable. But, "at least they could say they were married," and they had children. Many people today, women as well as many men, long for the simplicity they associate with an idealized past in which relationships were supposedly easier to find and keep. Marriage may have been perceived as a prison by many career women who resisted it in earlier decades, but today it is often perceived as liberation from the eternal quest for a perfect relationship that many have found frustrating.

Nora Ephron has continued to make very successful romantic comedies, most notably *Sleepless in Seattle* (1993) and *You've Got Mail* (1998), both of which starred Meg Ryan and Tom Hanks. In the former, the couple does not even meet until the end of the film, and having met it is assumed that they will live happily ever after. This amazingly unrealistic notion is supported intrafilmically by references to the romance *An Affair to Remember*, as the couple meets atop the Empire State Building just as Cary Grant and Deborah Kerr did, but of course in the latter film they had already spent some time together.

You've Got Mail is ostensibly a remake of *The Shop Around the Corner* (1940), in which two people who despise each other are unwittingly anonymous pen-pal sweethearts. The newer film not only updates this situation by changing the medium to email, but also makes the two business competitors rather than coworkers in the same shop. The net effect is to make a film that is considerably more sexist than the original, as the man has considerable power over the woman from the start because he represents the large corporation and she the little bookstore. Joe (Tom Hanks) invokes the classic line from *The Godfather*, "It's not personal, it's business," in reference to their corporate war, and eventually gets Kathleen (Meg Ryan) to overcome her animosity toward him for putting her out of business.

It seems odd that Kathleen would decide to marry someone who had destroyed her livelihood, even though she wonders at times if she would prefer doing something else. Joe encourages her to forgive him by reminding her that Elizabeth forgave Mr. Darcy in *Pride and Prejudice* (her favorite book); however, readers of the book will recall that Mr. Darcy risks his own social standing by associating with Elizabeth, and that he also goes to considerable effort and financial expense to rescue her sister from poverty and disgrace. Joe makes no such effort to redeem himself in the eyes of Kathleen, except that he is nice to her. There seems to be no basis for their relationship, even in its email form, as their chatroom talk is "meaningless nothing," as she puts it. In *Shop Around the Corner*, the pen pals shared a love of literature and poetry; in this version, the man does not even like *Pride and Prejudice*. *When Harry Met Sally* at least had a basis for the couple's relationship in the friendship they developed; in Ephron's later films, the romances seem to be based on nothing at all, neither substantial intellectual sharing nor physical attraction. What all three films share is the idea that sexual attraction should not be the basis for a relationship, making them appear to invoke "old-fashioned" ideals of romance. Even older viewers like this sort of film, perhaps because it offers gentle comedy and romance without explicit sexuality or violence.

Not all romantic comedies convey the same sexist stereotypes, such as the view that all men fear commitment and all women seek it, or that the goal of all women is to "catch" a man. *Runaway Bride* (1999) featured Julia Roberts as a woman who has almost been married four times, but whose fear of commitment always causes her to bolt at the altar. She finally ends up with Richard Gere, as he teaches her that she is trying to find her own identity through a husband rather than in herself; what she actually fears is that she will lose herself in her perpetual attempt to please a man. Her lack of identity is signified by the fact that she doesn't even know how she likes her eggs cooked, always deferring to the taste of her current fiancé until she decides to try every recipe to find out for herself. Empowered to be an individual rather than an appendage to a man, and to have her own views, she can freely choose to be with Gere.

In *Notting Hill* (1999), Roberts also played a woman afraid to commit to a man who cares about her, this time because she is a movie star and he is ordinary; she has to overcome her own class prejudice to realize his worth, so that it is the woman who controls the action more than the man. We also see sexual stereotyping flouted to some extent in *The Truth About Cats and Dogs* (1996), in which a woman is afraid a man will not like her because she is not beautiful enough, and so she convinces her beautiful friend to pretend to be her. In the end, she realizes that the man loves her mind more than her body, and it does not matter what she looks like, suggesting that men value other traits besides a woman's sexual attractiveness. (This film reversed the gender roles in *Roxanne* [1987], in which the man fears his ugliness will prevent a woman from loving him; the story is a comic version of Edmond Rostand's tragic play *Cyrano de Bergerac*.) Films like these depict the man as completely willing to commit, and it is the attitude of the woman that provides the obstacle to their relationship, not his reluctance to fall into "the tender trap."

At the same time, the standard myth of the romantic comedy remains alive and well. *Serendipity* (2001), for example, perpetuates the notion that a unique soulmate is there for each one of us, and that love is a matter of fate that transcends time and place. The two lovers in this movie spend one evening together (without sex), then spend years searching for each other as they "know" they belong together. Love is depicted as a matter of magic and moment, not a matter of a relationship that must develop with time. Such an unrealistic notion of romance is fun at the movies, but it reinforces the idea that first impressions are accurate and that people should get married because they had a nice time together. People obviously like to believe in this romanticism, but such a myth does not get one through a real relationship.

Romantic comedies, then, do not tend to subvert conventional ideas about love and romance. Even people who are already in relationships like these films because they reinforce for them the idea that lovers can be united and remain together forever. Unrealistic and sometimes harmful as this myth may be, it remains immensely popular for women and men due to its ability to convey the hope that true love will be found by all who seek it. The myth of romantic perfection is one that people seem to long for, especially in an age when so few seem to find it.

10

Children's Films and Fantasy

One might wonder whether children's films constitute a genre because they are defined by their targeted audience more than by structure or subject matter. But as we have seen, most genres seek a particular audience and are designed with it in mind, whether we look to the action movies designed for young men or romantic comedies and tearjerkers designed for young women. This does not mean that other groups cannot enjoy these films, but that the expectations of a particular group may govern the construction of the films. Children's films are clearly made for children, as well as for the parents who take them to the movies. These films therefore often move at two levels—including, for example, some slapstick humor for the kids and some more sophisticated references that will be understood mainly by the adults. There are also so-called family films that may sometimes be distinguished from children's films because they may offer a bit more for the adults in the way of character development and plot while also entertaining the children; they also tend to be live-action rather than animated. Sometimes a movie is defined as a "family film" simply because it is rated G, "suitable for all audiences": it has no sex, violence, or profanity, even though it may not be of any particular interest to children.

Films that are targeted toward children and their parents, however, must offer more than simply the absence of the sort of scenes one finds in R-rated films. Furthermore, not all children's films are rated G today; quite a few are PG and include the sort of mildly risqué humor that will attract preteens and parents. It is also worth noting that not all films that feature children in them are meant for children, and not all films meant for children have kids in them. Still, there are usually kids or other small beings in such films with which the younger generation can identify, whether they be animals, toys, or magical creatures.

An extraordinary number of films are made for children, as kids and their families constitute a large market. Any attempt at a comprehensive theory of children's films may therefore overreach itself in an effort to fit all into the same mold. At the same time, there are certain formulaic elements, as with other genres, that one often finds in children's films. I have linked this genre with fantasy, as such films tend either to be set in a fairy-tale world or other setting that allows magical action or talking animals. Not all fantasy is directed at children, but much of it is, as it is assumed that kids like imaginary settings with stark struggles between good and evil that they can understand and appreciate. The magical powers of the characters tend to highlight their ability to choose either good or evil in unambiguous ways (e.g., "should I rescue the princess or run away?"), rather than in the more subtle forms that most real-world adult choices are framed. In addition, the main characters usually have to demonstrate that they are "honest, brave, and unselfish," as *Pinocchio* (1940) did, in order to earn the privilege of being a "real boy," marrying the prince or princess, or being accepted as a valuable member of the family. They also need to face up to their responsibilities, like *Aladdin* (1992) or *The Lion King* (1994). The Disney Corporation's feature-length cartoons are particularly formulaic, although there are variations and a certain development that has occurred over time—for example, there are more strong-willed heroines who do not simply wait to be rescued. Thus *Mulan* (1998) saves her family's honor and the kingdom by entering the military disguised as a man and using certain unorthodox combat techniques, and *Pocahontas* (1995) prevents a war by convincing her father not to kill John Smith. The majority of Disney's films are more sexist, however, as they are modeled on traditional fairy tales that give the heroine little to do but wait for the prince to come—whether she is Snow White, Sleeping Beauty, Cinderella, or the Little Mermaid. *Beauty and the Beast* (1991) put a slightly different spin on this formula in that the beauty has to kiss the beast in order to rescue him, but it is still based in the conventional hope for a princely husband.

Children's films also often feature small and normally powerless creatures with whom children will easily identify in positions of role-reversal that allow them to be in charge. Disney's *101 Dalmatians* (1961/1996) and *The Rescuers* (1977) fit this model, as did two "insect" computer-generated fantasies released in 1998, *a bug's life* (Pixar) and *Antz* (Dreamworks). The former is essentially a remake of the western *The Magnificent Seven* (1960), itself a remake of Akira Kurosawa's classic samurai film, *Seven Samurai* (1954). In the kids' version, a group of ants hires a group of bugs to protect them from rapacious grasshoppers who take all their food, not realizing that they are really a group of circus performers rather than warriors. In spite of their underdog status, they manage to triumph over the bandits. In *Antz*, a nonconformist ant (voiced by Woody Allen, complete with neuroses) helps to foil a military coup by a megalomaniac soldier ant who wanted to destroy all the workers. And in Pixar's two *Toy Story* films (1995, 1999), toys rescue one another from a sadistic child and a greedy collector, learning along the way the value of friendship as well as the importance of accepting your role in life. In their case, it is to make children happy as playthings, rather than to be real spacemen (as Buzz Lightyear thought he was) or museum pieces (as Woody is tempted to be, in the second film). Children no doubt liked the idea that their toys enjoy being subordinate to them (as long as they are not tortured), but the message is actually more poignant for adults, who may realize that career and fame are less important than being there for their children.

Parents often learn to be better parents in children's films. This process fulfills the children's ideal as well as offering the grownups a moral about the importance of quality time with their kids. The moral includes not indulging their every whim simply in order to please them. In *Willy Wonka and the Chocolate Factory* (1971), for example, the audience is instructed by the singing Oompa-Loompas that the spoiled and selfish children who don't make it through the factory have their parents to blame for failing to teach them correct values. On the other hand, a temporarily neglectful parent may offer children a chance to assert their own power and show that they can take care of themselves, at least in the fantasy world of film. In *Home Alone* (1990), a bratty young boy is inadvertently left behind when his family goes to Europe, and before they can make it back he learns enough responsibility to take care of himself, even shopping for groceries and doing laundry. Via a series of traps that involve cartoonish violence, he also manages to capture the burglars who aim to rob his house. Although many adult critic (myself included) found the violence sadistic and were repelled by the idea of making child neglect humorous, many children (including my own) enjoyed the fantasy of freedom and power over adults the film offered. Thus, we can see that adults and children will perceive different things in a film, and that they may receive different messages depending on whether they identify with the adults or the children.

Children's films subvert some conventions of the child-parent relationship when they give children powers they do not normally have, but they are also conventional in usually asserting the value of the family as well as offering up a host of traditional morals. Dorothy of *The Wizard of Oz* (1939) manages to exert enough power while she is "over the rainbow" to destroy two witches and debunk a wizard, but all her actions are motivated by the desire to return home and atone for her desire to run away. The liminal nature of children's films allows children both to temporarily fantasize about stepping outside their normal roles, and to return to them afresh afterwards. Usually their subversion of their normal role has a noble purpose, so that they are serving a higher moral cause in their temporary revolt, and this cause may even help them readjust to their normal status afterwards, accepting their proper place in the family. This structure is found in what may be the most successful children's film of all time, *E.T., The Extra-Terrestrial.*

E.T., The Extra-Terrestrial (1982)

Steven Spielberg does not only make children's films, by any means, but many of his greatest commercial successes have been essentially targeted at a youth market. Because his early movies in particular tended to be "escapist" and fun, critics sometimes reacted with animosity to his work, as if it was not serious enough or as if his tendency to manipulate viewers through a range of simple emotions (fear, sentimentality, suspense) was entertainment but not art. Directors like Francis Ford Coppola or Alfred Hitchcock, who also utilize audience manipulation techniques, have ultimately succeeded better with critics as they also clearly incorporate some confrontation and challenge to the audience in their films. Spielberg, on the other hand, seems so much a "feel-good" director that some critics have an almost moral objection to his tendency to indulge the audience in what it wants to see. Even his more serious films such as *Schindler's List* (1993) have been criticized for having endings that are too "happy" and unambiguous, as good tends to triumph over evil and hope wins out over despair.

Stories that people like, however, tend to have happy endings, and this is true of religious stories as well. A story may deal with darkness that is finally conquered by the light, which tends to be the structure of Spielberg's best films. Some filmmakers (notably Hitchcock) have focused on the dark side in an effort to understand its place in our psyche and deal with its reality there, but Spielberg tries to exorcise the demons through creating a world of fantasy and hope. This does not make his films less artistic or less worthwhile; it simply means that his films have dealt with suffering and evil in a way that is ultimately more optimistic than the filmmakers we tend to label "challenging." To appreciate what his films offer, one has to begin by putting aside elitist prejudices that assume a film can only be "good" if it leaves the viewers unsatisfied or disturbed in some way.

E.T., The Extra-Terrestrial broke all box-office records when it came out, so it remains a good example of a children's film that connected extremely well with audiences, both adults and children. It might seem that this film ought to be categorized as science fiction, as it is a "first contact" story of an alien visiting Earth—a staple plot among science fiction films. I have chosen to treat it as an exemplar of children's films, however, as it is clearly directed toward children and has more themes in common with films of this genre than with other science fiction films. The latter focus more on humans' fears of aliens as well as of our own technological creations, and they do not tend to be directed at children to the same extent. This is not to say that the film has no science fiction themes, but that these themes do not predominate. As a story of interspecies friendship, it deals more with the impact the alien has on one boy and his family than on the significance of this meeting for humanity.

The film begins with the landing of E.T.'s ship on Earth, apparently on a peaceful mission to collect samples of plant life. Point-of-view (POV) shots identify us with his character immediately, as he wanders too far from the ship in his curiosity about this planet. Scientists who have spotted the ship suddenly appear in a car, shot from a low angle to maintain E.T.'s POV, and we see their lower bodies and the keys that jangle on the belt of one, but not their faces. It is the humans that appear frightening here, not the small and vulnerable alien. When they hear his "heart-light" beep (a signal from his ship to return), they shine their flashlights on him, and he screams and runs in terror. We hear his fast and panicked breathing during a POV tracking shot that follows his flight through the forest to the ship, but the spaceship takes off before he gets there because his comrades fear detection by the humans. He has been left alone.

This scene cuts to another small person, ten-year-old Elliot, whose name begins and ends with "E" and "T," indicating his similarity to the alien. Although he is with his fifteen-year-old brother and his friends, he is essentially alone as well because he is being ignored in his desire to join their "Dungeons and Dragons" role-playing game. They agree to let him join if he waits outside for the pizza they have ordered. After it arrives, he hears a sound in the tool shed and goes to investigate. He rolls a baseball into the shed, and E.T. throws it back at him—though Elliot cannot see him. In fright, he runs inside to tell his mother and the boys, who follow him outside to "check it out." Of course, they find nothing, though the audience sees two of E.T.'s fingers after they leave. Late that night, Elliot goes outside again and finds E.T. eating in the cornfield by their house, much to the surprise of both of them. Each of them screams and E.T. runs away, still not clearly seen by us.

In these scenes, Spielberg mimics the style of horror movies that do not show the "monster" early in the film but only fully reveal him later. Such films also tend to use POV shots for the "monster," only later shifting to shots in which the creature is the object of view rather than identified with the camera. Although in horror movies this revelation usually signals the ultimate control of the monster through the gaze of the viewer and the characters who subdue the monster, in this film we are gradually given more to see of E.T.—not to subdue him, but to subdue our fears of him as "other" because we realize he is not a threat and was initially just as scared as Elliot. This full view is revealed the following night when E.T. approaches Elliot as he sits outside waiting, chiefly because Elliot left some "Reese's Pieces" candy in the forest for him, and he has come for more. Sharing candy signals friendship for children, and apparently this is an intergalactically accepted sign. When E.T. comes into the house to Elliot's room, we are at last privileged to view him fully as he mimics Elliot's gestures. Elliot suddenly falls asleep, and from this time on they seem to be joined emotionally via E.T.'s mental powers, so that Elliot feels what E.T. feels.

The next day Elliot manages to feign illness so he can remain home from school by himself. He and E.T. spend the day together and he teaches E.T. about such crucial cultural matters as toys and junk food. After school, he plans to introduce E.T. to his brother Mike, but their five-year-old sister Gertie runs in and screams in fright; soon all of them are screaming, but miraculously Mom does not hear. They manage to conceal E.T. from her, with Elliot making his siblings promise to keep the alien's presence a secret. Elliot tells Gertie that "only little kids" can see E.T., to which his savvy sister responds, "Give me a break." The joke is that it seems adults really cannot see him, as noted when Gertie later breaks her promise and tries to show E.T. to her mom, but the preoccupied parent manages to miss seeing him even as he walks by her in the same room.

When Elliot returns to school and leaves E.T. home alone, the alien drinks several beers by mistake and gets drunk. Due to their emotional linkage, Elliot vicariously experiences this intoxication himself while he is at school, resulting in a lot of humor as the inhibitions of both relax. Influenced by E.T.'s feelings of vegetarian pacifism, Elliot frees the frogs in his classroom that were to be dissected and also manages to kiss the girl who is always looking at him (while E.T., at home, is watching a similar scene from John Ford's 1952 film, *The Quiet Man*). Meanwhile, E.T. learns to talk (aided by Gertie and *Sesame Street*) and develops a plan to "phone home" by constructing a signaling device that will call his spaceship back. Interspersed with the narrative of the children, however, are ominous scenes of the scientists following his trail, to the point that their listening devices pick up a suspicious conversation between Elliot and Mike in their garage as they discuss E.T. In the meantime, the alien is also getting sick: although Elliot denies it when Mike asks him about it, we see the flowers that E.T. had caused to bloom are now wilting, indicating that his powers are waning.

On Halloween, they dress E.T. in a white sheet and pretend that he is Gertie so he can get out of the house; their mother, of course, is easily fooled. Elliot and E.T. go to the forest to set up the signaling device, and Elliot discovers to his delight that E.T. can make his bicycle fly with his powers—he has already seen him move other objects and heal a cut finger, indicating some "magical" abilities. When the spaceship does not return immediately, Elliot tries to get E.T. to go back to his house, telling him, "You could be happy here. . . . I wouldn't let anybody hurt you. We could grow up together, E.T." But E.T. only looks at the sky and says "ouch" to indicate his feelings of abandonment and loss. He sees Elliot crying, however, and realizes that he is not alone in his feelings. Alternating close-ups of them help us to feel the emotions of both; we temporarily forget that E.T. is a construct designed by the filmmakers as we see his face convey pain and sadness.

When Elliot and his siblings do not return home, their mother becomes anxious and goes out to look for them. While the house is empty, we see the dark-suited scientists enter with equipment designed to uncover evidence of the alien. By the next day, Elliot returns, having lost E.T. in the forest after falling asleep; he tells Mike to find E.T. and bring him home. Mike finds E.T. lying in a river, pale and sick. Once he is home, the children decide they must tell their mother; when she sees E.T., Elliot says to her, "We're sick. I think we're dying." She reacts with understandable fright and pulls Elliot away from E.T., though they do not want to be separated. At this moment, the scientists enter the house in space suits. Now *they* have clearly become the invading monsters, as they enter through doors and windows with arms outstretched (in "monster" fashion) and prevent the escape of the family. The house is turned into a laboratory as the scientists take over. Elliot and E.T. are in hospital beds, side by side, as both are hooked to medical monitors, which show that their lives are linked. Elliot screams that they should leave E.T. alone, that they are scaring and hurting him, while they are seeking with traditional medical technology to analyze and save E.T. At last we see the face of the scientist with the keys who approaches Elliot by tapping with two fingers (similar to E.T.) on the plastic case in which Elliot is held. He asks him about the device in the forest and tells Elliot that he's glad E.T. came to him first, and that "you did the best that anybody could do," as he holds Elliot's hand. He is clearly a compassionate scientist, though he is still part of the adult world. That night, Mike sleeps in the room where E.T. slept, a closet full of stuffed animals, and he seems to have returned to his own childhood in this setting, just as the adult viewers have.

The next morning, the life signals for E.T. and Elliot separate on the medical monitors, and it is clear that E.T. will die but Elliot will live. Elliot tells him to stay, that "I'll be right here," and E.T. says simply "Stay, Elliot," as if he knows that his death will not be permanent. The scientists make one last attempt to save him as Elliot yells, "You're killing him!" Gertie stares in horror as they use electroshock on his heart to force it to beat, in vain. Though the scientists are trying to help, their efforts are perceived as invasive and violent from the children's point of view. Elliot is allowed to say good-bye to the lifeless body of E.T. as it rests in a coffin of ice. He tells him, "You must be dead, because I don't know how to feel. . . . I can't feel anything anymore." He also tells him, "I'll believe in you all my life, every day. E.T., I love you." As he closes the lid to the coffin, we see E.T.'s heart-light turn red; as Elliot walks out, he sees the flowers in the pot come to life, and he runs back to the coffin to see a now fully alive E.T. telling him that his people are returning for him. The assumption is that he has been rejuvenated by their "return phone call," but the film also makes it seem as if Elliot's profession of love and faith brings E.T. to life. Earlier in the film, we saw Gertie and her mother reading the part of *Peter Pan* in which Tinkerbell comes to life after they clap their hands and say, "I believe in fairies." When E.T. dies, Gertie and her mother, like Tinkerbell, express their wish that E.T. could come back to life, and indeed, he does come back to life precisely when Elliot says he "believes" in E.T.

Elliot tells Mike that E.T. is alive, though they keep this a secret from the scientists so that they might help him return to his ship. There is quite a bit of fun and excitement derived from the successful effort of the children to outwit the grownups in this effort, and the audience enjoys being fully identified with this effort. Mike's friends even help out by joining in on their bikes, and they manage to evade the authorities until a roadblock seems to have them trapped. We see shots of men with rifles[1] and Elliot's terrified reaction as he bikes toward them with E.T. on his handlebars. At the last possible second, E.T. levitates all of the bikes away from them into the forest, where his ship is landing.

Gertie and her mom arrive in their car, with "Keys," the scientist, just behind. Each of the children has a chance to say good-bye to him. E.T. asks Elliot to "come," but Elliot must "stay." Each indicates his pain on parting ("ouch"), but E.T. tells him that "I'll be right here" as he touches his magical finger of healing to Elliot's forehead. E.T. will be with him emotionally and spiritually, if not physically. As the ship flies away and leaves its rainbow trail of hope, the final shot of the film is a close-up of Elliot's face, reinforcing the idea that E.T. is within him and not in some distant place.

There is a clear use of Christian imagery by Spielberg in this film, as it includes a savior with healing powers who comes from the heavens, dies, and is resurrected to ascend to heaven once more. He also leaves behind his spirit with his faithful disciples. But we should be wary of "baptizing" the film as if it simply repeated the Christian message, for Spielberg is not Christian, but Jewish. His use of Christian imagery reflects his ability to utilize images that are familiar to our culture and appropriate them for his own purposes. In this case, he has used the images of Christian salvation and applied them to the situation of a family suffering from an absent father. We are told early in the film that the father has left his wife for another woman ("He's in Mexico with Sally"). It is clear that the mother is not having an easy time raising three children by herself, as she admits to the police officer who comes to the house when Elliot does not return on Halloween night. She is unable to work at a job and also be aware of all that the kids are doing, this being one of the reasons they find it easy to conceal E.T. from her for so long. All of them miss their father, and we see Mike and Elliot recall some of the fun they had had with him. Elliot's attachment to E.T. arises from his need for a father, although E.T. is also perceived by him as a friend and playmate. "Keys" is also a sort of father figure to Elliot, as he praises Elliot for his care of E.T. and even comes to the spaceship to see E.T. depart. Still, he is no substitute for E.T., who allows Elliot to truly "feel" and helps him reconnect with his family. We see the reconnection first as the siblings work together to help E.T., and later even the mother joins them in their concern for him as she comforts Gertie and Elliot when E.T. is dying. Furthermore, in the final scene, when Elliot and E.T. hug each other, we see Elliot's mother kneel as if in reverence, but then we see Elliot looking at his mother over E.T.'s shoulder, and the reaction shot of her meeting his gaze. The mother and the son are reconnected through E.T., so that even though the spaceman leaves, the family remains unified—even without a father.

Spielberg utilized the fantasy of a boy meeting a friendly alien as a device for reuniting a family suffering from divorce, in part because he had suffered the divorce of his own parents and sought to escape this situation in the fantasies that ultimately led him to be a filmmaker.[2] This film connected so well with audiences presumably because they also could identify with the family and its sufferings, whether they had experienced the loss of a parent or not, and they also believed in the power of love to overcome whatever tribulations they met. Spielberg created this mythic narrative to achieve catharsis for himself and his audience, to give hope, and to convey a belief in the value of family. One could hardly find a better example of the "religious" power of cinema, achieved through overt sentimentality and an almost viscerally simple script.

Many of Spielberg's films are equally personal, arising from experiences of his own life and his attempt to deal with them. Such humanity is one of the reasons his films are so popular, as they express genuine emotions about real situations that people face. Although he sometimes uses the medium of fantasy to convey this reality, it serves to deepen our sense of the ordinary conflicts of everyday life rather than to distance us from them—as any good myth does. In *Hook* (1991), for example, he tells the story of a grownup Peter Pan who must recall his true identity in order to win back his children from Captain Hook, who has captured them. Peter has become a ruthless corporate lawyer with little time for his children, and he must recapture the child within himself in order to be a decent parent. His children also gain new respect for him as he shows he truly loves them and has the ability to rescue them from harm. The rest of us do not need to "fly, fight, and crow" like Peter Pan in order to be good parents, but we need to remember to spend time with our children, to remember that they are more important to us than our jobs—and we need to be sure that our children know this as well.

A movie like this one has as much to say to parents as to children, although it also shows children the importance of family and the fantasy of omnipotent parental love. Families do not always experience such perfection, as Spielberg himself did not as a child; families do not always stay together, and parents are not always there to deliver "quality time." Sometimes parents just want their children to go to bed so that they can be by themselves, as Hook tells Peter's incredulous children. Faced with the contradictions between the ideal of parenthood and the reality, parents don't always measure up. Spielberg has been divorced himself, and is trying to balance a rather significant career with the effort to be a father to the children of his two marriages (including adoptees). In *Hook* he holds out an ideal of familial perfection for himself and others, not because he believes this is literally attainable, but because the fantasy invokes an image of the world as we would like it to be—an image that he hopes will rub off on reality.

All of us like such images of hope and ideality, even though we know they are fantasies, because they inspire us with the idea that things could be better. Religions offer us the hope of a better world not by describing the world as it is but by describing it as it could be. In this way we begin to believe that religions' models *for* reality could be our models *of* reality as well. The simplicity and innocence of children's films, Spielberg's in particular, offer this religious hope in a powerful and convincing way.

11

Science Fiction

Like the western, science fiction is a genre that existed in literature prior to film. There is, however, greater diversity in science fiction literature than in western literature, in that one does not always find the same setting or props as signifiers in science fiction settings. Spaceships, laser guns, mad scientists, and monstrous aliens appear in a certain type of science fiction, but not all. Science fiction may be set in the future, or in the present—sometimes even in the past.

The attempt to find a definition of science fiction and its conventions is also confused by the fact that it has a certain overlap with both horror and fantasy, and these genre confusions spill over into film as well. If a film features a monster on the loose, is it science fiction if it is from another planet, but horror if its origin is supernatural? Similarly, is the only distinction between fantasy and science fiction that in the former extraordinary powers come from "magic," and in the latter, from "technology"? If so, then the distinction between these genres would seem thin, because (as science fiction author Larry Niven has pointed out) a sufficiently advanced technology may look just like magic to those who don't understand it; for example, telekinesis and telepathy may be explained either magically or technologically/scientifically, depending on the narrative.

I would suggest that science fiction is not defined simply by the presence of scientific as opposed to supernatural explanations, but rather by the distinct set of issues it is usually focused upon, linked to the fact that technological explanations can be given. In fantasy, heroes show their virtue by battling and conquering inexplicable ("magical") powers, and an attempt to explain the origin of those powers is unnecessary; the world is simply viewed as a place where good and evil powers struggle, and we must choose which side we will pick. Thus I have considered *E.T.* to be a fantasy, rather than science fiction. One could also include a movie like *Groundhog Day* (1993), in which it is never explained why the hero has to relive the same day over and over again; the only question is whether he will make the best of the situation, and improve himself as a result.

In horror movies, also, we do not really need to explain the origin of the monster, as this is irrelevant—it may be supernatural (*Dracula, The Wolf Man*) or natural (*King Kong, The Creature from the Black Lagoon*). Films such as these suggest that the monster represents our own evil nature, often as it is understood in relation to unchecked sexual power, which is projected onto another as an object of fear and sometimes of sympathy. In contrast to both fantasy and horror, in science fiction the origins of extraordinary phenomena can be explained, at least in part, as being from our own technology or beings from another world. The significance of this lies not so much in the fact that an "explanation" is provided as in the fact that the extraordinary is attributed to powers that humans may someday have—for even 'aliens' usually represent a more advanced form of ourselves, what we may become, for better or worse.[1]

Science fiction then deals with our hopes and fears for ourselves as a species in that it projects either utopian (perfectionistic) or dystopian (catastrophic) futures, or often a combination of the two. Technological developments per se may or may not be a significant part of this formula, as we see in Terry Gilliam's *Brazil* (1985), about a totalitarian society in the "near future." The sets and costumes are made to look more like they are from the 1950s than the twenty-first century, presumably in order to make it clear that this kind of dystopia is already very possible. In a similar way, Philip Dick's classic science fiction novel *The Man in the High Castle* imagined a dystopian world, set in 1962 (when Dick wrote the book), in which Germany and Japan won the Second World War. This world is in some ways technologically behind our own, but it still represents the threat of what our own future might become.

The lines between the genres still remain fuzzy even with this definition, and there is a certain amount of hybridization between them. Thus *Alien* (1979) and its sequels are structured like horror movies in which the monster sneaks up on the unsuspecting, and only female warrior Ripley can defeat it. Finally, she begins to share the nature of the monster after being impregnated by it (and ultimately cloned from it), and in this way the films implicate the heroine and the viewer into the evil, as horror movies do. But the *Alien* movies are also set in a future world in which a malevolent corporate government seeks to use the monsters for biological warfare, and this corporation frequently frustrates Ripley's efforts to exterminate the creatures. In this sense, the narratives suggest a dystopian world in which all is done for profit and power, and compassionate human relationships are all but impossible. This situation makes the films more than horror, as a science fiction setting provides the message that it is society that perpetuates the monsters (through an unwillingness to destroy them), and the individual who fights them will have to stage a heroic quest without any real help from that uncompassionate society.

I would also classify *Invasion of the Body Snatchers* (1956) as science fiction in that it represents a dystopian future. The monsters in this film look and act exactly like the people they replace, except that they are unable to show any emotion; in this way, they represent what we may all become if we lose the ability to love and care for one another and instead become part of an emotionless, societal "organism." As the protagonist and narrator (Dr. Miles Bennell) puts it, all of us are losing our humanity, bit by bit, as "we harden our hearts" toward others, but the process is so gradual that we don't even notice it. In contrast, *I Married a Monster from Outer Space* (1958), which has almost the same story of aliens impersonating humans, deals less with fears about what may happen to society than it does with the anxieties of a wife about her strangely distant husband (who is really an alien that looks like him). This plot is more like a horror movie in that it focuses on the female fear of the male "monster" but the story has a happier ending than many horror movies: the wife gets her real husband back in the end.

Science fiction thus expresses our dystopian fears of what we may become if our destructive tendencies triumph, as well as our utopian hopes that we might overcome those destructive tendencies. The popularity of the original *Star Trek* show was in no small part due to the perception that it described a utopian future in which Earth has overcome poverty and war, so that we can zip around the galaxy discovering "strange new worlds." The episodes never took place on Earth, of course, so the civilizations visited each week tended to be dystopias that required some fixing by the *Enterprise* crew (in spite of the "prime directive" that told them not to intervene). By itself, utopia is uninteresting, so it is only from the threat of dystopia that stories can develop. In the later *Star Trek* shows and movies, it was made more clear that much of the galaxy was not a utopia, including much of Federation space.

The hope for utopia and the threat of dystopia are expressed through a variety of elements and plot devices. Dystopia may be depicted as an unfeeling and repressive totalitarian regime, but our fears about the future are also sometimes expressed through the fear that our technology will destroy us. This may take the form of nuclear or biological holocaust, brought about by environmental carelessness, the development of dooms-day weapons that destroy all life, or general scientific hubris about the extent of human powers. Mary Shelley's *Frankenstein* is usually regarded as the first science fiction novel, for when she decided to make the monster a product of science (rather than magic) it became a cautionary tale about the dangerous temptation of scientists to play God as they invent things they cannot control. Similarly, during the Cold War, science fiction movies expressed the fear that we might inadvertently destroy ourselves by nuclear weapons. One finds this fear expressed realistically in *Fail-Safe* (1964), and as an object of black comedy in *Dr. Strangelove or: How I Learned to Stop Worrying and Love the Bomb* (1964). In *The Day the Earth Stood Still* (1951), an alien visits Earth to warn us that we must control our violent tendencies or risk annihilation from the other planets; in *Planet of the Apes* (1968), the hero discovers at the end of the movie that what he thought was another planet is in fact the Earth of the future, as humans destroyed themselves and the environment in a nuclear war. Since the fall of the Soviet Union and the apparent lessening of the nuclear threat, more films have dealt with fears about biological holocaust, such as *Twelve Monkeys* (1995), in which a scientifically engineered virus decimates the human population and banishes the few survivors below the surface of the Earth.

More specifically, a form that science fiction inherited from *Franken-stein* is the "robot story" in which human-created artificial intelligence becomes a threat to human survival. In *Colossus: The Forbin Project* (1970), a superintelligent computer takes over the world, demonstrating that humans may become slaves of the machines they have created. The *Termina-tor* films (analyzed below) were based on the same concept, except that the robots seek the total obliteration of humans, much like the "Borg" of the television series *Star Trek: The Next Generation* that were featured in *Star Trek: First Contact* (1996). A similar theme was developed in *2001: A Space Odyssey* (1968) when the spaceship's computer, HAL, tries to kill all the astronauts aboard after it realizes they are planning to disable it. Such stories reflect our fear that we may not be able to control our own technology, that it might begin to control us instead.

There is also the more optimistic possibility, however, that machine intelligence might prove benevolent and protective of humanity. The robots of Isaac Asimov's stories who are programmed so they are unable to harm humans fall into this category. They are not only unthreatening, but actually more virtuous than humans. The character "Data" on *Star Trek: The*

Next Generation and the associated movies is this sort of robot, even though his evil twin is not; in a similar way, the robot played by Arnold Schwarzenegger in the second *Terminator* film is benevolent, in contrast to the one he played in the first film of the series. Similarly, in *Blade Runner* (1982), most of the androids are homicidal, but at least one is not, and even those who kill ostensibly do so in self-defense. This duality of the robot nature reflects the hope that our technology may be used for good along with our fear that it may be used for evil. These two sides in turn reflect our own nature and its twin sides; which side will win in the end is up to us as we create our own future in addition to the machines that will express the nature of this future.

A similar duality is played out in respect to aliens, as they may be represented as demons or angels, a threat to our survival or virtuous saviors. Just as robots represent us in our technological abilities, so do aliens represent our possible future as they tend to be more "advanced" than we are— at least they can fly across interstellar space more easily. Most of the movies of the 1950s represented aliens as threatening, as we projected onto them fears of our own destructive abilities, recently unleashed through atomic power. Klaatu of *The Day the Earth Stood Still* was an exception, as he came in peace to warn us to curb our fear and violence; we were the real enemy in this film, as humans reacted with fear to Klaatu and tried to destroy him, demonstrating that humans are just as violent as he had said we were. In this case, it is the humans in the film who project their own violence onto the alien, imagining that he is the threat. But the viewer of the film can see that the alien is not to be feared and that he represents our better nature, what we might become if we control our violence. At the same time, he threatened that unless we learned to be nonviolent, we would be destroyed by the invincible race of robots represented by his companion Gort. In suggesting that the only real way to curb violence is with the threat of violence, the movie oddly enough sanctioned the very stockpiling of nuclear weapons that it was ostensibly criticizing.

When aliens are evil, they also tend to reflect our worst side as they exaggerate our own faults, through being excessively violent and genocidal and perhaps through other traits that relate to our current fears about our future. In *Independence Day* (1996), for example, the aliens intent on destroying Earth move from planet to planet, using up natural resources with no concern about pollution or conservation, even as many humans fear we will do with our own planet. Their selfish consumerism is a parody of human behavior, so that we can see ourselves in them.

Another element that science fiction utilizes to express the duality of our hopes and fears about the future is time travel. The possibility of knowing what will happen and having the chance to try to change it invites the question of whether we are destined to doom ourselves or whether we can, by strength of will, create a different future. In *Twelve Monkeys* the hero thinks that he can prevent a biological holocaust, but he can't, as his efforts to do so simply make him a pawn in the schemes of the future government that manipulates him for its own purposes. The sequels to *Planet of the Apes* toyed with the idea that the nuclear holocaust was not predestined, especially if apes and humans could learn to live together in peace. *Terminator 2: Judgment Day*, as we shall see, makes a similar proposal, and in this way plays with the question of whether the future will reflect our worst fears or our finest hopes.

The Terminator (1984) and Terminator 2: Judgment Day (1991)

The *Terminator* films have elements of both action movies and horror, but can be classified as science fiction in that their essential theme is the threat and promise of technology. Director James Cameron updates the Frankenstein theme, suggesting that in our hubris we may place too much trust in our abilities to create perfection, and this overconfidence may prove to be our own undoing when our technological creation turns on us. As we have seen, he would later develop this theme in a somewhat different form in *Titanic*.

The *Terminator* (1984) begins with a scene of Los Angeles in the year 2029, a post-Holocaust world in which the remaining humans fight for survival against the machines. Images of countless human skulls on the battlefield recall images of the Nazi death camps and the bodies of their victims. Text on the screen tells us, however, that the final battle will be fought "here, in our present—tonight." After the credits, the action shifts to 1984 Los Angeles, as the Terminator (Arnold Schwarzenegger) arrives naked via a time machine and kills three street youth for their clothes. Next we see his human nemesis arrive from the future, and he also has to steal clothes and weapons. He looks up Sarah Connor in the phone book; the next day, we see Sarah at her job as a waitress. She seems to be fairly incompetent, getting orders wrong and spilling coffee on a customer. Meanwhile, the Terminator steals a number of weapons from a gun store and begins killing all the Sarah Connors in the phonebook.

After the police realize that two women with the same name have been killed, they try to warn the "real" Sarah that a pattern killer may be looking for her. Sarah, however, is not at home but at a bar, where she sees television coverage of the murders and realizes she is in danger. As the bar's phone is out of order, she goes onto the street and realizes she is being followed. Although she doesn't know it, it is the human from the future, Kyle Reese. She enters a club at which she tries to phone the police, with no success ("all lines are busy"). Meanwhile, the Terminator enters Sarah's apartment and kills her roommate and the roommate's boyfriend. He also hears Sarah leaving a message for her roommate on the answering machine, telling her where she is, and sees a photo of her, enabling him to identify her. When he reaches the club where she is, there is some suspense until he spots her; as he is about to shoot her, Reese shoots him but does not kill him. Considerable carnage follows as the Terminator shoots at everyone with his submachine gun while he is trying to hit Reese. Reese's shotgun knocks the Terminator out the window; in the moment it takes the Terminator to recover, Reese grabs Sarah and says, "Come with me if you want to live."

During the subsequent chase scene, Reese manages to tell Sarah (and the audience) what is going on. The Terminator has been sent from the future to eliminate Sarah, and Reese is there to stop it. The Terminator may look like a man, but "it doesn't feel pity or remorse or fear" and "it absolutely will not stop ever, until you are dead." He tells her that in a few years, the world she knows will be gone, as the machines will develop a "new order of intelligence" and will seek to exterminate all humans in an effort to eliminate any threat to the machines' existence. A few humans will be kept alive to load bodies into disposal units, he tells her—another reference to the procedures of the Nazi death camps (and, as in the concentration camps, the prisoners are given identifying tattoos on their arms). These survivors manage to fight back, however, led by John Connor, Sarah's yet unborn son; that this savior has the same initials as Jesus Christ is obviously no coincidence. With his leadership, they will destroy the defenses of the machines. The Terminator, who has been sent back in time, seeks to kill Sarah before she can give birth to the savior of the human race in order to insure that the machines will win. Reese is there to make sure the effort fails, to protect her at all costs.

Reasonably enough, Sarah believes that Reese is totally crazy, and after she and Reese are taken into police custody, this diagnosis is confirmed by the police psychologist, Dr. Silverman. The Terminator, however, smashes into the police station and begins killing everyone in his path to get to Sarah. Reese manages to rescue her again, and they escape. He tells her that it was she who taught her son to fight so well, which she finds hard to believe: "Do I look like the mother of the future? I can't even balance my checkbook." Reese also tells her that he loves her, that he always has, that he "came across time" for her; then they have sex. The Terminator finds them at their motel, as Sarah had phoned her mother and told her where she was—but it was really the Terminator at the other end, impersonating her mother's voice. In the final chase and battle, there are a number of points at which it seems the Terminator should really be dead, but he keeps coming back to life, finally being reduced to a metallic skeleton with no human appearance. Reese sacrifices himself to blow up the Terminator, but its upper torso still snakes after Sarah, who is also reduced to crawling, by her injuries. She manages to crush the Terminator in a metal press and by now has begun to embrace her warrior future as she shouts, "You're terminated!" to the machine as she kills it.

The final scene of the film is six months later, as we see a pregnant and more self-assured Sarah with her own handgun, driving a jeep and stopping at a gas station near the Mexican border. She records a message for her unborn son on a cassette tape, and we realize that Reese is the father—creating one of those time travel paradoxes in which it seems that the past and the future form a loop, as Reese came to the past to conceive a son who will later send him back. Sarah, having shed her earlier lack of confidence in her abilities, has also embraced her mission to raise a son tough enough to help the human race survive.

Terminator 2: Judgment Day (1991) is set in 1994. The film begins with Sarah's voice-over narration, noting that three billion people died when the machines that ran the defense networks rebelled and began a nuclear war on August 29, 1997. She tells us that in addition to the Terminator being sent into 1984 to kill her, another was sent into 1994 to kill nine-year-old John, and once again the adult John of 2029 sent a protector. "It was just a question of which would reach him first." As in the first film, we see the two visitors from the future arrive—one is Arnold Schwarzenegger portraying another terminator, the other is apparently a human (played by Robert Patrick). Each of them needs to get a disguise and weapons once again. Although Schwarzenegger's character is still very violent, this time he does not kill anyone to steal a motorcycle and biker clothes, and there is some humor generated about his appearance as the soundtrack plays "Bad to the Bone." Meanwhile, Sarah is in a mental hospital as the result of her "delusions" about the coming destruction. She has become much tougher than before, as we see her doing pull-ups in her cell; the actress, Linda Hamilton, also got into rather muscular shape for this movie and projects a totally different persona. Despite her physical and emotional strength, however, Sarah is haunted by the certainty that the war will come and that there is nothing she can do to stop it. Evidence of this is her recurring dream in which she watches a playground full of children incinerated from a nuclear blast before her eyes while she stands behind a fence, unable to warn them.

When the two beings from the future find John at the same time in a shopping mall, it is revealed for the first time that the Terminator, played by Schwarzenegger, is this time the protector, and the being whom we had thought was human is in fact an even more sophisticated terminator. This "T-1000" is made of "liquid metal," and can change its shape to resemble anything as well as heal itself from any injury, making it more or less invincible. It is also a considerably more advanced model than the old "T-101," which resembles Schwarzenegger in both films. Many people who went to see the film probably had some idea that Schwarzenegger was a "good" terminator this time (e.g., some of the preview materials punned, "This time he's back, for good"), but it is only at this point that the audience and young John know for certain who is the good guy and who is the bad. We are further confused by the fact that we do not see the T-1000 kill anyone prior to this scene, and it takes the form of a policeman, whom we would presumably trust because he is there "to protect and serve" (as his police car logo states). In fact, however, it is the one who looks like a biker, a nonconformist outcast from society, that is the protector, while the apparent "authority" figure is there to harm. This is one of the ways in which the film inverts the status quo, as do many action movies that empower the underdog and depict those in charge as the enemy (cf. *Die Hard*); young John himself is a juvenile delinquent who wears a shirt that reads "Public Enemy," an homage to the controversial rap group but also a statement about his own status in society.

The T-101 rescues John and explains that he has been programmed to save John by John's future self, the adult John Connor of the year 2029. At this point, the boy realizes that his mother has not been crazy all these years, and that she really has wanted to protect him. He discovers that the T-1000 has already killed his foster parents, and decides he must save his mother before the T-1000 kills her too. The T-101 believes this is too dangerous but is programmed to obey John and so cannot dissent. John also programs the T-101 not to take any human lives, as he makes him hold up his hand and repeat, "I swear I will not kill anyone." John also tells him, "You're not a Terminator anymore. You just can't go around killing people." Meanwhile, Sarah escapes from her cell because she learned that John's foster parents have been murdered and believes this was done by a T-101, because she has seen photos of him taken by the cameras at the shopping mall where John was intercepted by both terminators. On the loose in the mental hospital, she runs straight into the T-101 and reacts with terror until he inexplicably rescues her, repeating the same line Reese used in the first film: "Come with me if you want to live." She also realizes that the T-1000 is an even greater threat than the T-101 she encountered before, as she sees its ability to change its shape and heal from any injury.

Sarah is not as quick to accept the T-101 as her son: she has learned to hate and distrust all terminators as representatives of the destruction of humanity. She has a hard time accepting the fact that John risked his life to save hers, believing he is more important to the future than she is. She rebukes him for taking this risk but also does not show any gratitude or even love for him. When she reaches for him after their escape, for example, he assumes he is about to be hugged but she only checks his body for wounds. His importance to her seems to be abstract. She sees him as the key to humanity's survival but does not show any concern for him as an individual, and she cannot understand why he showed such concern for her. In her quest to destroy the terminators, she has begun to take on their emotionless nature, doing everything for the survival of her species rather than out of genuine compassion for individuals.

The T-101, on the other hand, is moving toward becoming more human. This was actually explained in a scene cut from the 1991 theatrical release but restored for the special edition issued on videotape in 1993. In this scene, when John asks the T-101 how it might become more human, it reveals that it has had limits placed on its ability to mimic humans but the limitation could be removed by turning off and rebooting its CPU. Sarah and John proceed to open its head and remove the CPU chip; John then has to convince Sarah to replace rather than destroy it while she has the chance. Sarah fears all terminators, but John insists that this one is his "friend" and that they need it to help them. In the end, she says, "We'll play it your way," and they replace the CPU. With the limits on its learning removed, the T-101 can now mimic humans, John in particular. His repertoire includes the use of Hispanic colloquialisms ("no problemo," "hasta la vista, baby") and attempts to smile, as well as a certain amount of compassion for others. Ultimately, his concern for John is accepted even by Sarah, as she shows when she reflects in an interior monologue:

> Watching John with a machine, it was suddenly so clear. The Terminator would never stop—it would never leave him. It would never shout at him, or get drunk and hit him, or say it was too busy to spend time with him. It would always be there. And it would die to protect him. Of all the would-be fathers who came and went over the years, he was the only one who measured up. In an insane world, it was the sanest choice.

Sarah recognizes that the machine is better than humans, that it demonstrates the ideal qualities humans would like to think they have but don't. Machines can reflect the creative as well as the destructive possibilities of human nature, the best or the worst. This point is reinforced by a conversation John has with the T-101 just a few scenes earlier when they see two children playing war with toy guns. John asks, "We're not going to make it, are we? People, I mean." The T-101 responds, "It is in your nature to destroy yourselves." Here it is explicitly recognized that it is humans who destroy themselves by creating doomsday weapons, and the blame cannot be projected onto the terminators that only reflect our own violent nature. Frankenstein's monster said the same thing to his creator.

In this case, the creator is Dr. Miles Dyson, who is designing the technology that will eventually lead to a self-aware computer. After Sarah destroyed the first terminator in the previous film, enough was left of it to be salvaged and researched by scientists, including Dyson. The computer chip they found will be the basis for the artificial intelligence that will ultimately turn against them. Here we see another paradox of time travel: that a visitor from the future leaves a piece of technology that provides the clue for the invention of that same technology. The T-101 tells Sarah about Dyson, and she develops a plan to kill him before he can invent the technology that will lead to the nuclear holocaust. She comes to her decision to do so after she once more dreams of a nuclear holocaust (and the audience for the first time sees the nightmare as well). Singlemindedly and without emotion, she arms herself and drives off, looking very much like a terminator herself—right down to the sunglasses, black leather jacket, and boots. This signifies that, without her being aware of it, she has become like the terminators, willing to sacrifice individuals for the sake of the species. John races to stop her from murdering Dyson, the T-101 at his side; when the latter points out that perhaps Sarah is right, that her murder of the scientist might prevent the nuclear holocaust, John replies, "I don't care! Haven't you figured out why you can't kill people? Maybe you don't care whether you live or die, but everybody's not like you. We hurt. We have feelings. We're afraid. You gotta learn this stuff—I'm not kidding, it's important." The T-101 has not yet learned why he can't kill people, but John has. He refuses to lose the essence of humanity, the ability to feel for others, in a quest for the mere physical survival of the species. To do so would be to sacrifice the soul for the body, so to speak, and to live the kind of despiritualized material existence the terminators represent.

Sarah realizes in time, however, that she is becoming the very thing she hates. Her first shot at Dyson misses as he bends down to pick up his son's remote-control (robot) car. Sarah shoots up the house indiscriminately with her automatic rifle, entering with her cold terminator persona intact; but when she sees Dyson cowering on the floor with his wife and young son, she cannot go through with the murders. John and the T-101 enter at that moment, and she repents the attempted murder and confesses her love to John for the first time. Dyson is convinced that they are from the future when the T-101 shows him the metallic inside of his arm, which is identical to the arm (now owned by Dyson's company) that remained from the first T-101. Although he accepts their story, Dyson does not want to accept responsibility for the destruction of humanity. "You're judging me on things I haven't even done yet," he says. "How were we supposed to know?" Faced with this standard excuse of scientists who don't consider the practical (and destructive) consequences of their research, Sarah replies, "Men like you built the H-bomb. Men like you thought it up. You think you're so creative! You don't know what it's like to really create something—to create a life. To feel it growing inside you . . . all you know how to do is create death and destruction." Although only a few moments before, Sarah was ready to kill Dyson, she now proclaims an eco-feminist ethic based on birth and creation rather than death and destruction, suggesting that womb-envy is at the heart of the violent tendencies of males. It may seem odd to find this philosophy expressed in the middle of a movie that caters to similar desires to see violence. As we have seen, however, the products of popular culture may temporarily indulge certain fantasies even while they suggest that these fantasies should not be the basis for our everyday life. This is part of the liminal nature of film, to allow audiences vicarious experience of the forbidden so that they can return to societal structure afterwards. In this film, through the decision the characters make to destroy the lab that houses Dyson's research without killing a single human, the critique of violence is incorporated into the film narrative itself.

This decision also represents a belief of the main characters (Dyson, Sarah, John) that the future is not set, that there is "no fate but what we make." The first film had made it seem as if the future can't be changed by time traveling to the past, as one will only end up creating that same future—aspects of which could not even exist without the time traveler (e.g., John Connor would not exist but for Reese, sent back in time by John himself to father him). The second film, however, suggests that all is not predestined, and specifically that the nuclear holocaust can be averted. Sarah muses while they drive to Dyson's lab, "The future, always so clear to me, had become like a black highway at night. We were in uncharted territory now, making up history as we went along." They do manage to destroy the lab, as well as the T-1000, and the only human life lost is that of Dyson, who seems to sacrifice himself in part to atone for his "sin" of developing the technology that could (or did, in one future) lead to holocaust. The T-101, however, realizes that he must sacrifice himself as well so that no trace of the destructive technology of the terminators remains. John has grown to love him as the "perfect father" described earlier by Sarah, and so resists this plan, but the terminator reminds him that he is not human: "I know now why you cry, but it is something I can never do." The T-101 also takes the burden of being humanity's "savior" off John ("J.C.") by taking the sins of humanity on his own sinless self. He dies so that we might live, even though it is really humans and not machines who created the possibility of destruction. Even Sarah recognizes the value of the sacrifice, as her final monologue indicates: "The unknown future rolls towards us. I face it for the first time with a sense of hope. Because if a machine, a terminator, can learn the value of human life, maybe we can too."

Sarah has discovered the basic point of the tale: the enemy is within us rather than in our machine creations. We must decide what we should do with our technology, as in itself it is morally neutral, possessing either the capacity to create or to destroy depending on what we bring to it. There is no point in projecting our evil intentions onto our technological "monsters" as if these were the real threat; the threat is in our own ability to do evil with our technology. Thus, the film does not argue against technology so much as it poses a question to humanity, asking whether we will use technology for good or for evil. This ambiguity reflects the ambivalent relationship of science fiction films to technology. They are themselves the product of elaborate technological tools and special effects, and to a certain extent celebrate them, but there is also a fear of technology that gains expression in the depiction of dystopian futures. We are especially ambivalent about the meteoric rise of computers: they have given us the ability to do creative and beneficial work, including the unprecedented possibilities to communicate on the Internet, but they have also brought addiction, pornography, and a certain invasion of privacy into our homes. Computers, like all our technology, will express both our good and our evil nature, and we must choose which side of our nature will dominate our use of them and all our other tools.

The original director's cut of *Terminator 2* ended with less ambiguity, as it depicted a child's playground in 2029, this time not one destroyed by a nuclear blast but one populated by the adult John Connor, now a U.S. senator who seeks to make the world a better place, playing with his children. The elderly Sarah speaks into a recording device, telling us that "Judgment Day" was averted. This scene was cut from the final version of the film to allow the future to be more open ended (and of course, to allow for more sequels). The utopian image worked against the dystopian elements of the film that suggest it is still an open question whether or not we will destroy ourselves. The threat of apocalypse (expressed by the "Judgment Day" subtitle) still hangs over us, as we may suffer "judgment" for our sins if we do not repent and change our ways. In 1991, when the film was made, the Soviet Union had just collapsed and the threat of total nuclear destruction was still real enough to most people to have some relevance. Young John Connor does at one point say to the T-101, "But aren't the Russians our friends now?" as if to note that the threat should be lessened, but the T-101 reminds him that enough weapons are still out there to destroy the world—as they can still do, today. Still, it is probably not the threat of nuclear war that most viewers would focus upon, but the more generalized threat that our technology can be used destructively, whether in war or to cause environmental degradation. Many people feel we ought to be behaving more responsibly with our technology, and this film connects with that hope even as it also suggests what could happen if we do not act with more caution and compassion. While most people enjoy the benefits of technology, they also fear the negative effects it may bring. Science fiction films express this duality and suggest that we should consider carefully how we negotiate our relationship with our technological creations.

Ideological criticism of this film might suggest that any cautionary message about violence or technology is muted by the celebration of violence and technology expressed by its action-movie format, that most viewers will not come away with any real challenge to their value systems. But this assumes that viewers are unable to notice the elements in films that suggest dystopia and critique, which are central to many science fiction films. Any viewer could see that Sarah was wrong to want to kill Dyson, that the T-101 is to be admired for not killing anyone, that scientists ought to think about the power of what they are inventing. As another example, ethnographic studies of the audiences for *Judge Dredd* (1995) showed that audiences understood the dystopian challenge of this film, which depicts a future world in which authoritarian law enforcement has eliminated the rights of the accused in a draconian effort to curb crime. Some were so disturbed by this message that it ruined their enjoyment of the film, so obviously even in an "action" science fiction movie the dystopian challenge cannot be entirely ignored.[2]

The Matrix (1999) was another popular science fiction film that contained much entertaining violence. But it also suggested a challenge to authoritarianism: that people should be free to know the truth about their lives and their world. In this film, a computer keeps humans alive in a "virtual" computer-generated reality to tap their energy, rather than letting them live free in the real world. This message was hardly lost on the younger generation that liked the film so much, as I have found out myself in conversations with students about it. Perhaps their own rebellions against the status quo will not be so dramatic, but viewing the film allows them to temporarily engage in a liminal questioning of technology and society. Indeed, much of their enjoyment of the film comes from its youth-culture challenge to the status quo. Even if the young continue to enjoy watching the possibilities of hyper-real combat within the matrix, they are aware that they would not like to live in it all the time, and that losing the distinction between reality and fantasy could be deadly to our humanity.

The Original Star Wars Films (1977, 1980, 1983)

I have included two extended film analyses in this chapter rather than one, because the *Star Wars* movies represent a somewhat different but immensely popular form of science fiction.[3] And while the *Terminator* films are easily recognized as science fiction, the *Star Wars* movies have sometimes been deprived of this label. This may be because they seem to be more "space opera" than genuine science fiction, much like the old *Flash Gordon* and *Buck Rogers* serials of the 1930s they mimic, in which the technology seemed almost irrelevant to the plot. These serials resembled swashbucklers set in space, in which displaced aristocrats battled despots for the throne, and *Star Wars* utilizes aspects of that genre as well as of westerns and samurai films, making it hard to identify it by the conventions of any one genre.

In spite of its cross-genre identity, however, the *Star Wars* saga is clearly science fiction because it deals with what I have defined as the central issue of science fiction, the use and misuse of technology. Like the *Terminator* movies, the *Star Wars* films argue that we need spirituality and not just technology, and that in order to keep our souls we must not be absorbed by our machine creations. The religious themes of the *Star Wars* films are also often remarked upon, largely because of the well-known influence of myth theorist Joseph Campbell on George Lucas and his original script. Lucas actually claimed to have been entirely without direction until he stumbled upon Campbell's *The Hero with a Thousand Faces*, with its formula for the hero's journey.[4] And the plot of the original *Star Wars* film does seem to reproduce the stages Campbell discusses: the hero (Luke) is called to the adventure; he initially refuses the call; supernatural aid is supplied (Obi-Wan), which enables the adventure to proceed; he passes the threshold (Mos Eisley spaceport) and enters the "belly of the whale" (the Death Star); he meets the goddess (Leia) he must rescue, and loses the father figure (Obi-Wan), who then becomes a spiritual presence to him. After escaping the Deathstar, he must return to it, this time to destroy it.[5]

After the release of the original trilogy of *Star Wars* (*Episode IV: A New Hope*, 1977; *Episode V: The Empire Strikes Back*, 1980; *Episode VI: Return of the Jedi*, 1983), Lucas invited Campbell to Skywalker Ranch to view all three films in a single day. Campbell could clearly see Lucas's use of his ideas on myth, and also gave his own interpretation of the films. As was noted in chapter 3, Campbell had a tendency to reduce the subject matter of myth to an internal psychological struggle rather than an external one, and he also denied the existence of any transcendent reality apart from the psyche. In his view, the Force is "what best fosters the flowering of our humanity" and as such it is not a "first cause" or "higher cause" but a "more inward cause." He goes so far as to say that "higher is just up there, and there is no 'up there.' We know that. That old man up there has been blown away. You've got to find the Force inside you."[6]

But this reductive psychological monism may not represent the mythology of *Star Wars* accurately, unless all the battles with the Dark Side of the force are merely internal battles. There is certainly a crucial element of the battle that is waged internally, but there are also real enemies in the story—unless, that is, Campbell is right in his view that all our problems are psychological rather than external, and the Force is nothing transcendent but merely a symbol for our internal psychological powers. This, however, represents a particular religious view, one that need not be shared by every viewer of the films.

Arguing against Campbell's view, I would suggest that we not interpret *Star Wars* simply as a mythology of internal psychological struggles. For, while Campbell would like to reduce all religious mythology to this strife, it may not fairly represent all mythology (as I suggested in chapter 3). For this reason, we need not accept his reductionistic view of the mythology of *Star Wars* any more than we need to accept his view of other religions, which belittles the belief in a transcendent reality and the notion of a responsibility to it (as opposed to just responsibility to one's own inner conscience). George Lucas seems open to the possibility of such an interpretation, in that he speaks of the Force as the "greater mystery out there," and even as "God," in a way that Campbell avoids. Lucas has also noted that he never intended the mythology of his films to be a replacement for traditional religion so much as a generalized spirituality to which someone of any religious background might relate.[7] The mythology of *Star Wars*, then, can be understood as one that deals with our own internal battles, but also our struggles with technology and our need to believe in something bigger than ourselves. In what follows, I will try to unpack some of the diverse elements of this mythology.

Besides the original trilogy, the series includes at this time two more episodes of a projected six-part cycle: *Episode I: The Phantom Menace* (1999) and *Episode II: Attack of the Clones* (2002). The third episode is due in 2005 and will complete the prequel trilogy dealing with the transformation of Anakin Skywalker into Darth Vader. The heart of the series, however, remains the original trilogy. In this, the overall plot concerns a cosmic battle between good and evil, between an authoritarian evil empire and virtuous rebels, and the fate of the whole galaxy hangs on the outcome. Ultimately, the rebels will win not through superior weaponry, but through trusting in the Force, the divine power that "binds the galaxy together." Sometimes it may seem as if luck is what allows these underdogs to survive, but as Jedi master Obi-Wan Kenobi says, "In my experience, there's no such thing as luck." The Force helps those who trust in its power, which can enable good to win out over evil.

The central hero of the saga, Luke Skywalker, is brought into the plot when two robots, C-3PO and R2-D2, end up (by "luck") in his possession on his home planet of Tatooine, which is far from the rebellion (or so he thinks). R2 contains the plans to the Imperial Death Star, a massive battle station that can destroy a planet with a single blast, and which represents the empire's "final solution" to the rebellion. The rebels hope that with these plans they will be able to destroy it, although this is clearly a long shot. Luke knows nothing of this until R2 runs away into the Tatooine desert and finds Obi-Wan, apparently retired from Jedi service, to whom R2 delivers a message from Princess Leia that he must get the plans to the rebel leaders on the planet Alderaan. After Luke's aunt and uncle are killed by Imperial stormtroopers searching for the robots and the plans, he agrees to join Obi-Wan on his quest and "become a Jedi like my father." Obi-Wan has told Luke that his father was a great Jedi who was "betrayed and murdered" by Darth Vader, a former Jedi now in the service of the empire who was seduced by the "Dark Side" of the Force. Obi-Wan introduces Luke to the idea of the Force and the notion that Jedis can tap into its power, but he also teaches him that such power should only be used for defense and knowledge rather than the selfish goal of power associated with the dark side.

Their mission does not go as planned, however, as the Death Star destroys Alderaan and captures the *Millennium Falcon*, the ship hired by Obi-Wan and Luke to take them to Alderaan. The pilot, Han Solo, is a mercenary and a smuggler who tends only to look out for himself and is unhappy to be enlisted into the rebels' struggles. They hide in the ship and escape detection, after which Obi-Wan goes to release the "tractor beam" that holds their ship prisoner in the Death Star; meanwhile, Luke finds out that Princess Leia is a captive there, and he convinces Han to help with her rescue as the reward will be "more wealth than you can imagine." Han indicates that he can "imagine quite a lot," but he agrees to help; once rescued, the princess proves to be as acerbic and difficult as he is. Much of the fun of the movie comes from watching these three interact throughout their adventures.

Obi-Wan sacrifices himself in a light saber battle with Darth Vader, his former pupil, in order to allow the others to escape. The Death Star follows them to the rebel base, where the final battle occurs in which Luke makes a "one in a million" shot to destroy the Death Star. He does so without the benefit of the targeting computer on his spacecraft, after hearing the voice of Obi-Wan directing him to "trust his feelings." We are not quite sure if he is imagining this voice, nor is he, so it is only on the basis of faith in Obi-Wan and the Force that he can make the seemingly reckless decision to use instinct and feeling rather than technology to shoot. Faith is of particular importance in this film, as Luke has not yet learned (as he does in later films) how to communicate with spirits, use telekinesis, or see the future. About all he directly experiences of the power of the Force, other than hearing Obi-Wan's voice after his death, is Obi-Wan's "Jedi mind trick" (used on dim-witted stormtroopers to evade capture), and his own developing ability to fight a combat droid without seeing it. Han Solo, always the skeptic, dismisses all such instances as "simple tricks and nonsense," for, as he says to Luke, "Kid, I've flown from one end of this galaxy to the other; I've seen a lot of strange stuff. But I've never seen anything to make me believe there's one all-powerful force controlling everything. There's no mystical energy field controlling my destiny." Han would rather trust in his own abilities than invisible transcendent powers to get out of a tough situation. ("Hokey religions and ancient weapons are no match for a good blaster at your side.") At the same time, he can fight alongside those who do believe, as he comes to embrace their cause and their friendship, even though he has not seen enough to believe in the Force. He is not as selfish as he seems: for examples, he changes his mind about leaving with his reward money to help Luke blow up the Death Star; in fact, he shows up just in time to cause Darth Vader to miss shooting Luke, and to force him to retreat. We might categorize Han as a sort of "anonymous Jedi" who fights for and with the Force without realizing it.

Darth Vader is also depicted as a figure who paradoxically bears witness to the power of faith in the Force. When his "ancient religion" is ridiculed by one of the Imperial officers as inadequate next to the technological power of the Death Star, he uses the Force to choke him and asserts that he finds his "lack of faith disturbing." Throughout episode four, Vader appears to be an anachronism in the Empire, as no one else among the Imperials seems to believe in the mystical dimension he does; his faith is a peculiarity in the otherwise secularized and technologized Empire. As Governor Tarkin puts it to him, "The Jedi are extinct; their fire has gone out in the universe. You, my friend, are all that is left of their religion." Of course, Tarkin is incorrect in this assumption, which costs him his life when the Death Star is destroyed by the powers of that "ancient religion."

Several things are different beginning in episode five (*The Empire Strikes Back*), which includes the demolition of the rebel base and the desperate flight of Han and Leia from Vader, who plans to use them as bait to lure Luke to himself and thereby to the dark side. We also encounter the emperor for the first time in this film and discover that he represents the Dark Side of the Force more powerfully than Vader; he is not simply a bureaucrat as Governor Tarkin was. In addition, Vader seems to have more power. In episode four, Leia makes a crack about Tarkin "holding Vader's leash," likening him to a henchman; now, Vader has his own star cruiser and crew just for the purpose of chasing Luke's friends, and he is free to execute Imperial officers whenever they disappoint him. Also in episode five, Luke begins to discover the power of the Force (with the help of Master Yoda) and actually sees some of the things he has only believed up to this point. Obi-Wan appears to him and delivers messages; Yoda shows him how to move objects and see the future. At the same time, Luke lacks the total belief required to be a Jedi. He believes it is impossible by mental powers to lift his ship out of the Dagobah swamp, as it is too big, so Yoda demonstrates it is not impossible by doing it for him. Luke can only say, "I don't believe it!" to which master Yoda replies: "That is why you fail." Luke also confronts the power of the Dark Side in a new way, not only through Vader's attempt to capture him but through the revelation that Vader is his father. In this way, Luke confronts the possibility of evil in himself, in that even his Jedi father turned to the Dark Side. Luke's dream-vision in the cave on Dagobah, in which he kills Vader only to find he wears Luke's own face, reinforces this idea that the only evil one needs to fear is the hatred and anger that lurks within oneself—for as Yoda keeps telling him, anger, fear, and aggression can only lead to the Dark Side. This may seem to support Campbell's interpretation that both sides of the Force are within us, but we should note that although the temptation to the Dark Side resides within, the Dark Side also has a powerful external side in the presence of the real Darth Vader and the emperor. The film ends with a confused and injured Luke barely escaping, and Han in the clutches of the gangster Jabba the Hutt.

Episode six of the saga (*Return of the Jedi*) brings all its elements to a conclusion. After Han is rescued, we see the final apocalyptic battle between the rebels and the Empire (working with a second Death Star), and Luke faces Vader again. He now accepts Vader as his father and attempts to redeem him by appealing to his former nature as Anakin Skywalker. In this Luke fails, and he is brought before the emperor for a final testing. Can he resist hate and anger, even when confronted with the destruction of his own friends and the rebel cause? His attempt to remain noncombative breaks down when Vader threatens to turn his sister to the Dark Side. In a fit of anger, he chops off his father's hand, just as Vader had chopped off Luke's hand at the end of the previous film. But when the emperor exhorts Luke to kill Vader and "take your father's place at my side," Luke throws down his weapon. "I am a Jedi, like my father before me," he says. He is able to come to this decision, as he sees himself about to suffer the same fate as his father. In particular, he looks at the stump of Vader's electronic hand and then at his own machine hand, which he was given after he lost his own. Here, the robot limbs and form of Vader represent the loss of real humanity and compassion to a technologized and depersonalized identity.

Luke's decision not to fight may appear to be borrowed from Eastern religious notions of *ahimsa*, nonviolence. But there is a significant difference between his actions and the ethic of the Bhagavad Gita in which the Hindu notion of ahimsa is developed. In that text, Krishna advises Arjuna to fight to preserve the world order of *dharma*, but to do so without selfish desire or hatred. This is basically the same advice Yoda and Obi-Wan give to Luke: to kill his father, but without giving in to hate or anger. Yet Luke ignores their counsel and refuses to fight him at all. He abandons the Eastern philosophy of detachment advocated by Ben and Yoda for a more Christian ideal of attachment to those whom one loves; here we see Lucas's ability to combine religious ideas from numerous religious traditions in his own polyglot invention. Oddly enough, Luke's attachment saves them all, as the pitiful sight of Luke's torture at the hands of the emperor causes Vader to remember his own attachment to Luke, and to rescue him and destroy the emperor.

Here again, Christian concepts of redemption clearly take center stage, as Luke's willingness to sacrifice himself nonviolently (much like Obi-Wan's self-sacrifice in episode four) becomes the key to turning his father back. Granted, in his "conversion" Vader does use violence against the Emperor (by throwing him down an air shaft), but in so doing he eschews the path of hatred and power he has been following since he turned to the Dark Side. As Vader dies, he asks Luke to remove his mask so that he can see Luke with his "own eyes" rather than the technological apparatus of his helmet. This also allows Luke, and the audience, to see the face of Anakin for the first time, which conveys compassion and vulnerability—quite unlike the frightening visage of Darth Vader. His human nature has won out over his machine nature, and he tells Luke that he has been "saved" from the Dark Side. In the final scene of the film, Luke and the audience see the spirit of his father reunited with those of Obi-Wan and Yoda; he now appears in his form as Anakin, rather than as Vader, having recovered his true human nature.

Ideological analysis of the *Star Wars* films has suggested that they work to support the political status quo, in spite of the fact that the heroes are the "rebels."[8] Citizens of the United States, in particular, tend to see themselves as vanquishing "evil empires" around the globe in order to establish a "new republic" in which democracy rules the planet. It can be observed that the uniforms of the Imperials resemble both those of Stalinist Russia and Nazi Germany, so that we will easily identify with those who fight against their totalitarianism. Certainly, there are probably few Americans who would identify the evil empire with the United States or seek to act as "rebels" against a power so close to home, and in this way the film supports the status quo rather than political self-critique.

But audiences do not really view the message of the film as a political one, as can be seen by the fact that they did not agree whether the Empire resembled a right-wing dictatorship or communism, or whether the rebels resembled right-wing freedom fighters more than left-wing revolutionaries.[9] The real enemy, in the films, is not a political ideology (as the political details of the Empire and the republic are never articulated) but the threat we pose to ourselves, that we may give in to our own "dark side" by losing our human nature to greed and selfish desires for power. It is not coincidental, either, that this dark side is expressed by monstrous technological creations that represent massive human power without ethical boundaries: gigantic Imperial walkers demolishing the rebel base on Hoth, Vader's star cruiser chasing the tiny *Millennium Falcon*, the Death Star, and of course Vader's own oversized and menacing robot body. (Obi-Wan notes about Vader that "he's more machine than man now, twisted and evil.") In contrast, the rebels (although they also use technology) rely on friendship, trust, courage, and a faith in something greater that will aid them. We also see them aided by "primitive" Ewoks who, without the benefit of superior technology, are able to best the stormtroopers in combat. These scenes are humorous because we enjoy the role-reversals that allow the underdogs to vanquish the powerful, as when two Ewoks and hairy Chewbacca hijack a "chicken walker" and use it to win the ground battle as well as to gain entry to the shield generator that protects the unfinished Death Star. The fact that it is hairy "beasts" that manage this critical victory also indicates the preference the films show for the "natural" over the technological, even as they favor the "spiritual" over technology.

As with the *Terminator* films, we can see how the *Star Wars* films operate both to celebrate technology (via special effects and spaceship battles) and to critique a technology that is unchecked by ethics and religion. Viewers spend much time admiring the technology, which may suggest they have lost the other message, but the essential popularity of the films is due to more than the special effects. There are plenty of science fiction films that do poorly at the box office, even with fairly good effects, if they lack an appealing story. In contrast, the original *Star Wars* film is still enjoyed by audiences, though its effects look rather primitive by today's standards. Even at the time of its initial release, its story was the primary basis for its phenomenal success (as its profits easily topped those of other special-effects-laden films like the thankfully forgotten *Logan's Run* [1976] or even *Close Encounters of the Third Kind* [1977], which was pretty to look at but had a rather thin story).

The story of *Star Wars* focused on the need to preserve our humanity (natural, spiritual, ethical) even in this technological age, to avoid giving in to hatred or fear, and to look to the value of family and friendship, faith and loyalty, as well as the redeeming virtues of love and forgiveness. Although these may seem like banal values, they are what many viewers are anxious to see on the screen as they depict for them an ideal they would like to follow in their own lives. Many religious critics seemed upset by the films' popularity, as they worried that the "Star Wars cult" will replace "real" religion in our society.[10] But they might be less worried if they accepted the fact that the values supported by *Star Wars* are not entirely negative, even if the "religion" it represents is not identical with Christianity or any other traditional religion. Lucas has said that he designed the "religion" of *Star Wars* by "taking all the issues that religion represents and trying to distill them down into a more modern and easily accessible construct," which did not represent "any particular religious system" but rather a syncretistic mix of ideas.[11] Traditional religions don't usually have a great deal of tolerance for such popular syncretism, as they tend to believe it fails to take any religion seriously, but this criticism fails to note that all religions have been formed by the processes of syncretism, borrowing and stealing from various other philosophies and religions to create a new system.

As we have seen, traditional religions do not like the competition they feel from movies like the *Star Wars* films, but they might relax a bit if they saw that such films do not really celebrate selfish consumerism or materialism (often taken as the content of all popular culture) but rather critique it. Although cultural criticism may point to the immense profits derived from associated toy sales as the real motivating values for the filmmakers, this does not reduce the film's message to materialism any more than the greed of a hypocritical televangelist can reduce his Christian message to materialism. Traditional religions are having enough trouble trying to get their own members not to give in to all the values of materialism that they might be able to use an ally like *Star Wars*, which promotes a different set of values that people might apply in their daily lives. As George Lucas has put it:

Heroes come in all sizes, and you don't have to be a giant hero. You can be a very small hero. It's just as important to understand that accepting self-responsibility for the things you do, having good manners, caring about other people—these are heroic acts. Everybody has the choice of being a hero or not being a hero every day of their lives. You don't have to get into a giant laser-sword fight and blow up three spaceships to become a hero.[12]

12

Thrillers and Horror Movies

These two genres are not normally linked together in discussions, but I have found the issues they deal with to have more similarities than differences, and often the line between the two is genuinely blurry. Horror movies mean to horrify, not so much through the depiction of blood or violence (these may be included, but they are not essential) as through the depiction of evil. We may be horrified by some of the violent acts in gangster or action films (if they are not presented sympathetically or comically), but the basic purpose of these genres is not to horrify or terrify as it is for horror films per se. A "thriller" might be distinguished from a horror film in that it does not aim to horrify so much as to invoke suspense (which is then cathartically released), but both genres seek to create terror through the depiction of frightening situations from which individuals attempt release.

Furthermore, the man who more or less created the "suspense thriller" as we know it, Alfred Hitchcock, can also be credited with inventing the modern psycho-killer "slasher" film in *Psycho* (1960). Slasher films are usually considered a subgenre of horror, possibly the most popular form of horror today, as they replace the traditional monster of supernatural origin with a monster that is all the more frightening for being fully human (although he is sometimes imbued with a superhuman ability to survive). Clearly, there is not so great a difference between horror and thrillers as is sometimes assumed, except perhaps for the fact that those of us with weaker stomachs are often more comfortable with films we label "suspense thrillers" as they feature less overt terror and violence than their grosser cousins. In any case, all such films evoke pleasure for viewers who like to be scared, and all create a presence of evil that is both disturbing and titillating to those who enjoy such films.

Violent thrillers and horror movies also have more critics than any other genre (except perhaps pornography) as their excessive violence, and their exploitation of our fears about violence, assault many viewers as immoral. The fact that people enjoy them is even more disturbing than the films themselves, since such pleasure suggests viewers are "getting off" on this exploitation. Feminist criticism has railed against the victimization of women in horror movies, who may become screaming victims of bloodthirsty killers who dismember them in apparent displays of misogyny. Psychological interpretations have been wedded to feminist analyses in suggesting that male castration anxiety is at the root of the need to see women dismembered and destroyed. As for the female viewers of such films, they can only be pitied as masochists who are complicit in their own destruction.

But not all feminists have accepted this view, precisely because some of them actually like horror movies and believe that such films are not as misogynistic as is often believed. It has been pointed out that, contrary to conventional wisdom, about half of the audience of many horror films is made up of women, and it seems unlikely that all of them are there just because their misogynist boyfriends made them go. Brigid Cherry has noted that audience studies show women receive pleasure from watching these films for some of the same reasons that male viewers do—in particular, they are able to express and master their fears. In fact, some studies have suggested that women *pretend* to be more afraid than they really are, as this is expected of them, especially in the presence of boyfriends who like to think their girlfriends require their comfort and strength. While this shows adolescents acting in accordance with gender stereotyping, it also shows that it is a façade, for the women may be having just as much fun as the guys—they just can't admit it.[1]

It seems that it was more socially permissible for women to show interest in horror movies earlier in the history of cinema. When the film version of *Dracula* (1931) was released, it was marketed to female viewers, partly because Bela Lugosi was viewed as a sexually seductive and attractive vampire. Such "gothic" horror, whether in novels or films, has long been of interest to women, even as gothic romances are. We even see gothic romance and horror mixed in a novel like *Jane Eyre*, which features a crazy first wife in the attic and a mysteriously distant but attractive man. Women surveyed by Cherry admit to the "romantic" attraction of horror in, for example, vampire stories. One respondent claimed that the vampire is depicted as having "an uncanny knowledge of how to give pleasure," giving a figure like Lugosi the same exotic appeal as a silent film star like Rudolf Valentino.[2]

The traditional movie monster was always depicted rather sympathetically, whether as a seductive stranger (Lugosi) or as a tragic figure who is the victim of his own baser instincts. *Frankenstein* (1931) represented the monster not as the embittered but eloquent creature of Mary Shelley's novel, but as an almost mute and clumsy oaf whose every effort to achieve friendship backfires. He seems almost childlike in his desire for companionship and in his inability to understand the consequences of his actions, as when (in a scene cut from some prints) he tosses a little girl into a pond to see if she can float, and she drowns. The monster is not a bad one at heart, but becomes violent because others regard him as such—this much the film had in common with the novel. In a somewhat different way, *The Wolf Man* (1941) becomes a tragic figure in that he cannot control his necessity to kill when he changes into the monster, and his awareness of this during the time he spends as a human causes him tremendous pain. He realizes his next victim will be his own true love unless he is stopped, and it is ultimately his own father who unwittingly kills him in his monstrous form with a silver-headed cane.

Frankenstein and the Wolf Man, as well as Dracula, could all be viewed as examples of male sexual desire without appropriate limits placed on it, the violent and aggressive tendencies of which must be domesticated in order to protect women from them. One could also add *The Mummy* (1932) as well as *King Kong* (1933) to this list, as both of them are drawn to women they cannot have due to their monstrous natures. It is "tragic" that the monsters must be destroyed to the extent that the audience empathizes with them in their pain and exclusion, mirroring the pain and exclusion of adolescence for both males and females. It is not only young men who feel drawn to such monsters, which mirror their own struggles with their sexual desires; young women also struggle with such desires and are also drawn to the monsters out of pity and compassion.[3]

More recent horror movies lack the tragic and moralistic form of classic horror films as the monster is not always domesticated by the end but is still on the loose somewhere; there is less narrative closure, and more surprise. But even the classic horror films allowed the monster to come back via numerous sequels, so audiences could reflect on the fact that the monster can never be completely extinguished. All horror films, classic and modern, wrestle with the continued existence of evil in the world and allow the viewer to wrestle with this fact as well.

Isabel Pinedo has written about recent horror films (which she calls "postmodern") from the perspective of a feminist who is also a fan of modern horror. The mutilation of the body is shown more explicitly in re-cent horror films than in their classic counterparts (surely in large part due to the demise of censorship), which may make it seem as if such films are exploitative and gratuitously violent. Pinedo, however, suggests that there are pleasures related both to seeing and to not-seeing violence on screen, both of which are featured in modern horror films. Sometimes we are not allowed to see the monster or its violence in full, which protects the viewer from the overwhelming emotions associated with the murders it commits, but at other times we are treated to a great deal of on-screen gore. Such screen violence and blood allow the audience to deal with their own fears of bodily violation and mutilation in a "safe" way, often accom-panied by humor as audiences laugh at mediocre special effects that do not seem "real." Although such scenes of realistic violence are sometimes compared with hard-core pornography in their attempt to show some-thing that is both "real" and inappropriate or gross, the difference is that horror movie fans *know* that the violence is in fact fake, and they generally have no desire to go out and simulate the activities they have seen in "hard-core" horror (as fans of hard-core pornography might).[4]

Pinedo speculates that viewers of horror films achieve a certain mastery of their fears in surviving the ordeal of the film, as they can return to nor-mal life afterwards. This experience obviously has similarities to what I have termed the liminal nature of filmgoing. It allows us temporarily to step into a "forbidden" area by putting ourselves into the world of the film, so that we can return to our world more able to deal with it. Horror film director Wes Craven has said that he does not believe people watch horror films because they want to be scared, but because they *are* scared, or have been scared, and they try to deal with these fears at the movies—both by submitting to the fear, and by mastering it.[5] This mastery is also shown to a large extent, especially for women, in films in which a woman (the so-called final girl who survives) kills the slasher at the end. Ultimately, the viewer is led to identify with "final girl" as we see shots from her point of view, not the monster's, as the film nears its conclusion. Such films can serve as an expression of "female rage" against male aggression, as the woman refuses to be made a victim and is able to fight back effectively in the end.[6]

One sees the same phenomenon of the woman who refuses to become a victim in classic suspense thrillers like Hitchcock's *Dial M for Murder* (1954), in which Grace Kelly foils her husband's plan to have her killed by jabbing a large scissor into her attacker, and in *Wait Until Dark* (1967), in which blind Audrey Hepburn manages to knife her attacker to death after pulling the plug on the lights in order to make him sightless as well. Male viewers also identify with the woman in such a situation, as we all cheer for an apparently powerless victim who effectively strikes back against an aggressor. Pinedo admits that many horror films are misogynistic in, for example, punishing women for being sexually active, but she also sees horror films as having the opportunity to challenge the misogynistic status quo by providing models of strong women—some of the strongest in popular film, oddly enough.

In this chapter we will examine two films of the thriller/horror genre that were both extremely popular and well received critically—one classic, one more recent. Each film connects the viewer with a killer in such a way as to invite an uncomfortable identification with him, raising questions about the evil within each of us, but also allowing a partial mastery of our fears of that evil. But first, a brief examination of the work of Alfred Hitchcock will give us more insights into his films, in particular *Psycho* (1960). I have not given such an extended analysis of any of the other film directors, but Hitchcock merits being an exception.

Alfred Hitchcock

It is impossible to overemphasize the influence of Alfred Hitchcock on the history of cinema. Immensely popular with both audiences and critics, his prolific career spanned five decades and produced dozens of films, many of which are regarded as classics. His ability to manipulate viewer emotions is legendary, and he has been the inspiration for many of the techniques of other popular directors, such as Steven Spielberg and Francis Ford Coppola. While critics seem annoyed at Spielberg's use of manipulation insofar as it is viewed as too comforting, less challenging, and hence supposedly less "artistic," Hitchcock's films are uncomfortable enough to please any critic in search of work that challenges and disturbs the viewer. The odd alliance of his ability to please and excite audiences and his capacity to disturb and unsettle them, sometimes in the same shot, has led to his almost unique status as a perpetually profitable filmmaker who is also regarded as a genius and an innovator without parallel.

In addition, although all of Hitchcock's films could be considered "thrillers" in some sense, his work never became formulaic or boring. Audiences expected to be continually thrilled by new surprises in his films, and they were, at least through the appearance of *The Birds* (1963). The work that took audiences and critics most by surprise is probably *Psycho* (1960). Many critics initially panned the film, viewing it as a "blot on an honorable career," only to change their minds later as they realized its greatness (e.g., *New York Times* critic Bosley Crowther).[7] Audiences did not suffer from such ambivalence, as the film made more money than any previous Hitchcock film. It is often viewed as being his most terrifying and disturbing film, and it probably most shocked those who had come to associate Hitchcock with his adventure/romantic comedies that went back at least to *The Lady Vanishes* (1938) and were as recent as *To Catch a Thief* (1955) and *North by Northwest* (1959). In films like these, a romantic and witty hero is mistaken for a criminal and drawn into an adventure that makes his life more exciting; it usually ends with romantic fulfillment, and along the way the hero survives a series of thrilling but fun ordeals. But even some of Hitchcock's "romantic comedies" have disturbing aspects, like the fact that the female lead essentially prostitutes herself as a lover for the villain in *North by Northwest* and *Notorious* (1946), and in the latter film the hero actually encourages her to do so; neither the hero nor the heroine is "pure" or untainted by sin.

Throughout his career, Hitchcock made many disturbing films, and even the less unsettling ones tend to have disturbing elements. Just a few years before *Psycho*, he had made *Rear Window* (1954), which utilizes some of the elements of the romance/adventure, but confines the hero to a wheelchair from which he engages in an unsettling obsession with voyeurism. And in *Vertigo* (1958), Hitchcock had invented a genuinely tragic situation in which a man becomes obsessed with a dead woman he believes he can re-create through her look-alike, only to find that he has been twice deceived, and his anger effectively leads to her murder at his hands.

The unsettling aspect of Hitchcock's films may be connected with his ability to implicate the viewer into the evil being depicted, as we are led to identify with characters who cannot avoid their own darker side. The use of doubles in films like *Strangers on a Train* (1951) and *Shadow of a Doubt* (1943) illustrates this well. In the former, Guy (Farley Granger) wants to be rid of his unfaithful wife in order to marry a senator's daughter, and Bruno (Robert Walker) wants to be rid of his father. When they meet by chance on a train, Bruno suggests that they commit each other's murders to avoid suspicion; Guy thinks this is a big joke until Bruno kills his wife, and then Guy is effectively implicated in his scheme. Although

Guy is exonerated (just barely) in the end, along the way we are uncomfortably reminded of the fact that Bruno represents his "evil" side that acts on Guy's desires. Guy shares the guilt of his wife's murder with Bruno, and we share it as well through our identification with someone who is just a "regular guy" with desires he knows should not be actualized. In *Shadow of a Doubt* (Hitchcock's personal favorite) small-town girl Charlie (Teresa Wright) is visited by her beloved Uncle Charlie (Joseph Cotton) only to discover that he is a psychotic serial killer. As his alter ego, Young Charlie covers for him to avoid the upset such a revelation might cause her mother, the sister of the killer. Young Charlie survives his attempt to kill her even as he becomes a victim of his own murderous plan, and after his death no one in the family but Young Charlie knows the truth about his evil nature. She has found evil in a Charlie who is not herself, but she shares in his secrets and is indirectly his accomplice in allowing his murderous side to escape detection.

Hitchcock continually asserted the complicity of his characters, and therefore the audience as well, in crimes of evil and violence. Audiences who enjoyed such films obviously enjoyed identifying with a killer, if only for a short time, just as fans of horror films often sympathize or identify with the monster. The fact that the monster must be restrained or brought to justice, and that we identify also with those who restrain him, does not necessarily lessen our attachment to the evil or our fascination with it. Closer examination of *Psycho* will reveal how Hitchcock was able to identify the audience with evil more effectively than ever before, for although implicating audiences in the crime was not new to him, this film made the identification with the killer more complete and more disturbing than ever before. At the same time, the film was not made to be serious like *Vertigo*: it was a comedy, so that it was "fun" to be made an accomplice of the murderer, as Hitchcock brings the viewer from one surprise to another before the chilling resolution.

Psycho (1960)

The film begins with an aerial shot of Phoenix, Arizona, after which a tracking shot (actually two shots) brings the viewer through a hotel window into a room where Sam and Marian are in a state of semidress, clearly having just had sex during Marian's lunch hour. Marian indicates that she does not want to meet in secret anymore, that she wants to get married;

Sam, however, is in debt and is paying alimony to his ex-wife, and so insists they cannot get married until he has more money. Trapped by the need for respectability, Marian desperately wants the money they need to escape their predicament.

The way out is offered when she returns to work and a wealthy boor pulls out $40,000 in cash to purchase a house for his daughter as a wedding gift. "I buy off unhappiness," he says to Marian, which reminds her once again of the usefulness of money in solving her own problems. Uncomfortable with such a large amount of cash, Marian's boss asks her to put it in the bank before the weekend; ostensibly, she is to stop by the bank on her way home to sleep off a headache. But Marian goes home with the money instead and puts it on her bed, where both the camera's and Marian's gaze continually return. (Marian is now in black underwear, incidentally, rather than the white of the first scene, as if to indicate a change in her own nature as she gets further implicated in sin.)

The next thing we see, she is on the road in her car, imagining Sam's surprise at seeing her. Unfortunately, her boss sees her while driving and she waves nervously. During her trip to see Sam, we are given many close-ups of her worried face, and there's little talking but tense music. After she stops the car to sleep in it for the night, a state trooper finds her and wakes her up to question her. He is suspicious, and although she manages to get away from him, he follows her into town. She buys another car and sells her old one to hide her trail, but when the trooper arrives at the car dealer while she is concluding the transaction, she becomes worried and takes off. As she drives in the dark and the rain, she imagines the suspicions of the car salesman, the trooper, and her boss, so that it seems like her ill-conceived scheme is doomed to fail. At this point she comes across the Bates Motel.

For quite some time now in the film, we have been entirely identified with Marian, as the action and the camera have followed her without a break. We have been made accomplices in her crime, and feel her anxiety about detection of it. Now we are introduced to the character of Norman Bates, who is friendly and helpful to her. He invites her to join him for dinner at his house near the motel, along with his mother. As she unpacks in her room and hides her stolen cash in a newspaper, we hear an argument between Norman and his mother, who finds the thought of his invitation to Marian "disgusting." Norman yells at her to "shut up" and returns to the motel. Marian apologizes for having caused him some "trouble" and he answers (in one of those lines that becomes memorable on repeat viewings) that his mother "isn't quite herself today."

Marian and Norman share a sandwich for dinner in the parlor adjacent to the motel office, which is filled with stuffed birds of prey. It turns out that his hobby is taxidermy, and that he prefers birds because they seem so "passive" that they still look good when stuffed. They don't look so passive, however, when we see one particularly menacing bird poised in simulated flight above Norman's head; Norman may either be its prey, or another predator like it, depending on whether one views Norman as victim or not. Whether Norman *is* a victim or a predator is genuinely unclear at this point—and in some ways, this remains true even at the end of the film, as he speaks of his controlling mother and of being "trapped" by her. "We're all in our private traps, and none of us can ever get out. We scratch and claw, but only at the air, only at each other . . . we never budge an inch." Marian seems to feel she has stepped into a trap of her own making, but Norman says, "I was born in mine." It is not his fault that he has a domineering mother; Hitchcock offers much evidence in his films of a belief in original sin, perhaps drawn from his Roman Catholic background, in that we are implicated from birth in a web of evil from which we cannot choose to escape—we are predestined by factors beyond our control. In Norman's case, his mother has doomed him from the start to be trapped by his relationship with her, a relationship that he cannot escape even with her death (as the audience finds out).

When Marian gently tries to suggest that Norman put his mother "someplace," he correctly understands this euphemism to refer to an insane asylum. As he balks at this suggestion, he tells Marian that his mother needs him, that she's "not a maniac" (in fact, he adds that "she's as harmless as one of those stuffed birds," another ironic remark on repeat viewings), but that "she just goes a little mad sometimes," as we all do, and he asks Marian if she has not done so herself. She knows she has, in stealing the $40,000 still sitting in her room. No one is pure, and Norman knows this as well as anyone. Their conversation ends with Marian telling him her real name, and that she has decided to return to Phoenix the next day. She also tells him she needs "to pull myself out of my private trap" while she still can. Norman checks the motel register and realizes she gave a false name initially: Marie Samuels, showing her desire to share Sam's name. He also observes her undressing through a peephole. Hitchcock reminds viewers of their own voyeuristic nature in this way, and also demonstrates that Norman has more desires than he has admitted. After he goes up to the house, Marian subtracts the cost of the car from the stolen money on a piece of paper, and then rips it up and tries to flush it down the toilet.

The famous shower scene follows, in which Marian is stabbed to death by "mother." This scene is shocking not because it is particularly bloody (we actually never see the knife enter her body, though we hear it) but because it is unexpected; we have been entirely identified with the character of Marian for almost half of the film, and suddenly she is as dead as can be, taken by surprise at her most vulnerable. That she is dead is not in question, as we see her dead, unseeing eyes and her face unnaturally pressed against the floor where she fell, the shower still gushing as blood swirls down the drain. The camera moves slowly from her face into the bedroom, where it lingers momentarily on the newspaper containing the money. Hitchcock seems to be mocking our concern with the "little matter of $40,000" that we had thought the film was about, as our own greed, like Marian's, has come to nothing after the violence we have just witnessed. The primary function of the money is now that of a "MacGuffin," Hitchcock's own term for an arbitrary something that motivates the action of the characters who desire it.

Norman, of course, has no idea that the money is even there. He enters the scene after we hear his cry from the house, "Mother! Oh God, Mother! Blood! Blood!" and we see him rush into Marian's room. Initially horrified and nauseated by what he sees, he quickly gains his composure enough to systematically dispose of all the evidence that indicates anyone was ever there. Here is the second shock: after losing our identification with Marian, we are now led to identify with Norman, as we stay with him through the entire scene in which he drags her body out, puts it in the trunk of her car with all her possessions (including the newspaper, which he remembers at the last second), mops the floor, and dumps the car in the swamp. There is an uncomfortable moment during which it looks like the car will not sink, but it does, much to his relief. We are horrified by his calm during this process and by his efficiency, which seem to suggest he has had to "clean up" after his mother before this, but also by the fact that we are made to be part of this clean-up as he is the only character onscreen. Just as we had no choice about our identification with Marian, in spite of her imperfections, so we cannot choose to avoid "being" Norman—just as he cannot. It is also worth noting that even his concealment of the crime seems motivated by a boy's desire to protect his mother, and so cannot be completely condemned by us—not even on repeat viewings, when we know the identity of the "mother."

Once Marian is at the bottom of the swamp, the film temporarily moves into the form of a more conventional detective drama, as private investigator Arbogast meets with Sam and Lila (Marian's sister), who are also looking for Marian by now. Arbogast has been hired to find the money, which he assumes he will do if he finds Marian. We are now led temporarily if superficially to identify with Arbogast in his search, which leads him to the Bates Motel and Norman. He identifies the signature of "Marie Samuels" in the register book as being in Marian's handwriting, and so Norman cannot avoid telling him something. Norman insists that Marian left early in the morning and that nothing remarkable happened. Arbogast wants to talk with Norman's mother, as he has seen her sitting in the window, but Norman refuses. Arbogast leaves in order to phone Sam and Lila with this information, then returns to the Bates Motel to attempt again to speak with Norman's mother. His mistake is to go up to the house, where he is also knifed to death by Mom.

Now that we have been deprived of Arbogast as a point of identification, we are left once again with Sam and Lila. They go to the local deputy sheriff, from whom they learn that Norman's mother has been dead for ten years, victim of a "murder-suicide" in which she and her lover were poisoned. Since Arbogast and Sam have seen "Mom" sitting in the window, and the audience and Marian have heard and seen "her," we are left with the sheriff's question of who is buried in the cemetery, and if in fact it is Norman's mother who is stabbing all their visitors. Next, we see Norman enter his mother's room and hear a conversation between them in which he insists she hide in the fruit cellar for a few days. Over her protests, he has to carry her down there. For a woman who just stabbed a man to death, she seems surprisingly passive in his arms.

In the next scene, the sheriff insists that Norman is alone, and that he doesn't "believe in ghosts." He shares this belief outside a church, which invokes a sense of reassurance and normality that is (of course) false, for the audience knows that somebody is knifing people to death up there. Sam and Lila decide to investigate on their own and check into the motel as husband and wife. They find the fragments of Marian's subtraction efforts in the toilet (apparently Hitchcock enjoyed putting such scatological references throughout the film), which convinces them that she was there. Sam agrees to keep Norman busy while Lila goes up to the house to talk to Mrs. Bates, for as she says, "I can handle a sick old woman." Of course, we know that she really can't handle this "woman," so there is considerable tension generated when, after investigating the house, she heads downstairs to the fruit cellar to escape Norman (who has just knocked Sam unconscious and run to the house to stop Lila from finding his mother).

Here all is revealed, as she finds Mom is a skeleton. Norman, in drag, dashes in with a knife, stopped just in time by Sam, who has regained consciousness. The skeleton rocking in the chair, and the light from a swinging bulb casting shadows on the skull's empty eye sockets, creates a horrifying impression that Mom is still alive or that we should believe in ghosts.

The postlude to this scene has often been referred to as a disappointment, as a pompous criminal psychiatrist analyzes Norman's pathology in the police station. This scene functions partly to give the audience some relaxation after a very tense scene, and partly to explain some of the mysteries of the film—such as the motivation for the murders, and why Norman assumed his mother's identity. But it also serves to "excuse" Norman's actions by indicating that he really was as trapped as he thought he was. It would be easy, in the wake of discovering that he was the murderer all along, to move from our original supposition that he was protecting his crazy mother to a moralistic condemnation of Norman as the murderer not only of Marian and Arbogast, but also of his own mother and her lover (as well as two other young women he killed prior to the film narrative). But the psychiatrist suggests that the possessiveness of Norman's mother created his pathological dependence on her, which was challenged when she took a lover, creating a jealousy in Norman that could only be relieved by her murder. To deal with his own guilt, he kept her alive by "becoming" her, complete with clothes and voice, and used his taxidermic skills to preserve her body like one of his stuffed birds. In a sense, the psychiatrist tells us, it was not Norman but Mrs. Bates who committed the murders, as "she" became jealous of Norman's attachment to the young women who came to the motel. As the "dominant personality" has now taken over, Norman is only his mother now, and we cannot blame him as he no longer exists; in fact, "he only half existed to begin with." Norman truly was "born" into his trap, and he never had any choice about it (as Marian may have had about her situation).

Hitchcock, however, has no intention of letting the psychiatrist have the last word, as this might leave us with too much sympathy for a murderer, and we might forget the horrific nature of his/her violence. It is Mrs. Bates who gets the last word, as she (in Norman's head) suggests that Norman is trying to blame her for the killings, that it was really him, for it should be obvious that she can't "do anything but sit and stare, like one of his stuffed birds." As she concludes that she "wouldn't even hurt a fly," we see a sick grin spread across Norman's face, the most menacing we have seen it, and a brief, not-quite-subliminal image of her skull is superimposed on it before a jump to the last quick shot of his victim's car being pulled out of the swamp.

This jarring ending prevents us from resting easily with any of the "explanations" of the murders, for all of them fail to convey their full horror.[8] We can neither fully blame nor fully excuse Norman or his mother, for both of them helped to create the situation even as both were trapped and destroyed by it—Norman in personality, his mother in body. It would be more comfortable if we could blame someone, as in an action movie, where it is usually pretty clear who the good guys and the bad guys are, but in a horror movie we are implicated into the evil more effectively. We become both victim and killer by our identifications with them, and we realize the evil is part of our own nature. This evil can never really be expelled, certainly not by neatly projecting it onto an "other" who is not also ourselves in some sense. The moral of the story is not "don't be like murderous Norman, or greedy Marian," for we are already like them. The moral, if there is one, could be that we should recognize the evil in ourselves and in others, not to deny it or to give it free rein, but to contain it and express it in "acceptable" ways. One of the acceptable ways is to go to horror movies, where we receive catharsis of our sins by participating in the acts of those on-screen rather than acting on our own baser instincts outside the theater.

The fact that Hitchcock always turns the accusing finger back at the audience is his genius, and although no one else did this as well as he did, it is a basic principle of all horror insofar as this genre forces us to look at the evil in human nature, a nature we all share. Some critics have accused Hitchcock of misogyny, as if his women tend to get blamed or punished for being assertive or sexual; one could point to Norman's mother, or to Marian, who has tried to assert herself through her theft, and who is depicted sexually both as she enjoys her shower and in the first scene with Sam. But Hitchcock does not mean to suggest that Marian deserves to die, for the audience identifies with her and understands that she is just trying to get out of her own "private trap." The fact that she does so through a poorly planned theft does not merit her murder, in the eyes of the audience or anyone else, just as the fact that she sleeps with Sam does not merit her murder. She is a completely sympathetic character. It should be recalled that it is her conventional desire for respectability that motivates her theft, not sexual desire. But any notion that Hitchcock suggests his victims "deserve" to die surely misses the point, as he continually makes it clear that no one is pure, all are trapped, and we are no different. Whether they are men or women, we cannot project the blame onto any of his characters without recognizing our own complicity in the crimes we help them commit.

Recall the discussion of ritual in chapter 4 in which characters are "sacrificed for our sins," which means that we participate in their sufferings just as they participate in ours, for their sins *are* ours. We cannot simply transfer guilt to a "scapegoat" without also feeling some connection to that guilt, and Hitchcock's films make this more clear than anyone's. Some rituals or films may not make this connection as clear, trying instead to project the guilt onto someone else without us also taking responsibility for it, but the most effective rituals or dramas will not do so. *Oedipus Rex*, for example, is a great tragedy because it implicates us in its evil and makes us feel both horror for the crime as well as sympathy for the criminal. Hitchcock toyed with oedipal themes throughout his films, so that those who enjoy looking for them will find no end of material to work with. Often his characters have unnatural attachments to domineering mothers or mother-figures who have effectively emasculated them, and this again may suggest that Hitchcock is a misogynist or that he is working out his own frustrations against a controlling mother. But Hitchcock also did this with a tremendous sense of humor, as if it were a great private joke the audience might share if they looked for it. And those who take the oedipal themes too seriously or become too pompous (like the psychiatrist in *Psycho*) will not share the joke but may become the butt of it.

Psycho, in particular, ought not to be reduced to a serious moral message, for it was a film that Hitchcock clearly regarded as a piece of "fun" for the audience as he leads them from one character to another without a sense of where things will end. They enjoy this disorientation in the same way that people enjoy amusement park rides that create both excitement and fear. The key component is that the ride ends, so that we can realize it was "only a game"—and therein lies the pleasure of the experience. Thomas Leitch has argued that Hitchcock's films are best understood as a kind of playing where the things that normally cause pain are mastered through humor and the ability to "wake up" from the nightmare afterwards. We can let ourselves go and ride with the characters through the funhouse, as we believe that stepping outside the norm in this way will allow us to better deal with the everyday when we return to it.[9] This view relates to the idea that movies offer an experience of liminality, that they allow us entry into an imaginary world in order to take on "forbidden" roles so that we can return to the real world refreshed and renewed.

The fact that Hitchcock's films offer "ludic pleasure," however, does not mean they do not have serious moral points to make.[10] They make their points in the form of play, but that does not lessen the importance of those points. Games are very serious things in that, like humor, they allow us to deal with that which is too frightening to face directly. Hitchcock allows us to deal with our own evil impulses, to reflect on them as well as to gain cathartic release from them, just as religions do.

The Silence of the Lambs (1991)

The Silence of the Lambs shares with *Psycho* the distinction of having been both immensely popular and receiving critical acclaim. Like *Psycho*, it is viewed by its fans as terrifying and disturbing, and yet at the same time as "fun" entertainment. People like to be scared, perhaps, but they also like to master their fears through films such as this one. Another similarity between the two films is that we begin with a female protagonist with whom we are invited to identify; she later becomes connected with a male serial killer with whom we are also invited to identify. One difference is that the heroine of *Lambs* survives through the end of the film rather than becoming a victim halfway through it, so she remains a strong point of identification, especially for female viewers. *Lambs* is a film in which a woman confronts her fears and masters them, and this can provide a model for women as well as the men in the audience who wish to do the same.

The film begins with Clarice Starling (Jodi Foster), an FBI trainee, working out on an obstacle fitness course; we see a group of signs on a tree that reads "Hurt-Agony-Pain—Love it." While this can be taken as a typical macho military message about the value of getting in shape, it also speaks to the fascination of Clarice (and the audience) with criminal pathology; we "love" to look at the suffering and pain inflicted by evildoers as a way of mastering and controlling them. Clarice wants to do this by going to work for Dr. Crawford in the Behavioral Sciences Division of the FBI, which investigates serial killers, among other things. Crawford recruits Clarice to speak with Hannibal Lecter (Anthony Hopkins), a brilliant psychiatrist turned cannibalistic serial killer, who is now serving a life sentence. While Crawford says this is just a routine interview, in fact he is using her as a way to get to Lecter, who just might open up to an attractive young female trainee. In particular, Crawford is hoping to learn something from Lecter that might help them catch "Buffalo Bill," a serial killer on the loose who kills and skins women.

When Clarice visits the prison, she first meets its warden, Dr. Chilton, who compliments her on her appearance and asks her out. Throughout the film, we constantly see men looking at Clarice with sexual desire, failing to respect her as a professional and behaving inappropriately as a result. We are also clearly identified with Clarice to the point that we cannot but see such attentions as intrusive, whether the viewer is male or female. Clarice manages to brush Chilton off before being admitted to see Lecter, who is housed in a cellblock with other deviant killers such as Miggs, who makes an obscene remark about Clarice as she passes. Unlike the others, Lecter initially seems polite and dignified, but has a controlling gaze that is almost overpowering. He asks her about Miggs's remark, and about "Buffalo Bill," and then analyzes her as someone who is "one generation from poor white trash" who just had to get away from those who would reduce her to a sexual object. Not one easily cowed, Clarice answers him by asking if he ever turns his gaze on himself, or whether that is too frightening. Rather than answering, he suggests he does not like questions, as he once ate the liver of a census taker "with some fava beans and a nice Chianti." He dismisses her, and as she leaves she panics when the inmates again reduce her to the object of their own deviant sexual fantasies; Lecter calls her back, apologizes for the others, and gives her a clue—she should seek out his old patient, "Miss Moffett." Outside by her car, she bursts into tears as she recalls her father running to greet her when she was a child; she no longer has the luxury of that sort of comfort when she is faced with the evil of the world.

But Clarice is too tough to give up. We see her return to her training, but also investigating Lecter on the side. Crawford phones her to let her know that Miggs committed suicide by swallowing his own tongue after Lecter verbally abused him. It seems that Clarice has an odd sort of friend in Hannibal the Cannibal. Clarice is also clever enough to find a storage facility rented in the name of "Hester Mofet," which she realizes is Lecter's anagram for "the rest of me." Here she finds the head of Lecter's former patient, and she immediately visits Lecter to let him know; he assures her that he did not kill him, only "tucked him away," suggesting that the dead man's lover killed him and that he might also be the serial killer "Buffalo Bill." Lecter offers her a psychological profile of "Buffalo Bill" if she will get him transferred to another institution in which he can have a window view.

The next scene shows the kidnapping by "Bill" of Catherine Martin, who (it will turn out) is the daughter of U.S. senator Ruth Martin; this is followed by the discovery of one of his earlier victims, and Clarice is invited by Crawford to go along for the autopsy. At the funeral home, Clarice is at first excluded from the proceedings because she is a woman, and although Crawford later suggests to her this was just "smoke" to get rid of the local sheriff, she challenges him for modeling sexist behavior to other officers. She also has a flashback of her father's funeral and sees herself once more as a young and vulnerable girl. But she then joins the group at the autopsy, and in spite of feeling a great deal of emotion upon seeing the skinned corpse of a woman, she manages to give a thorough and clinical description of her condition. In order to deal with evil, she must be able to face its effects and be able to analyze them; but she also fears losing her human feeling for the victims through such analysis.

This fear is shown a few scenes later when Senator Martin appears on television to appeal to the kidnapper, talking about her daughter and showing pictures of her as a child. In close-up, Clarice notes that the senator is trying to make the killer see her daughter "as a person and not as an object," for then it is "harder to tear her up." She clearly is thinking of her own experience with the autopsy, in which the victim had been depersonalized just as effectively as when she was skinned by "Bill." Her challenge is to have enough distance to be tough, yet maintain her ability to feel for the victim so that she does not become the very thing she is fighting against. In this way, she models for women a way to survive and fight evil while at the same time preserving the feminist mandate to feel for and avoid objectification of persons.

Clarice, acting on Crawford's instructions, presents to Lecter a phony offer from Senator Martin in which he is promised a move to a better location in exchange for information leading to the capture of Buffalo Bill. Lecter offers information on a quid pro quo basis, asking her to answer questions about her childhood in exchange for information about the killer. She reveals that her father was a town marshall killed by two burglars when she was a child, and he offers that "Billy" wants to be a transsexual but is always refused surgery as he does not demonstrate true transsexual tendencies. Instead, he simply wants to be something other than he is, as he hates the person he became through a childhood of systematic abuse. During this scene, Lecter's face is reflected in the glass that separates them, so that his image is superimposed on hers, indicating that they are becoming joined. Through Clarice, we are also being joined to a killer, becoming his companion. Before their exchanges can go further, however, Chilton discovers that the offer from Senator Martin is a fraud, and he tells Lecter, who agrees to deal directly with Martin if they bring him to Memphis. Confined in a corset and face mask like an animal, he is brought to the senator and offers her the real name of her daughter's kidnapper; he then insults her and reminds her of the torture that awaits her daughter, as if he would rather be viewed by her as a monster than pitied.

Clarice visits Lecter in his new temporary "home," a cage in the middle of a large room in the police station. Although the bars make him seem more like a dangerous confined animal, he now is no longer behind glass as in the other facility, so that physical contact is possible (and he manages to touch Clarice before she leaves). Clarice knows that he has given a fake name to the authorities and begs him to tell her the real name of the killer. Lecter no longer trusts her, however, and has no reason to; still, he agrees to give her more clues in exchange for a story from her childhood, in particular, why she could not remain on her cousin's sheep farm after the death of her father left her orphaned. Lecter wants to know what she "covets," as this is the secret to knowing her, just as it is the secret to knowing Buffalo Bill and everyone else. "Billy" kills not out of sadism or sexual frustration, but because of what he covets, what he "sees every day." He asks her if she has not seen men covet her body as they gaze at her (and indeed this is what we have seen throughout the film); but what does she covet? She reveals that one morning she heard the screaming of the lambs ("like a child's voice") as they were being slaughtered, and that she tried to run away with a lamb, in order to save "just one." She was caught and sent away to an orphanage. Lecter sees that this desire to save the "innocent lambs," to stop their screaming, is what motivates her desire to enter law enforcement—to save the victims she could not save on the sheep ranch, to save those she can, since she could not save her own father.

After she leaves, Lecter escapes his cage, brutally murdering several people along the way. Clarice realizes that his remark about Buffalo Bill coveting what he sees every day suggests that his first victim was someone he knew, and she visits the victim's hometown to search for clues. She also realizes that because he covets being a woman, he is killing women to make a suit made of real women's skin. She calls Crawford, but he has already figured out who the killer is through discovering one Jame Gumb, who was refused for transsexual surgery numerous times and who also has brought rare moths into the country such as were found in his victims' throats—a symbol of his own desire to change from caterpillar to butterfly, male to female. He tells Clarice "we couldn't have done it without you," and then his plane flies out of radio range, leaving Clarice out of his plan to arrest Gumb (as the "boys" are meant to handle this).

Ironically, however, Gumb is not at the address they have, but is instead found accidentally by Clarice as she interviews the denizens of the victim's small town. She manages to kill him by pursuing him through his basement (along the way finding Catherine Martin confined in a hole) and ultimately shoots him dead in the dark, even though he has infra-red goggles and she doesn't. In this scene, Clarice is clearly terrified, as her hands shake while she swings her gun around in the dark, but she is also tough enough to find and shoot him when she hears his gun being cocked, before he can shoot her. (Incidentally, Catherine Martin also shows herself to be a strong woman who refuses to accept the status of a victim, as just prior to her rescue she managed to lure Gumb's beloved poodle into her hole, threatening to "break her neck" if Gumb didn't bring her a telephone.)

The last scene in the film is Clarice's graduation. She has at last earned the respect of Crawford, who congratulates her and shakes her hand; she has proven that she can compete in a man's profession, and he accepts her as an equal. But she also receives a phone call from her other mentor, Dr. Lecter, who asks if the "lambs have stopped screaming" since her rescue of Catherine. Of course, they have not, as evil is still on the loose in the world—including Lecter. He tells her he will leave her alone, as "the world's more interesting with you in it," and asks that she do the same (though he knows she cannot promise that). Before he hangs up, Lecter says he's "having an old friend for dinner," and then we see him stroll after Dr. Chilton.

The figure of Lecter is an interesting one as he is made to be both horrific and sympathetic. He is a brutal killer with almost superhuman powers, yet he helps Clarice and seems to like her. He is not depicted as a sexual deviant like Miggs or Gumb, for that would lessen our ability to like him; his pathology (cannibalism) is so excessive that it invites a humorous response rather than the disgust we feel for Gumb. We also have no sense of the origin of his pathology, as we do with Jame Gumb. The latter is the "bad" serial killer who needs to be understood in order to be stopped, but not so that we may feel any sympathy for him—he is the villain of the film. Lecter's role is peculiar as he is aligned with the heroine, and so he is the "good" serial killer, but we do not gain sympathy for him through a story of how he became evil (as we do with Norman Bates). He represents evil pure and simple, but he also represents its attractiveness displayed by his seductive power. Anthony Hopkins essentially plays him as Faust's Mephistopheles, who tempts the heroine with greater knowledge in exchange for participation in his evil. In being able to deal with Lecter, Clarice (like Faust) confronts and deals with evil in order to be better able to contain it—to attempt to stop her private lambs from screaming, even though she knows they will never stop, for evil will always exist. All victories over evil are partial, it is shown, and there is also a recognition that the potential for evil is within us all, shown through Clarice's attraction (and ours) to Lecter, as well as in her own "covetous" drive. In her case and in the case of "well-adjusted" people, this drive does not become destructive but is channeled to socially acceptable pursuits. Yet we need to recognize that we all have such drives and desires. This film allows viewers to look within themselves and face what they covet, to better deal with the presence of evil both inside themselves and outside, in the world of chaos and sin that religions seek to address.

Conclusion

The purpose of this book has been to develop a method of studying film, informed by the insights of religious studies, which offers an alternative to the current range of approaches informed by theological and/or ideological criticism. I do not recommend the cessation of these approaches, but I support their supplementation by an approach that I believe can go further in understanding the power of film for its audiences. In order to understand film, one must try to understand how it functions for its audiences—the beliefs and values it conveys, and its ritual power to provide catharsis of the emotions associated with a range of life problems and situations. If we are to make value judgments on popular culture, as I believe we should, such value judgments should be based on an understanding of the phenomenon in question and not simply on one's own theological or ideological agenda. Total objectivity is never possible, of course, but this insight does not give scholars carte blanche to assume a film functions in a certain way without making some effort to check their hypotheses.

I applaud the nascent ethnographic studies that seek to determine what audience members actually say about films, as this is one way of checking our assumptions. At the same time, readers will note that I have not made extensive use of them—partly because such studies are currently in short supply, and partly because such studies do not always tell you what you would like to know. Although it is crucial to listen to what viewers say, sometimes they do not articulate very well the reasons a film has affected them, or they may not even realize why they liked one film better than another. For this reason, I do not apologize for engaging in textual analyses of the films in order to better understand how they do what they do, as this is not irrelevant to understanding audience appreciation of a film. Many of those who enjoyed Hitchcock's films, for example, probably could not articulate how his filmmaking managed to seduce them so effectively, but an examination of his art gives insights into that process and thereby into the ability of the films to reach a popular audience.

My interest in what is popular is also one of the reasons why I have focused on box-office hits, as these offer the clearest evidence of films that have managed to act "religiously" for a large number of people. This does not mean that only "popular" films have religious power, as "art films" may have just as much religious power for the intelligentsia who enjoy them. For myself, I have been affected "religiously" both by Hollywood "popular" movies (such as those I have discussed) and by more iconoclastic, less popular films (whether of foreign or domestic origin). This is one reason why I have rejected the effort to make a great distinction between these two types of films, as if one had value and the other did not. What I find most objectionable is the tendency to reject completely all films made in Hollywood, or all films that make a profit, as if these were too tainted to deserve any serious examination except as tools of the dominant ideology. This sort of elitism, which assumes that all that is popular must be bad, is unable to understand or even properly examine why something is popular, having decided at the outset that popularity discredits it from having any real value.

Although I have reacted against those who condemn all that is popular, however, this does not mean that I would accept without criticism all that is popular. I have made positive comments about most of the genres and films I examined in detail. This does not mean, however, that they are above criticism or that I could not comment on other films of which I might be considerably more critical. The important thing is to look at each genre and each film to determine what functions it serves, and then ideological criticism may be appropriate. For example, I was more judgmental about romantic comedies than the other genres I examined, not because I do not like them, but because their structure and appropriation suggest that they be more entrenched in sexist ideology than many of the other genres—even (oddly enough) horror or action movies. Of course, some romantic comedies are less sexist, but I chose to examine the most popular, which happen to be (in my view) among the most sexist. I am not suggesting that romantic comedies are by nature sexist, nor that elements of sexism or other hegemonic ideologies are absent from other genres or other films. Even in a film as artistic and morally complex as *The Godfather*, there is a disturbing amount of sexism as well as anti-Semitism that often go unidentified by the average viewer. The presence of these elements, however, does not discredit the film from performing other functions, perhaps even less objectionable ones, for its viewers.

Films are full of a variety of messages, and we should try to identify as many of them as possible in order to understand them better. We should also be able to appreciate and applaud the positive functions they perform (conveying hope, catharsis, and a range of societally supportive values) even as we may deplore some of the functions we perceive as more negative (perpetuating hegemonies, stereotypes, and antisocial values). Any given viewer may get any number of things out of a film, positive and negative, which is another reason to look for the range of things it may convey to different people. This disparity also means we should avoid blanket condemnation or approbation of a film, in that it may function in a variety of ways.

This approach, I believe, is even good for ideological criticism in that the ability to find ideology where it clearly is, rather than imagining it to be where it is not, would add credibility to the enterprise of ideological analysis. Students tend to be skeptical about ideological criticism, surely in part because they are threatened by it, but the often ill-supported generalizations of ideological critics also serve to fuel its skeptical rejection by students. If academic film analysis, or for that matter analysis of popular culture in general, could be more open to the positive benefits of cultural texts, then perhaps students would be better able to see the benefit of its criticism. They might be more willing to allow the negative aspects of their favorite films, and better able to identify such, if they were also told that the films might have other, more positive aspects and functions. In a similar way, the concerns of conservative social critics about sex and violence in popular films would gain credibility if they looked at the films in question to see how the objectionable images are being used and how they are being appropriated. Almost everyone would agree that children, at least, should not see certain images, and so we all approve of some restrictions on viewing. But this does not mean that one should reject altogether the depiction of sex and violence, or one might as well censor the entire history of literature as well.

Conservative theological analysis of popular culture also seems to have a tremendous blind spot in relation to its own formative texts, assuming that the Bible is clean and good while popular media are the opposite. Actually, the Bible is full of sexually explicit language (e.g., in the Song of Songs) as well as the depiction of a variety of sinful and violent behaviors that are not always condemned. Granted, such texts do not tend to feature prominently in the weekly lectionary, but it still seems to be a case of look-ing for the speck in the eye of popular culture rather than dealing with the beam in one's own scriptures. Sometimes criticism of popular films or books may have more to do with jealousy of their popularity than any real criticism of their content. For example, when J. K. Rowling's book *Harry Potter and the Goblet of Fire* (2000) came out (the fourth in the series), it was so popular that many conservative Christians attacked the Harry Pot-ter series for its sympathetic portrayal of witchcraft. In fact, the books deal largely with a conflict between those who would use magic for good and those who would use it for evil, so that its morality is quite traditional. The same sort of portrayal of a conflict between two types of magic in-forms *The Chronicles of Narnia*, written by popular Christian author C. S. Lewis, whom Christian readers do not tend to condemn. Indeed, the battle between Moses and Pharoah's magicians in the Bible is a similar sort of conflict between good and evil forces, and the evil magic is real enough even though it is weak when compared with the power of God. In their zeal to criticize popular culture, conservatives often refuse to see similari-ties even where they exist.

The approach I have utilized could also be applied to other texts of popular culture besides films, and in this way it might become possible to approach the study of popular culture in ways that are not as beholden to ideological criticism and its negative evaluations of popular culture. Again, this is not to suggest an uncritical approach that celebrates every aspect of popular culture, but a balanced approach that can assess the power of popular culture—why it appeals—and both appreciate and cri-tique the way it functions. We should be able to examine any religion or any cultural phenomenon in this way, seeking to understand it first but also reserving the right to make value judgments on it. These value judg-ments will inevitably be informed by our own perspectives, so that we will come up with different conclusions. But in this way we can begin a con-versation among a variety of viewpoints that is not based on blind rejec-tion of the other but rather on an attempt to understand the other. Con-sidered in relation to the history of sociology and social criticism, perhaps what is needed is a return to Max Weber's *Verstehen* (understanding) ap-proach to correct the excesses of Marxist social critique.

I have sought to begin such a conversation here, so that I do not claim to have offered the definitive view of any film so much as a suggestion of a method that can be further developed. If these provisional efforts are helpful to others seeking to understand the power of popular culture, then

I will be pleased if the dialogue among academics, religious leaders, and popular culture has been facilitated. It will not hurt traditional religion or academia to listen to the films that speak so strongly in our culture or to recognize that they may have something to say that is worth hearing; the only thing that may be damaged is our pride, as we may not be able to continue to assert our superiority to the texts we so confidently deride.

Notes

NOTES TO CHAPTER 1

1. M. Darrol Bryant, "Cinema, Religion, and Popular Culture," in John R. May and Michael Bird, eds., *Religion in Film* (Knoxville: University of Tennessee Press, 1982), 106.

2. Bryant, 105.

3. Conrad E. Ostwalt, Jr., "Conclusion: Religion, Film, and Cultural Analysis," in Joel W. Martin and Conrad E. Ostwalt, Jr., eds., *Screening the Sacred: Religion, Myth, and Ideology in Popular American Film* (Boulder, CO: Westview Press, 1995), 154.

4. Ostwalt, 157.

5. H. Richard Niebuhr, *Christ and Culture* (New York: Harper and Row, 1951), 45–82.

6. Niebuhr, 83–115.

7. Niebuhr, 116–148.

8. Niebuhr, 149–189.

9. Niebuhr, 190–229.

10. Paul Tillich, "On the Idea of a Theology of Culture" in James Luther Adams, ed., *What is Religion?* (New York: Harper and Row, 1969), 164.

11. Tillich, 162.

12. Tillich, 162–163.

13. Tillich, 169.

14. Niebuhr, 238.

15. John C. Cooper and Carl Skrade, eds., *Celluloid and Symbols* (Philadelphia: Fortress Press, 1970), ix.

16. Cooper and Skrade, 2–3.

17. James M. Wall, *Church and Cinema* (Grand Rapids, MI: Eerdmans, 1971), 13.

18. Wall, 44.

19. Robert Jewett, *Saint Paul at the Movies: The Apostle's Dialogue with American Culture* (Louisville, KY: Westminster/John Knox Press, 1993), 7.

20. Jewett, 8.

21. Jewett, 9–10.

22. Jewett, 11.

23. Robert Jewett, *Saint Paul Returns to the Movies: Triumph over Shame* (Grand Rapids, MI: Eerdmans, 1999).

24. Bernard Brandon Scott, *Hollywood Dreams and Biblical Stories* (Minneapolis: Fortress, 1994), x, 3.

25. Scott, 3–6.

26. Scott, 16.

27. Scott, 14.

28. Scott, 253–254.

29. Scott, 213–214.

30. Clive Marsh, "Film and Theologies of Culture," in Clive Marsh and Gaye Ortiz, eds., *Explorations in Theology and Film: Movies and Meaning* (Oxford: Blackwell, 1997), 21–34.

31. Marsh, "Film and Theologies of Culture," 31–32.

32. Marsh, "Film and Theologies of Culture," 33, also Clive Marsh and Gaye Ortiz, "Theology beyond the Modern and the Postmodern: A Future Agenda for Theology and Film," in Marsh and Ortiz, 254.

33. Robert K. Johnston, *Reel Spirituality: Theology and Film in Dialogue* (Grand Rapids, MI: Baker, 2000), 41–62.

34. Some other recent Protestant works seem to move similarly toward the Roman Catholic model, e.g.: Bryan Stone, *Faith and Film: Theological Themes at the Cinema* (St. Louis, MO: Chalice Press, 2000); William D. Romanowski, *Eyes Wide Open: Looking for God in Popular Culture* (Grand Rapids, MI: Brazos Press, 2001); Ken Gire, *Reflections on the Movies: Hearing God in the Unlikeliest of Places* (Colorado Springs: Chariot Victor, 2000).

35. Neil P. Hurley, *Theology through Film* (New York: Harper and Row, 1970), 8. Republished as *Toward a Film Humanism* (New York: Delta Paperbacks, 1975).

36. Neil P. Hurley, *The Reel Revolution: A Film Primer on Liberation* (Maryknoll, NY: Orbis Books, 1978), xii.

37. Neil P. Hurley, "*On the Waterfront*: Rebirth of a 'Contenduh,'" in John R. May, ed., *Image and Likeness: Religious Visions in American Film Classics* (New York: Paulist Press, 1992), 103.

38. John R. May, "Visual Story and the Religious Interpretation of Film," in May and Bird, *Religion in Film*, 29.

39. May, "Visual Story," 31.

40. May, "Visual Story," 35.

41. Michael Bird, "Film as Hierophany," in May and Bird, 3–4.

42. Bird, 5.

43. Bird, 11–13.

44. Bird, 13–22.

45. Paul Schrader, *Transcendental Style in Film* (Berkeley: University of California Press, 1972), 29.

46. Kevin Jackson, ed., *Schrader on Schrader* (London: Faber and Faber, 1990), 29.

47. May has recognized this in "Contemporary Theories Regarding the Interpretation of Film," in John R. May, ed., *New Image of Religious Film* (Kansas City, MO: Sheed and Ward, 1997), 30.

48. E.g., Ernest Ferlita and John R. May, *Film Odyssey: The Art of Film as Search for Meaning* (New York: Paulist Press, 1976).

49. Ernest Ferlita, "The Analogy of Action in Film," in May and Bird, 54.

50. Ferlita, "Analogy," 56.

51. Ernest Ferlita, "Film and the Quest for Meaning," in May and Bird, 118.

52. Ferlita, "Quest," 128.

53. Ferlita, "Quest," 131.

54. In addition to Miles's work, discussed below, a good example of this approach is found in S. Brent Plate and David Jasper, eds., *Imag(in)ing Otherness: Filmic Visions of Living Together* (Atlanta: Scholars Press, 1999). The authors engage in ideological critique of popular Western cinema in its portrayal of other cultures, and conversely analyze rather sympathetically non-Western or "alternative" cinema's challenge to cultural chauvinism and marginalization. See also David Jasper, "On Systematizing the Unsystematic: A Response," in Marsh and Ortiz, 235–244, in which he critiques the theological approach from an ideological perspective.

55. Margaret R. Miles, *Seeing and Believing: Religion and Values in the Movies* (Boston: Beacon Press, 1996), xiii.

56. Miles, 4.

57. Graeme Turner, "Cultural Studies and Film," in John Hill and Pamela Church Gibson, eds., *Film Studies: Critical Approaches* (Oxford: Oxford University Press, 2000), 197–198.

58. Lisa Taylor, "From Psychoanalytic Feminism to Popular Feminism," in Joanne Hollows and Mark Jancovich, eds., *Approaches to Popular Film* (Manchester, UK: Manchester University Press, 1995), 151–171.

59. Miles, 46.

60. Miles, 47.

61. Miles, 56–57.

62. Miles, 65–66.

63. Joanne Hollows, "Mass Culture Theory and Political Economy," in Hollows and Jancovich, 22.

64. This ideological approach to film is exemplified by Michael Ryan and Douglas Kellner in *Camera Politica: The Politics and Ideology of Contemporary Hollywood Film* (Bloomington: Indiana University Press, 1988). For a critique of the

ideological bias of popular film studies, see Hollows and Jancovich, especially 1–36, 123–150.

65. Joel W. Martin, "Introduction: Seeing the Sacred on the Screen," in Martin and Ostwalt, 6–7.

66. Martin, 9–11.

67. See Clive Marsh, "Religion, Theology, and Film in a Postmodern Age: A Response to John Lyden," *Journal of Religion and Film* 2:1 (April 1998): http://www.unomaha.edu/~wwwjrf/marshrel.htm. This was a response to my article, "To Commend or to Critique? The Question of Religion and Film Studies," *Journal of Religion and Film* 1:2 (October 1997): http://www.unomaha.edu /~wwwjrf/tocommend.htm. In my response to Marsh, "Continuing the Conversation: A Response to Clive Marsh," *Journal of Religion and Film*, Reader Discussion: http://www.unomaha.edu/~wwwjrf/disctopc.htm, I made it clear that I agreed with him on this point.

NOTES TO CHAPTER 2

1. Jonathan Z. Smith, *Imagining Religion: From Babylon to Jonestown* (Chicago: University of Chicago Press, 1982), xi.

2. Friedrich Schleiermacher, *The Christian Faith*, ed. H. R. Mackintosh and J. S. Stewart (Philadelphia: Fortress Press, 1976), 17.

3. Rudolf Otto, *The Idea of the Holy*, trans. John W. Harvey (New York: Oxford University Press, 1958), 10.

4. Otto identifies the Buddhist concept of "emptiness" with an experience of the "wholly other" (30, 39); he also associates it with Taoism (201, n. 2). It is noteworthy that he says almost nothing about Confucianism, which is perhaps not surprising as it seems to lack that sense of radical transcendence.

5. Mircea Eliade, *The Sacred and the Profane: The Nature of Religion*, trans. Willard R. Trask (New York: Harcourt, Brace, Jovanovich, 1959); also *Patterns in Comparative Religion*, trans. Rosemary Sheed (New York: World Publishing, 1958).

6. John Hick, *An Interpretation of Religion* (New Haven: Yale University Press, 1989).

7. Paul Tillich, *Systematic Theology* (Chicago: University of Chicago Press, 1967), 11–15; also *Dynamics of Faith* (New York: Harper and Row, 1957), 1–4.

8. Paul Tillich, *Ultimate Concern: Tillich in Dialogue*, ed. D. Mackenzie Brown (New York: Harper and Row, 1965), 8.

9. Tillich, *Dynamics of Faith*, 11–12, 16–18; *Systematic Theology*, 13.

10. Paul Tillich, "The Significance of the History of Religions for the Systematic Theologian," in *The Future of Religions*, ed. Jerald C. Brauer (New York: Harper and Row, 1966), 80–94; see esp. 88–89. Tillich gave this talk on October 12,

1965, ten days before his death. See also Paul Tillich, *Christianity and the Encounter of the World Religions* (New York: Columbia University Press, 1963).

11. Rodney Stark and William Sims Bainbridge, *A Theory of Religion* (New York: Peter Lang, 1987), 22–23.

12. This debate was recently revisited by theologian David Ray Griffin, who argues for a theological explanation, and J. Samuel Preus and Robert A. Segal, who favor naturalistic explanations, in an exchange of articles in the *Journal of the American Academy of Religion* 68:1 (March 2000): 99–149.

13. There is technically a distinction between the claim that religion can be naturalistically explained and the claim that religion is basically hegemony-promoting ideology, but in practice the two ideas have tended to be joined in the reductionist critiques of many social scientists.

14. Clifford Geertz, *The Interpretation of Cultures* (New York: Basic Books, 1973), 23.

15. Geertz, 7.

16. Geertz, 90.

17. Geertz, 93.

18. Geertz, 96–97.

19. Geertz, 98–99.

20. Geertz, 100.

21. Geertz, 108.

22. Geertz, 112.

23. Geertz, 114.

24. Geertz, 116.

25. Geertz, 118.

26. Geertz, 121.

27. Geertz, 122.

28. For a summary and critique of this view, see Joanne Hollows, "Mass Culture Theory and Political Economy," in Joanne Hollows and Mark Jancovich, eds., *Approaches to Popular Film* (Manchester, UK: Manchester University Press, 1995), 15–23.

29. Geertz, 116.

30. Here I must disagree with Margaret Miles when she claims that films lack the religious power of icons precisely because they are not viewed repeatedly: "Most people see a film only once. A few people see 'cult' films again and again, but most of us buy the video of a film we have enjoyed, only to let it collect dust" (Miles, 190). This statement represents to me people who do not really like movies, but not me or those whom I would consider movie lovers. Although some people act as she claims, many people do not, and it is not clear that we should let those who are less involved with movies define how they function for the more "religious." Surely it would be a mistake to conclude that Christianity

lacks religious power in our culture simply because most members do not attend church weekly and many 'Christians' only attend on Easter and Christmas. The more involved people will define the nature of the religion, and there may well be many more people who repeatedly view films than Miles realizes.

31. Geertz, 111–112.

32. Siegfried Kracauer, "Basic Concepts," in Leo Braudy and Marshall Cohen, eds., *Film Theory and Criticism*, 5th ed. (New York: Oxford University Press, 1999), 173–177.

33. Tim Bywater and Thomas Sobchack, *An Introduction to Film Criticism* (New York: Longman), 165–169.

34. This was noted by Jean Mitry. See Bywater and Sobchack, 170.

35. Colin McCabe, "Realism and the Cinema: Notes on Some Brechtian Theses," *Screen* 15:2 (Summer 1974): 21–27.

36. Jean-Louis Baudry, "Ideological Effects of the Basic Cinematographic Apparatus," in Braudy and Cohen, 345–355.

37. Jean Baudrillard, *Simulacra and Simulation*, trans. Sheila Faria Glaser (Ann Arbor: University of Michigan Press, 1994).

38. Tom Gunning, "An Aesthetic of Astonishment: Early Film and the (In)credulous Spectator," in Braudy and Cohen, 818–832.

39. Noel Carroll, "Jean-Louis Baudry and 'The Apparatus,'" in Braudy and Cohen, 778–794.

40. Richard Allen, *Projecting Illusion: Film Spectatorship and the Impression of Reality* (New York: Cambridge University Press, 1995), 4.

41. Allen, 100–106.

42. Allen, 134.

43. Sam Gill, *Native American Religions: An Introduction* (Belmont, CA: Wadsworth, 1982), 71–73.

NOTES TO CHAPTER 3

1. Wendy Doniger O'Flaherty, *Other People's Myths* (New York: Macmillan, 1988), 26–27.

2. See Daniel L. Pals, *Seven Theories of Religion* (New York: Oxford University Press, 1996), 16–53, for a summary and critique of Tylor and Frazer. One of the things they neglected was the fact that a belief in magic and mythology persists even in modern technological societies, suggesting that a scientific worldview has not displaced it and may be compatible with such beliefs.

3. Stefan Arvidsson, "Aryan Mythology as Science and Ideology," *Journal of the American Academy of Religion* 67:2 (June 1999): 327–354.

4. This section is a revision of a portion of my article, "The Apocalyptic Cosmology of *Star Wars*," *Journal of Religion and Film* 4:1 (April 2000): http://www

.unomaha.edu/~wwwjrf/LydenStWars.htm. Some of this material is also used in chapter 11. I am grateful to the *Journal of Religion and Film* for allowing me to use this material.

5. C. G. Jung, "Archetypes of the Collective Unconscious," in C. G. Jung, *The Collected Works of C. G. Jung*, ed. Sir Herbert Read et al., vol. 9, pt. 1, *The Archetypes and the Collective Unconscious*, 2nd ed., trans. R. F. C. Hull (Princeton: Princeton University Press, 1968), 3–41.

6. Jung, *Archetypes*, 6.

7. C. G. Jung, "A Psychological Approach to the Dogma of the Trinity," in C. G. Jung, *Psychology and Western Religion*, trans. R. F. C. Hull (London: Routledge, 1988), 3–96.

8. C. G. Jung, "Jung and Religious Belief," in C. G. Jung, *Psychology and Western Religion*, 278.

9. C. G. Jung, "Religion and Psychology: A Reply to Martin Buber," in *The Gnostic Jung*, ed. Robert A. Segal (Princeton: Princeton University Press, 1992), 155–163.

10. This critique is made by Michael Palmer in his *Freud and Jung on Religion* (London: Routledge, 1997), especially 184–187.

11. E.g., James F. Iaccino, *Jungian Reflections within the Cinema: A Psychological Analysis of Sci-Fi and Fantasy Archetypes* (Westport, CT: Praeger, 1998); Janice Hocker Rushing and Thomas S. Frentz, *Projecting the Shadow: The Cyborg Hero in American Film* (Chicago: University of Chicago Press, 1995).

12. Joseph Campbell, *The Hero with a Thousand Faces* (Princeton: Princeton University Press, 1949), especially 49–243.

13. "Campbell typically ignores the story in myths—most ironic for someone lauded as a master storyteller." Robert A. Segal, "The Romantic Appeal of Joseph Campbell," in *Theorizing about Myth* (Amherst: University of Massachusetts Press, 1999), 141. Segal does note that in *Hero*, Campbell pays more attention to plot details than in his other works, but even here Campbell does not give extended analyses and quickly goes to comparisons.

14. Joseph Campbell with Bill Moyers, *The Power of Myth* (New York: Doubleday, 1988), 161. Campbell speaks of "loving one's fate" even if it involves suffering, and quotes Nietzsche in support of this ideal. He also quotes the Buddha's dictum that "all life is suffering," ignoring the fact that the Buddha sought an escape from this, not an affirmation of it.

15. Here I must agree with Maurice Friedman against Robert Segal. "Campbell seems to want a unity of inner and outer, as Segal says, yet it is not the actual outer but a mysticized and universalized outer that comes from his projection of his inward philosophy on it." Maurice Friedman, "Psychology, Psychologism, and Myth: A Rejoinder," *Journal of the American Academy of Religion* 67:2 (June 1999): 471.

16. "The Biblical image of the universe simply won't do anymore." Joseph Campbell, *Myths to Live By* (New York: Viking, 1972), 89ff.

17. This claim privileges one group's proximity to the divine, whereas (in his view) all have the divine within them already. Since Judaism seeks a relationship with a named God rather than identity, it claims this relationship is only available "through membership in a certain supernaturally endowed, uniquely favored social group." Campbell, *Myths to Live By*, 95–96.

18. Robert A. Segal, *Joseph Campbell: An Introduction* (New York: Garland, 1987); Maurice Friedman, "Why Joseph Campbell's Psychologizing of Myth Precludes the Holocaust as Touchstone of Reality," *Journal of the American Academy of Religion* 66:2 (June 1998): 385–401.

19. Geertz, 119.

20. Geertz, 120. Also see 142–144, where Geertz faults Durkheim for reducing culture to society, and Malinowski for reducing society to culture. Geertz favors a dialectical model for the interaction between culture and society, well expressed in the supporting article, "Ritual and Social Change: a Javanese Example," 142–169.

21. Jonathan Z. Smith critiques the tendency of anthropologists (especially Lévy-Bruhl) to mystify "primitives" as alien and prelogical in "I am a Parrot (Red)," 265–288, in *Map Is Not Territory: Studies in the History of Religions* (Leiden: E. J. Brill, 1978). I must disagree, however, with his attempt to tar Geertz with the same brush (282, 286), as I believe that Geertz does not separate mythical language from ordinary language (as "absurd" or "illogical") but simply distinguishes them in order to show their dialectical interaction.

22. Clifford Geertz, "The Cerebral Savage: On the Work of Claude Lévi-Strauss," 345–359, in *The Interpretation of Cultures*.

23. Geertz, 355.

24. Mircea Eliade, *The Sacred and the Profane: The Nature of Religion*, trans. Willard R. Trask (New York: Harcourt, Brace, Jovanovich, 1959), 85–87, 105; also see Eliade, *Patterns in Comparative Religion*, trans. Rosemary Sheed (Cleveland: World Publishing, 1958), 388–408, and *Cosmos and History: The Myth of the Eternal Return*, trans. Willard R. Trask (New York: Harper and Row, 1959).

25. Mircea Eliade, *Rites and Symbols of Initiation: The Mysteries of Birth and Rebirth*, trans. Willard R. Trask (Dallas: Spring Publications, 1958).

26. Eliade, *The Sacred and the Profane*, 110–113.

27. Eliade, *Cosmos and History*, 147–159.

28. Mircea Eliade, *Myth and Reality*, trans. Willard R. Trask (New York: Harper and Row, 1963), 170–174.

29. Eliade, *Myth and Reality*, 185.

30. Eliade, *Myth and Reality*, 192; *The Sacred and the Profane*, 205.

31. Eliade, *The Sacred and the Profane*, 203.

32. See Eliade, *Myth and Reality*, 21–38, where he argues that all myths of origin are based in the cosmogony. Eliade later softened this claim by distinguishing myths of ancestral-anthropological origins from myths of world creation to a

greater extent, in "Cosmogonic Myth and 'Sacred History,'" found in *The Quest: History and Meaning in Religion* (Chicago: University of Chicago Press, 1969), 72–87.

33. Francisca Cho Bantly, "Archetypes of Selves: A Study of the Chinese Mytho-Historical Consciousness," in Laurie L. Patton and Wendy Doniger, eds., *Myth and Method* (Charlottesville: University Press of Virginia, 1996), 201.

34. Some critics have also pointed to Eliade's early relationship to Romanian fascism, and they feel that it may have affected his view of myth more than he admits. See, e.g., Ivan Strenski, *Four Theories of Myth in Twentieth-Century History* (Iowa City: University of Iowa Press, 1987), 70–103.

35. Smith, *Map*, "Sacred Persistence: Towards a Redescription of Canon," 96–103.

36. Jonathan Z. Smith, in *Imagining Religion: From Babylon to Jonestown* (Chicago: University of Chicago Press, 1982), especially 36–44.

37. Smith, *Map*, 296–297.

38. Smith, *Map*, 299–300.

39. Smith, *Map*, 302–308; *Imagining Religion*, 96–101.

40. Smith, *Imagining Religion*, 90–96; *Map*, 72–74.

41. Smith, *Map*, 309.

42. Smith, *Map*, 301.

43. Wendy Doniger O'Flaherty, *Other People's Myths: The Cave of Echoes* (New York: Macmillan, 1988), 28–33.

44. Wendy Doniger, "Minimyths and Maximyths and Political Points of View," in *Myth and Method*, 109–127; see especially 116–118. Also see her essay, "Postmodern and –colonial –structural Comparisons," in Kimberley C. Patton and Benjamin C. Ray, eds., *A Magic Still Dwells: Comparative Religion in the Postmodern Age* (Berkeley: University of California Press, 2000), 63–74. This book includes the reflections of a number of scholars on the validity of cross-cultural comparisons in the postmodern age; most are optimistic about the task although more cautious than their predecessors in the history of religions.

45. Doniger O'Flaherty, *Other People's Myths*, 32.

46. Wendy Doniger O'Flaherty, *Dreams, Illusions, and Other Realities* (Chicago: University of Chicago Press, 1984), 37–53.

47. Doniger O'Flaherty, *Dreams*, 132–135.

48. Doniger O'Flaherty, *Dreams*, 126.

49. Doniger O'Flaherty, *Other People's Myths*, 124.

50. Doniger O'Flaherty, *Other People's Myths*, 131–132.

51. Religion scholars have begun to devote serious attention to the "religion" of Star Trek fandom, e.g., in Jennifer E. Porter and Darcee L. McLaren, eds., Star Trek *and Sacred Ground: Explorations of* Star Trek, *Religion, and American Culture* (Albany: SUNY Press, 1999).

52. William G. Doty, *Mythography: The Study of Myths and Rituals*, 2nd ed.

(Tuscaloosa: University of Alabama Press, 2000), 89–104. Here Doty questions the "myth" of science and the alleged dichotomy between myth and science.

53. Doty, 107–112.

54. Doty, 7.

55. Doty, 436

56. Doty, 441.

57. Doty, 28.

NOTES TO CHAPTER 4

1. Ivan Strenski, "The Rise of Ritual and the Hegemony of Myth: Sylvain Lévi, the Durkheimians, and Max Müller," in Laurie L. Patton and Wendy Doniger, eds., *Myth and Method* (Charlottesville: University Press of Virginia, 1996), 73.

2. Catherine Bell, *Ritual: Perspectives and Dimensions* (New York: Oxford University Press, 1997), 93–137.

3. James George Frazer, *The Golden Bough: A Study in Magic and Religion*, 3rd ed., 12 vol. (London: Macmillan, 1911–1915). For a fine summary, see Daniel L. Pals, *Seven Theories of Religion* (New York: Oxford University Press, 1996), 32–44.

4. Sigmund Freud, *Totem and Taboo*, trans. A. A. Brill (New York: Vintage Books, 1946). Catherine Bell discusses the influence of Frazer on Freud in *Ritual: Perspectives and Dimensions*, 12–14.

5. Réne Girard, *Violence and the Sacred*, trans. Patrick Gregory (Baltimore: Johns Hopkins University Press, 1977). Girard has continued to refine and develop his thesis in more recent works.

6. On the development of the Hindu view, see Guy L. Beck, "Fire in the Atman: Repentance in Hinduism," in *Repentance: A Comparative Approach* (Lanham, MD: Rowman and Littlefield, 1997), 76–95.

7. Michael Wyschogrod, "Sin and Atonement in Judaism" in Frederick E. Greenspahn, ed., *The Human Condition in the Jewish and Christian Traditions* (Hoboken, NJ: Ktav, 1986), 124–125. On the continued role of sacrifice in Judaism and Christianity, also see John Lyden, "Atonement in Judaism and Christianity: Towards a Rapprochement," *Journal of Ecumenical Studies* 29:1 (Winter 1992): 47–54.

8. Godfrey Ashby, *Sacrifice: Its Nature and Purpose* (London: Macmillan, 1969), 36.

9. Vincent Taylor, *The Atonement in New Testament Teaching* (London: Epworth Press, 1940), 176 and passim. Although Taylor's work is not recent, his work still has value, as he remains one of the few biblical scholars to have devoted most of his career to the doctrine of the atonement. See also his *Jesus and His Sacrifice* (London: Macmillan, 1937) and *Forgiveness and Reconciliation* (London: Macmillan, 1941).

10. See Martin Hengel, *The Atonement: The Origins of the Doctrine in the New Testament*, trans. John Bowden (Philadelphia: Fortress Press, 1981), 63. On the link between Judaism and Christianity on this point, see Franz Mussner, *Tractate on the Jews: The Significance of Judaism for Christian Faith*, trans. Leonard Swidler (Philadelphia: Fortress Press, 1984), 90–94.

11. William G. Doty, *Mythography: The Study of Myths and Rituals*, 2nd ed. (Tuscaloosa: University of Alabama Press, 2000), 230–234.

12. Réne Girard, *Deceit, Desire, and the Novel: Self and Other in Literary Studies* (Baltimore: Johns Hopkins University Press, 1965), and *A Theater of Envy: William Shakespeare* (New York: Oxford University Press, 1991).

13. Aristotle, *The Basic Works of Aristotle*, ed. Richard McKeon (New York: Random House, 1941), 1460.

14. Aristotle, 1466–1467.

15. Francis Fergusson, "Oedipus Rex: The Tragic Rhythm of Action," reprinted in Robert A. Segal, ed., *Theories of Myth*, vol. 5, *Ritual and Myth* (New York: Garland Press, 1996), 67–95.

16. Herbert Weisinger, "The Myth and Ritual Approach to Shakespearian Tragedy," in Segal, *Ritual and Myth*, 392; also in Segal: Richard F. Hardin, "'Ritual' in Recent Criticism: The Elusive Sense of Community," 172.

17. Victor Turner, *The Ritual Process: Structure and Anti-Structure* (Ithaca, NY: Cornell University Press, 1969), 94.

18. Turner, 78.

19. Turner, 50.

20. Turner, 96–97.

21. Turner, 125–130.

22. Turner, 185–188.

23. Turner, 172–174.

24. Jonathan Z. Smith, "The Bare Facts of Ritual," in *Imagining Religion: From Babylon to Jonestown* (Chicago: University of Chicago Press, 1982), 53–65 (quotation from 65).

25. Bell, 139–155.

26. Bell, 157.

27. Bell, 160–161.

28. Bell, 164–165.

29. For Bell's own discussion of the scholarship on this point, see Bell, 197–202.

NOTES TO CHAPTER 5

1. Sam D. Gill, *Native American Traditions: Sources and Interpretations* (Belmont, CA: Wadsworth, 1983), 3–4.

2. Gill, *Native American Traditions*, 5–8; also Sam D. Gill, *Native American Religions: An Introduction* (Belmont, CA: Wadsworth, 1982), 6–7.

3. Jonathan Z. Smith, "Adde Parvum Parvo Magnus Acervus Erit," in *Map Is Not Territory: Studies in the History of Religions* (Leiden: E. J. Brill, 1978), 242.

4. George Catlin could thus observe in the 1830s that "I never saw any other people of any colour, who spend so much of their lives in humbling themselves before, and worshipping the Great Spirit, as some of these tribes do." In Gill, *Traditions*, 13.

5. Gill, *Religions*, 9.

6. Clifford Geertz, *The Interpretation of Cultures* (New York: Basic Books, 1973), 30.

7. There are some who hold this view and seem embarrassed by the negative connotations of the word "exclusivism" in that it suggests rejection based on cultural prejudice, and they may prefer a word such as "particularism" instead. However, all that the word really connotes is that truth is found exclusively in one tradition and that the truth of one excludes the truth of another. This seems to define the position better than "particularism," which might mean merely the recognition that everyone has a particular view or that they should be allowed one.

8. Karl Rahner, "Christianity and the Non-Christian Religions," in *Theological Investigations*, vol. 5 (Baltimore: Helicon Press, 1966), 128.

9. Rahner, "Non-Christian Religions," 132; see also Karl Rahner, "Observations on the Problem of the 'Anonymous Christian,'" in *Theological Investigations*, vol. 14 (New York: Seabury Press, 1976), 282–283.

10. John Hick initially developed this view in "The Copernican Revolution in Theology," in *God and the Universe of Faiths* (London: Macmillan, 1973), 120–147. His definitive formulation of his view is perhaps that given in *An Interpretation of Religion* (New Haven: Yale University Press, 1989).

11. Hick, *Interpretation*, 51.

12. Hick, *Interpretation*, 235.

13. S. Mark Heim, *Salvations: Truth and Difference in Religion* (Maryknoll, NY: Orbis Books, 1995), 96.

14. George Lindbeck, *The Nature of Doctrine: Religion and Theology in a Postliberal Age* (Philadelphia: Westminster Press, 1984), 55–63.

15. Lindbeck, 61.

16. John B. Cobb, Jr., *Beyond Dialogue: Toward a Mutual Transformation of Christianity and Buddhism* (Philadelphia: Fortress Press, 1982), 48.

17. Cobb, *Beyond Dialogue*, 42–45.

18. John B. Cobb, Jr., "Toward a Christocentric Catholic Theology," in Leonard Swidler, ed., *Toward a Universal Theology of Religion* (Maryknoll, NY: Orbis Books, 1987), 89.

19. John B. Cobb, Jr., "Beyond 'Pluralism,'" in Gavin D'Costa, ed., *Christian Uniqueness Reconsidered: The Myth of a Pluralistic Theology of Religions* (Maryknoll, NY: Orbis Books, 1990), 93.

20. Cobb, "Toward a Christocentric Catholic Theology," 100.

21. Cobb, *Beyond Dialogue*, 51–52.

22. Cobb mapped out a process-theology-oriented Christology in *Christ in a Pluralistic Age* (Philadelphia: Westminster, 1975), which sees the incarnation as a basic principle of the whole of creation, and therefore does not limit it to Jesus.

23. Cobb, "Beyond 'Pluralism,'" 86, 92–93; *Beyond Dialogue*, 48.

24. Raimundo Panikkar, "The Invisible Harmony: A Universal Theory of Religion or a Cosmic Confidence in Reality?" in Swidler, *Toward a Universal Theology of Religion*, 125.

25. Panikkar, "Invisible Harmony," 127.

26. Panikkar, "Invisible Harmony," 131.

27. Panikkar, "Invisible Harmony," 140.

28. Raimundo Panikkar, *The Unknown Christ of Hinduism*, rev. ed. (Maryknoll, NY: Orbis Books, 1981), 19.

29. Raimundo Panikkar, *The Intrareligious Dialogue* (New York: Paulist Press, 1978), xxiii–xxvii.

30. Raimundo Panikkar, "The Jordan, the Tiber, and the Ganges: Three Kairological Moments of Christic Self-Consciousness," in John Hick and Paul F. Knitter, eds., *The Myth of Christian Uniqueness: Toward a Pluralistic Theology of Religions* (Maryknoll, NY: Orbis Books, 1987), 109.

31. Panikkar, "Invisible Harmony," 135.

32. Panikkar, "Invisible Harmony," 144.

33. Panikkar, "Invisible Harmony," 145–147.

34. Heim, 219. On Cobb, see 143–144; on Panikkar, 170–171.

35. Heim, 38.

36. Heim, 220.

37. Heim, 146–149.

38. Heim, 152.

39. Heim, 154.

40. For example, Heim speculates that Christians or Buddhists may not correctly describe the final state metaphysically even while they might experience something like what they seek. Heim, 176–177.

41. Heim, 221.

42. Frank Walsh, *Sin and Censorship: The Catholic Church and the Motion Picture Industry* (New Haven: Yale University Press, 1996), 6–10.

43. Walsh, 12–16.

44. Gregory D. Black, *Hollywood Censored: Morality Codes, Catholics, and the Movies* (Cambridge, UK: Cambridge University Press, 1994), 39, 302–308.

45. Well documented by Thomas Doherty in *Pre-Code Hollywood: Sex, Immorality, and Insurrection in American Cinema, 1930–1934* (New York: Columbia University Press, 1999).

46. Black, 169–172.

47. Black, 216–217.

48. Black, 84–106.

49. Black, 278–281.

50. Walsh, 317–318.

51. It should be noted that ideological interpretations take on an inclusivist cast as well when they accept "art" films that support their own agendas; again, this approach relies on sharp distinctions between "artistic" (good) and "popular" (bad) films, which I have found indefensible in practice.

52. Jonathan Z. Smith, "The Devil in Mr. Jones," in *Imagining Religion: From Babylon to Jonestown* (Chicago: University of Chicago Press, 1982), 102–120. See especially 104–105 and 109–112.

53. Smith, "The Devil in Mr. Jones," 112–120.

54. Smith, "The Devil in Mr. Jones," 105.

55. See, for example, Melvyn Stokes and Richard Maltby, eds., *Identifying Hollywood's Audiences: Cultural Identity and the Movies* (London: British Film Institute, 1999).

NOTES TO THE INTRODUCTION TO PART II

1. Martin Barker with Thomas Austin, *From Antz to Titanic: Reinventing Film Analysis* (London: Pluto Press, 2000); pages 22–25 give Barker's critique of Leland Poague's psychoanalytic interpretation of *It's a Wonderful Life*.

2. Barker, 45–49. Barker's concept of the implied reader is based in part on that of Wolfgang Iser, though he finds Iser's approach overly intellectualized in its assumption that readers must consciously "make" meaning out of a text rather than achieving a cognitive and emotional relationship with it via largely unrecognized processes. The fact that Iser spoke of books rather than films is surely part of this difference between their approaches, as Barker acknowledges.

3. Barker, 177–190.

4. Jim Kitses makes this critique in "Authorship and Genre: Notes on the Western" (1969) in Jim Kitses and Gregg Rickman, eds., *The Western Reader* (New York: Limelight Editions, 1998), 63.

5. See Steve Neale, *Genre and Hollywood* (New York: Routledge, 2000), for a thorough study of the notion of genre and its uses in film criticism. Neale points out repeatedly that genres are fluid constructions and that hybridization has become increasingly common; also that film theorists have too often used fixed definitions of genres that have restricted the interpretation of particular films.

NOTES TO CHAPTER 6

1. Steve Neale, *Genre and Hollywood* (New York: Routledge, 2000), 136.

2. For a study of the history of how Native Americans have been depicted in movies, see Jacquelyn Kilpatrick, *Celluloid Indians: Native Americans and Film* (Lincoln: University of Nebraska Press, 1999).

NOTES TO CHAPTER 7

1. Gregory D. Black, *Hollywood Censored: Morality Codes, Catholics, and the Movies* (Cambridge, UK: University of Cambridge, 1994), 107–137.

2. Black, 305.

3. Robert Warshow, "The Gangster as Tragic Hero," published in *Partisan Review* 15:2 (February 1948), republished in Robert Warshow, *The Immediate Experience: Movies, Comics, Theater, and Other Aspects of Popular Culture* (New York: Doubleday, 1962), 127–133.

4. Jonathan Munby, *Public Enemies, Public Heroes: Screening the Gangster from Little Caesar to Touch of Evil* (Chicago: University of Chicago Press, 1999), 14–17.

5. Munby, 44.

6. Munby, 48.

7. Munby, 60–61.

8. Munby, 119.

9. Munby, 225.

NOTES TO CHAPTER 8

1. See Steve Neale, *Genre and Hollywood* (New York: Routledge, 2000), 179–204, for a discussion of the evolution of the term "melodrama" and its connections with the so-called women's film.

2. Jeanine Basinger, *A Woman's View: How Hollywood Spoke to Women, 1930–1960* (New York: Alfred A. Knopf, 1993), 23.

3. Basinger, 494–495.

4. This understanding is suggested by Isabel Cristina Pinedo, *Recreational Terror: Women and the Pleasures of Horror Film Viewing* (New York: SUNY Press, 1997), 86, also in reference to the "forbidden" pleasures of horror films for women, which I will discuss later. She also refers to Shere Hite, *The Hite Report* (New York: Macmillan, 1976), and Nancy Friday, *My Secret Garden: Women's Sexual Fantasies* (New York: Pocket Books, 1973).

5. Basinger, 438–444.

6. A study of this phenomenon is found in Mary Pipher, *Reviving Ophelia: Saving the Selves of Adolescent Girls* (New York: Ballantine Books, 1995).

NOTES TO CHAPTER 9

1. Martin Barker, with Thomas Austin, *From Antz to Titanic: Reinventing Film Analysis* (London: Pluto Press, 2000), 154.

NOTES TO CHAPTER 10

1. In the 2002 theatrical reissue of the film, certain changes were made that included the insertion of two previously deleted scenes and a computer-enhanced E.T. Spielberg also used computer technology to transform the guns of the FBI into walkie-talkies, as he now believes their use of guns is too frightening for young children. This change, however, deescalates the perceived threat to E.T. considerably, making the escape into the air seem almost superfluous; it also decreases the liminality of the children's revolt by making the adults seem less ominous. For these reasons, I did not consider it a helpful or particularly coherent change.

2. Philip M. Taylor, *Steven Spielberg: The Man, His Movies, and Their Meaning* (New York: Continuum, 1992), 57.

NOTES TO CHAPTER 11

1. A good discussion of the problems inherent in defining science fiction, and its distinction from horror, can be found in the first chapter of Vivian Sobchack, *Screening Space: The American Science Fiction Film* (New York: Ungar, 1987), 17–63.

2. Martin Barker and Kate Brooks, "Bleak Futures by Proxy," in Melvyn Stokes and Richard Maltby, eds., *Identifying Hollywood's Audiences: Cultural Identity and the Movies* (London: British Film Institute, 1999), 162–174.

3. This section represents a revision of my article, "The Apocalyptic Cosmology of *Star Wars*," *Journal of Religion and Film* 4:1 (April 2000), http://www.unomaha.edu/~wwwjrf/LydenStWars.htm. Portions of this article also appear in the discussion of Joseph Campbell in chapter 3. I am grateful to the *Journal of Religion and Film* for giving me permission to use this material here.

4. Phil Cousineau, *The Hero's Journey: The World of Joseph Campbell* (San Francisco: Harper and Row, 1990), 180.

5. This structure is clarified in Andrew Gordon, "*Star Wars*: A Myth for Our Time," in *Screening the Sacred: Religion, Myth, and Ideology in Popular American*

Film (Boulder, CO: Westview Press, 1995), 73–82. See also Joseph Campbell, *The Hero with a Thousand Faces* (Princeton: Princeton University Press, 1949).

6. Joseph Campbell with Bill Moyers, *The Power of Myth* (New York: Doubleday, 1988), 148.

7. Interview with George Lucas, "Of Myth and Men," *Time*, April 26, 1999, 92–94.

8. For one example, see Michael Ryan and Douglas Kellner, *Camera Politica* (Bloomington: Indiana University Press, 1988), 228–236.

9. Most viewers surveyed actually chose to view both the Empire and the rebels as right-wing, which seems rather contradictory if one is seeking to establish a political ideology through the film. See Ryan and Kellner, 235, for survey results.

10. When *The Phantom Menace* was released in May 1999, the popular press featured many interviews with those who had such worries; e.g., see "The Second Coming," *Maclean's*, May 24, 1999, 14–18.

11. "Of Myth and Men," *Time*, April 26, 1999, 92.

12. *Time*, 94.

NOTES TO CHAPTER 12

1. Brigid Cherry, "Refusing to Refuse to Look," in Melvyn Stokes and Richard Maltby, eds., *Identifying Hollywood's Audiences: Cultural Identity and the Movies* (London: British Film Institute, 1999), 188.

2. Cherry, 195.

3. Cherry, 196.

4. Isabel Cristina Pinedo, *Recreational Terror: Women and the Pleasures of Horror Film Viewing* (Albany: SUNY Press, 1997), 55–65.

5. Pinedo, 66.

6. Pinedo, 69–95.

7. Quoted in David Sterritt, *The Films of Alfred Hitchcock* (Cambridge, UK: Cambridge University Press, 1993), 100.

8. The inexplicable and irrational aspect of evil had long been a part of Hitchcock's films, but it may have achieved its high point in the postmodernism of *The Birds*, which made absolutely no attempt to explain why the birds are attacking. As in *Psycho*, there is an oedipal triangle in which a young woman comes between a man and his possessive mother, but it would be foolish to suggest that either woman has "caused" the attacks. At one point, a hysterical woman does accuse Melanie (the young woman) of being the cause, but because she faces the camera there is the suggestion that it is the *audience* that is actually the sadistic force "causing" the violence—which, in a way, they were, being the market for it! For a good discussion of these issues, see Robin Wood, *Hitchcock's Films Revisited* (New York: Columbia University Press, 1989), 152–172.

9. Thomas M. Leitch, *Find the Director, and Other Hitchcock Games* (Athens: University of Georgia Press, 1991), especially 260–261.

10. Robin Wood, e.g., has argued that Hitchcock only viewed *Psycho* as "fun" as a "means of preserving his sanity," as he could not face up to the depiction of horror he had created without a certain detachment (Wood, 151). He has emphasized the moral message of Hitchcock's films rather than the "fun and play" aspect emphasized by Leitch, but both are inextricably linked.

Bibliography

Allen, Richard. *Projecting Illusion: Film Spectatorship and the Impression of Reality.* New York: Cambridge University Press, 1995.

Aristotle. *The Basic Works of Aristotle.* Ed. Richard McKeon. New York: Random House, 1941.

Arvidsson, Stefan. "Aryan Mythology as Science and Ideology." *Journal of the American Academy of Religion* 67:2 (June 1999): 327–354.

Ashby, Godfrey. *Sacrifice: Its Nature and Purpose.* London: Macmillan, 1969.

Barker, Martin, with Thomas Austin. *From Antz to Titanic: Reinventing Film Analysis.* London: Pluto Press, 2000.

Barker, Martin, and Kate Brooks. "Bleak Futures by Proxy." In *Identifying Hollywood's Audiences: Cultural Identity and the Movies,* ed. Melvyn Stokes and Richard Maltby, 162–174. London: British Film Institute, 1999.

Basinger, Jeanine. *A Woman's View: How Hollywood Spoke to Women, 1930–1960.* New York: Alfred A. Knopf, 1993.

Baudrillard, Jean. *Simulacra and Simulation.* Trans. Sheila Faria Glaser. Ann Arbor: University of Michigan Press, 1994.

Baudry, Jean-Louis. "Ideological Effects of the Basic Cinematographic Apparatus." In *Film Theory and Criticism,* 5th ed., ed. Leo Braudy and Marshall Cohen, 345–355. New York: Oxford University Press, 1999.

Beck, Guy L. "Fire in the Atman: Repentance in Hinduism." In *Repentance: A Comparative Approach,* ed. Amitai Etzioni and David E. Carney, 76–95. Lanham, MD: Rowman and Littlefield, 1997.

Bell, Catherine. *Ritual: Perspectives and Dimensions.* New York: Oxford University Press, 1997.

Bird, Michael. "Film as Hierophany." In *Religion in Film,* ed. John R. May and Michael Bird, 3–22. Knoxville: University of Tennessee Press, 1982.

Black, Gregory D. *Hollywood Censored: Morality Codes, Catholics, and the Movies.* Cambridge, UK: Cambridge University Press, 1994.

Braudy, Leo, and Marshall Cohen, eds. *Film Theory and Criticism,* 5th ed. New York: Oxford University Press, 1999.

Bryant, M. Darrol. "Cinema, Religion, and Popular Culture." In *Religion in Film*, ed. John R. May and Michael Bird, 101–114. Knoxville: University of Tennessee Press, 1982.

Bywater, Tim, and Thomas Sobchack. *An Introduction to Film Criticism: Major Critical Approaches to Narrative Film*. New York: Longman, 1989.

Campbell, Joseph. *The Hero with a Thousand Faces*. Princeton, NJ: Princeton University Press, 1949.

Campbell, Joseph. *Myths to Live By*. New York: Viking, 1972.

Campbell, Joseph, with Bill Moyers. *The Power of Myth*. New York: Doubleday, 1988.

Carroll, Noel. "Jean-Louis Baudry and 'The Apparatus,'" In *Film Theory and Criticism*, 5th ed., ed. Leo Braudy and Marshall Cohen, 778–794. New York: Oxford University Press, 1999.

Cherry, Brigid. "Refusing to Refuse to Look." In *Identifying Hollywood's Audiences: Cultural Identity and the Movies*, ed. Melvyn Stokes and Richard Maltby, 187–203. London: British Film Institute, 1999.

Cho Bantly, Francisca. "Archetypes of Selves: A Study of the Chinese Mytho-Historical Consciousness." In *Myth and Method*, ed. Laurie L. Patton and Wendy Doniger, 177–207. Charlottesville: University Press of Virginia, 1996.

Cobb, John B., Jr. *Beyond Dialogue: Toward a Mutual Transformation of Christianity and Buddhism*. Philadelphia: Fortress Press, 1982.

Cobb, John B., Jr. "Beyond 'Pluralism.'" In *Christian Uniqueness Reconsidered: The Myth of a Pluralistic Theology of Religions*, ed. Gavin D'Costa, 81–95. Maryknoll, NY: Orbis Books, 1990.

Cobb, John B., Jr. *Christ in a Pluralistic Age*. Philadelphia: Westminster, 1975.

Cobb, John B., Jr. "Toward a Christocentric Catholic Theology." In *Toward a Universal Theology of Religion*, ed. Leonard Swidler, 86–100. Maryknoll, NY: Orbis Books, 1987.

Cooper, John C., and Carl Skrade, eds. *Celluloid and Symbols*. Philadelphia: Fortress Press, 1970.

Cousineau, Phil. *The Hero's Journey: The World of Joseph Campbell*. San Francisco: Harper and Row, 1990.

Doherty, Thomas. *Pre-Code Hollywood: Sex, Immorality, and Insurrection in American Cinema, 1930–1934*. New York: Columbia University Press, 1999.

Doniger, Wendy. "Minimyths and Maximyths and Political Points of View." In *Myth and Method*, ed. Laurie L. Patton and Wendy Doniger, 109–127. Charlottesville: University Press of Virginia, 1996.

Doniger, Wendy. "Post-modern and –colonial –structural Comparisons." In *A Magic Still Dwells: Comparative Religion in the Postmodern Age*, ed. Kimberley C. Patton and Benjamin C. Ray, 63–74. Berkeley: University of California Press, 2000.

Doniger O'Flaherty, Wendy. *Dreams, Illusions, and Other Realities.* Chicago: University of Chicago Press, 1984.

Doniger O'Flaherty, Wendy. *Other People's Myths.* New York: Macmillan, 1988.

Doty, William G. *Mythography: The Study of Myths and Rituals,* 2nd ed. Tuscaloosa: University of Alabama Press, 2000.

Eliade, Mircea. "Cosmogonic Myth and 'Sacred History.'" In *The Quest: History and Meaning in Religion,* 72–87. Chicago: University of Chicago Press, 1969.

Eliade, Mircea. *Cosmos and History: The Myth of the Eternal Return.* Trans. Willard R. Trask. New York: Harper and Row, 1959.

Eliade, Mircea. *Myth and Reality.* Trans. Willard R. Trask. New York: Harper and Row, 1963.

Eliade, Mircea. *Patterns in Comparative Religion.* Trans. Rosemary Sheed. New York: World Publishing, 1958.

Eliade, Mircea. *Rites and Symbols of Initiation: The Mysteries of Birth and Rebirth.* Trans. Willard R. Trask. Dallas: Spring Publications, 1958.

Eliade, Mircea. *The Sacred and the Profane: The Nature of Religion.* Trans. Willard R. Trask. New York: Harcourt, Brace, Jovanovich, 1959.

Fergusson, Francis. "Oedipus Rex: The Tragic Rhythm of Action." In *Theories of Myth,* vol. 5, *Ritual and Myth,* ed. Robert A. Segal, 67–95. New York: Garland Press, 1996.

Ferlita, Ernest. "The Analogy of Action in Film." In *Religion in Film,* ed. John R. May and Michael Bird, 44–57. Knoxville: University of Tennessee Press, 1982.

Ferlita, Ernest. "Film and the Quest for Meaning." In *Religion in Film,* ed. John R. May and Michael Bird, 115–131. Knoxville: University of Tennessee Press, 1982.

Ferlita, Ernest, and John R. May. *Film Odyssey: The Art of Film as Search for Meaning.* New York: Paulist Press, 1976.

Frazer, James George. *The Golden Bough: A Study in Magic and Religion.* 3rd ed. 12 vol. London: Macmillan, 1911–1915.

Freud, Sigmund. *Totem and Taboo.* Trans. A. A. Brill. New York: Vintage Books, 1946.

Friday, Nancy. *My Secret Garden: Women's Sexual Fantasies.* New York: Pocket Books, 1973.

Friedman, Maurice. "Psychology, Psychologism, and Myth: A Rejoinder." *Journal of the American Academy of Religion* 67:2 (June 1999): 469–471.

Friedman, Maurice. "Why Joseph Campbell's Psychologizing of Myth Precludes the Holocaust as Touchstone of Reality." *Journal of the American Academy of Religion* 66:2 (June 1998): 385–401.

Geertz, Clifford. *The Interpretation of Cultures.* New York: Basic Books, 1973.

Gill, Sam D. *Native American Religions: An Introduction.* Belmont, CA: Wadsworth, 1982.

Gill, Sam D. *Native American Traditions: Sources and Interpretations.* Belmont, CA: Wadsworth, 1983.

Girard, Réne. *Deceit, Desire, and the Novel: Self and Other in Literary Studies.* Baltimore: Johns Hopkins University Press, 1965.

Girard, Réne. *A Theater of Envy: William Shakespeare.* New York: Oxford University Press, 1991.

Girard, Réne. *Violence and the Sacred.* Trans. Patrick Gregory. Baltimore: Johns Hopkins University Press, 1977.

Gire, Ken. *Reflections on the Movies: Hearing God in the Unlikeliest of Places.* Colorado Springs, CO: Chariot Victor, 2000.

Gordon, Andrew. "*Star Wars*: A Myth for Our Time." In *Screening the Sacred: Religion, Myth, and Ideology in Popular American Film*, ed. Joel W. Martin and Conrad E. Ostwalt, Jr., 73–82. Boulder, CO: Westview Press, 1995.

Griffin, David Ray. "Rejoinder to Preus and Segal." *Journal of the American Academy of Religion* 68:1 (March 2000): 143–149.

Griffin, David Ray. "Religious Experience, Naturalism, and the Social Scientific Study of Religion." *Journal of the American Academy of Religion* 68:1 (March 2000): 99–125.

Gunning, Tom. "An Aesthetic of Astonishment: Early Film and the (In)credulous Spectator." In *Film Theory and Criticism*, 5th ed., ed. Leo Braudy and Marshall Cohen, 818–832. New York: Oxford University Press, 1999.

Hardin, Richard F. "'Ritual' in Recent Criticism: The Elusive Sense of Community." In *Theories of Myth*, vol. 5, *Ritual and Myth*, ed. Robert A. Segal, 170–186. New York: Garland Press, 1996.

Heim, S. Mark. *Salvations: Truth and Difference in Religion.* Maryknoll, NY: Orbis Books, 1995.

Hengel, Martin. *The Atonement: The Origins of the Doctrine in the New Testament.* Trans. John Bowden. Philadelphia: Fortress Press, 1981.

Hick, John. "The Copernican Revolution in Theology." In *God and the Universe of Faiths*, 120–147. London: Macmillan, 1973.

Hick, John. *An Interpretation of Religion.* New Haven: Yale University Press, 1989.

Hill, John, and Pamela Church Gibson, eds. *Film Studies: Critical Approaches.* Oxford: Oxford University Press, 2000.

Hite, Shere. *The Hite Report.* New York: Macmillan, 1976.

Hollows, Joanne. "Mass Culture Theory and Political Economy." In *Approaches to Popular Film*, ed. Joanne Hollows and Mark Jancovich, 15–35. Manchester, UK: Manchester University Press, 1995.

Hollows, Joanne, and Mark Jancovich, eds. *Approaches to Popular Film.* Manchester, UK: Manchester University Press, 1995.

Hollows, Joanne, and Mark Jancovich. "Introduction: Popular Film and Cultural Distinctions." In *Approaches to Popular Film*, ed. Joanne Hollows and Mark Jancovich, 1–14. Manchester, UK: Manchester University Press, 1995.

Hurley, Neil P. "*On the Waterfront*: Rebirth of a 'Contenduh.'" In *Image and Likeness: Religious Visions in American Film Classics*, ed. John R. May, 96–103. New York: Paulist Press, 1992.

Hurley, Neil P. *The Reel Revolution: A Film Primer on Liberation.* Maryknoll, NY: Orbis Books, 1978.

Hurley, Neil P. *Theology through Film.* New York: Harper and Row, 1970. Republished as *Toward a Film Humanism.* New York: Delta Paperbacks, 1975.

Iaccino, James F. *Jungian Reflections within the Cinema: A Psychological Analysis of Sci-Fi and Fantasy Archetypes.* Westport, CT: Praeger, 1998.

Jackson, Kevin, ed. *Schrader on Schrader.* London: Faber and Faber, 1990.

Jancovich, Mark. "Screen Theory." In *Approaches to Popular Film*, ed. Joanne Hollows and Mark Jancovich, 123–150. Manchester, UK: Manchester University Press, 1995.

Jasper, David Jasper. "On Systematizing the Unsystematic: A Response." In *Explorations in Theology and Film: Movies and Meaning*, ed. Clive Marsh and Gaye Ortiz, 235–244. Oxford: Blackwell, 1997.

Jewett, Robert. *Saint Paul at the Movies: The Apostle's Dialogue with American Culture.* Louisville, KY: Westminster/John Knox Press, 1993.

Jewett, Robert. *Saint Paul Returns to the Movies: Triumph over Shame.* Grand Rapids, MI: Eerdmans, 1999.

Johnston, Robert K. *Reel Spirituality: Theology and Film in Dialogue.* Grand Rapids, MI: Baker, 2000.

Jung, C. G. "Archetypes of the Collective Unconscious." In *The Collected Works of C. G. Jung*, ed. Sir Herbert Read et al., vol. 9, pt. 1, *The Archetypes and the Collective Unconscious*, 2nd ed., Trans. R. F. C. Hull, 3–41. Princeton, NJ: Princeton University Press, 1968.

Jung, C. G. *The Gnostic Jung.* Ed. Robert A. Segal. Princeton, NJ: Princeton University Press, 1992.

Jung, C. G. "Jung and Religious Belief." In *Psychology and Western Religion*, trans. R. F. C. Hull, 253–297. London: Routledge, 1988.

Jung, C. G. *Psychology and Western Religion.* Trans. R. F. C. Hull. London: Routledge, 1988.

Jung, C. G. "A Psychological Approach to the Dogma of the Trinity." In *Psychology and Western Religion*, trans. R. F. C. Hull, 3–96. London: Routledge, 1988.

Jung, C. G. "Religion and Psychology: A Reply to Martin Buber." In *The Gnostic Jung*, ed. Robert A. Segal, 155–163. Princeton, NJ: Princeton University Press, 1992.

Kilpatrick, Jacquelyn. *Celluloid Indians: Native Americans and Film.* Lincoln: University of Nebraska Press, 1999.

Kitses, Jim. "Authorship and Genre: Notes on the Western." In *The Western Reader*, ed. Jim Kitses and Gregg Rickman, 57–68. New York: Limelight Editions, 1998.

Kracauer, Siegfried. "Basic Concepts." In *Film Theory and Criticism*, 5th ed., ed. Leo Braudy and Marshall Cohen, 171–182. New York: Oxford University Press, 1999.

Leitch, Thomas M. *Find the Director, and Other Hitchcock Games*. Athens: University of Georgia Press, 1991.

Lindbeck, George. *The Nature of Doctrine: Religion and Theology in a Postliberal Age*. Philadelphia: Westminster Press, 1984.

Lopez, Donald S., Jr. "Jailbreak: Author's Response." *Journal of the American Academy of Religion* 69:1 (March 2001): 203–213.

Lopez, Donald S., Jr. *Prisoners of Shangri-La: Tibetan Buddhism and the West*. Chicago: University of Chicago Press, 1998.

Lucas, George (interviewed). "Of Myth and Men." *Time*, April 26, 1999, 92–94.

Lyden, John. "The Apocalyptic Cosmology of *Star Wars*." *Journal of Religion and Film* 4:1 (April 2000): http://www.unomaha.edu/~wwwjrf/LydenSt-Wars.htm.

Lyden, John. "Atonement in Judaism and Christianity: Towards a Rapprochement." *Journal of Ecumenical Studies* 29:1 (Winter 1992): 47–54.

Lyden, John. "Continuing the Conversation: A Response to Clive Marsh." *Journal of Religion and Film*, Reader Discussion: http://www.unomaha.edu/~wwwjrf/disctopc.htm.

Lyden, John. "To Commend or to Critique? The Question of Religion and Film Studies." *Journal of Religion and Film* 1:2 (October 1997): http://www.unomaha.edu/~wwwjrf/tocommend.htm.

Marsh, Clive. "Film and Theologies of Culture." In *Explorations in Theology and Film: Movies and Meaning*, ed. Clive Marsh and Gaye Ortiz, 21–34. Oxford: Blackwell, 1997.

Marsh, Clive. "Religion, Theology and Film in a Postmodern Age: A Response to John Lyden." *Journal of Religion and Film* 2:1 (April 1998): http://www.unomaha.edu/~wwwjrf/marshrel.htm.

Marsh, Clive, and Gaye Ortiz, eds. *Explorations in Theology and Film: Movies and Meaning*. Oxford: Blackwell, 1997.

Marsh, Clive, and Gaye Ortiz, "Theology Beyond the Modern and the Postmodern: A Future Agenda for Theology and Film." In *Explorations in Theology and Film: Movies and Meaning*, ed. Clive Marsh and Gaye Ortiz, 245–255. Oxford: Blackwell, 1997.

Martin, Joel W. "Introduction: Seeing the Sacred on the Screen." In *Screening the Sacred: Religion, Myth, and Ideology in Popular American Film*, ed. Joel W. Martin and Conrad E. Ostwalt, Jr., 1–12. Boulder, CO: Westview Press, 1995.

Martin, Joel W., and Conrad E. Ostwalt, Jr., eds. *Screening the Sacred: Religion, Myth, and Ideology in Popular American Film*. Boulder, CO: Westview Press, 1995.

May, John R. "Contemporary Theories Regarding the Interpretation of Religious Film." In *New Image of Religious Film*, ed. John R. May, 17–37. Kansas City, MO: Sheed and Ward, 1997.

May, John R., ed. *Image and Likeness: Religious Visions in American Film Classics*. New York: Paulist Press, 1982.

May, John R., ed. *New Image of Religious Film*. Kansas City, MO: Sheed and Ward, 1997.

May, John R., "Visual Story and the Religious Interpretation of Film." In *Religion in Film*, ed. John R. May and Michael Bird, 23–43. Knoxville: University of Tennessee Press, 1982.

May, John R. and Michael Bird, eds. *Religion in Film*. Knoxville: University of Tennessee Press, 1982.

McCabe, Colin. "Realism and the Cinema: Notes on Some Brechtian Theses." *Screen* 15:2 (Summer 1974): 21–27.

Miles, Margaret R. *Seeing and Believing: Religion and Values in the Movies*. Boston: Beacon Press, 1996.

Munby, Jonathan. *Public Enemies, Public Heroes: Screening the Gangster from Little Caesar to Touch of Evil*. Chicago: University of Chicago Press, 1999.

Mussner, Franz. *Tractate on the Jews: The Significance of Judaism for Christian Faith*. Trans. Leonard Swidler. Philadelphia: Fortress Press, 1984.

Neale, Steve. *Genre and Hollywood*. New York: Routledge, 2000.

Niebuhr, H. Richard. *Christ and Culture*. New York: Harper and Row, 1951.

Ostwalt, Conrad E., Jr. "Conclusion: Religion, Film, and Cultural Analysis." In *Screening the Sacred: Religion, Myth, and Ideology in Popular American Film*, ed. Joel W. Martin and Conrad E. Ostwalt, Jr., 152–159. Boulder, CO: Westview Press, 1995.

Otto, Rudolf. *The Idea of the Holy*. Trans. John W. Harvey. New York: Oxford University Press, 1958.

Palmer, Michael. *Freud and Jung on Religion*. London: Routledge, 1997.

Pals, Daniel L. *Seven Theories of Religion*. New York: Oxford University Press, 1996.

Panikkar, Raimundo. *The Intrareligious Dialogue*. New York: Paulist Press, 1978.

Panikkar, Raimundo. "The Invisible Harmony: A Universal Theory of Religion or a Cosmic Confidence in Reality?" In *Toward a Universal Theology of Religion*, ed. Leonard Swidler, 118–153. Maryknoll, NY: Orbis Books, 1987.

Panikkar, Raimundo. "The Jordan, the Tiber, and the Ganges: Three Kairological Moments of Christic Self-Consciousness." In *The Myth of Christian Uniqueness: Toward a Pluralistic Theology of Religions*, ed. John Hick and Paul F. Knitter, 89–116. Maryknoll, NY: Orbis Books, 1987.

Panikkar, Raimundo. *The Unknown Christ of Hinduism*. Rev. ed. Maryknoll, NY: Orbis Books, 1981.

Pinedo, Isabel Cristina. *Recreational Terror: Women and the Pleasures of Horror Film Viewing.* New York: SUNY Press, 1997.

Pipher, Mary. *Reviving Ophelia: Saving the Selves of Adolescent Girls.* New York: Ballantine Books, 1995.

Plate, S. Brent, and David Jasper, eds. *Imag(in)ing Otherness: Filmic Visions of Living Together.* Atlanta: Scholars Press, 1999.

Porter, Jennifer E., and Darcee L. McLaren, eds. Star Trek *and Sacred Ground: Explorations of* Star Trek, *Religion, and American Culture.* Albany: SUNY Press, 1999.

Preus, J. Samuel. "Response: Explaining Griffin." *Journal of the American Academy of Religion* 68:1 (March 2000): 127–132.

Rahner, Karl. "Christianity and the Non-Christian Religions." In *Theological Investigations*, vol. 5, 115–134. Baltimore: Helicon Press, 1966.

Rahner, Karl. "Observations on the Problem of the 'Anonymous Christian.'" In *Theological Investigations*, vol. 14, 280–294. New York: Seabury Press, 1976.

Romanowski, William D. *Eyes Wide Open: Looking for God in Popular Culture.* Grand Rapids, MI: Brazos Press, 2001.

Rushing, Janice Hocker, and Thomas S. Frentz. *Projecting the Shadow: The Cyborg Hero in American Film.* Chicago: University of Chicago Press, 1995.

Ryan, Michael, and Douglas Kellner. *Camera Politica: The Politics and Ideology of Contemporary Hollywood Film.* Bloomington: Indiana University Press, 1988.

Schleiermacher, Friedrich. *The Christian Faith.* Ed. H. R. Mackintosh and J. S. Stewart. Philadelphia: Fortress Press, 1976.

Schrader, Paul. *Transcendental Style in Film.* Berkeley: University of California Press, 1972.

Scott, Bernard Brandon. *Hollywood Dreams and Biblical Stories.* Minneapolis: Fortress, 1994.

"The Second Coming." *Maclean's*, May 24, 1999: 14–18.

Segal, Robert A. *Joseph Campbell: An Introduction.* New York: Garland, 1987.

Segal, Robert A. "Joseph Campbell as Antisemite and as Theorist of Myth: A Response to Maurice Friedman." *Journal of the American Academy of Religion* 67:2 (June 1999): 461–467.

Segal, Robert A. "Response: In Defense of Social Scientific Naturalism: A Response to David Ray Griffin." *Journal of the American Academy of Religion* 68:1 (March 2000): 133–141.

Segal, Robert A. *Theorizing about Myth.* Amherst: University of Massachusetts Press, 1999.

Smith, Jonathan Z. *Imagining Religion: From Babylon to Jonestown.* Chicago: University of Chicago Press, 1982.

Smith, Jonathan Z. *Map Is Not Territory: Studies in the History of Religions.* Leiden: E. J. Brill, 1978.

Sobchack, Vivian. *Screening Space: The American Science Fiction Film.* New York: Ungar, 1987.

Spoto, Donald. *The Art of Alfred Hitchcock: Fifty Years of His Motion Pictures.* 2nd ed. New York: Doubleday, 1992.

Spoto, Donald. *The Dark Side of Genius: The Life of Alfred Hitchcock.* Boston: Little, Brown, 1983.

Stark, Rodney, and William Sims Bainbridge. *A Theory of Religion.* New York: Peter Lang, 1987.

Sterritt, David. *The Films of Alfred Hitchcock.* Cambridge, UK: Cambridge University Press, 1993.

Stokes, Melvyn, and Richard Maltby, eds. *Identifying Hollywood's Audiences: Cultural Identity and the Movies.* London: British Film Institute, 1999.

Stone, Bryan. *Faith and Film: Theological Themes at the Cinema.* St. Louis, MO: Chalice Press, 2000.

Strenski, Ivan. *Four Theories of Myth in Twentieth-Century History.* Iowa City: University of Iowa Press, 1987.

Strenski, Ivan. "The Rise of Ritual and the Hegemony of Myth: Sylvain Lévi, the Durkheimians, and Max Müller." In *Myth and Method,* ed. Laurie L. Patton and Wendy Doniger, 52–81. Charlottesville: University Press of Virginia, 1996.

Taylor, Lisa. "From Psychoanalytic Feminism to Popular Feminism." In *Approaches to Popular Film,* ed. Joanne Hollows and Mark Jancovich, 151–171. Manchester, UK: Manchester University Press, 1995.

Taylor, Philip M. *Steven Spielberg: The Man, His Movies, and Their Meaning.* New York: Continuum, 1992.

Taylor, Vincent. *The Atonement in New Testament Teaching.* London: Epworth Press, 1940.

Taylor, Vincent. *Forgiveness and Reconciliation.* London: Macmillan, 1941.

Taylor, Vincent. *Jesus and His Sacrifice.* London: Macmillan, 1937.

Thurman, Robert A. F. "Critical Reflections on Donald S. Lopez Jr.'s *Prisoners of Shangri-La: Tibetan Buddhism and the West." Journal of the American Academy of Religion* 69:1 (March 2001): 191–201.

Tillich, Paul. *Christianity and the Encounter of the World Religions.* New York: Columbia University Press, 1963.

Tillich, Paul. *Dynamics of Faith.* New York: Harper and Row, 1957.

Tillich, Paul. "On the Idea of a Theology of Culture." In *What Is Religion?,* ed. James Luther Adams, 155–181. New York: Harper and Row, 1969.

Tillich, Paul. "Religion and Secular Culture." In *The Protestant Era.* Trans. James Luther Adams, 55–65. Chicago: University of Chicago Press, 1948.

Tillich, Paul. "The Significance of the History of Religions for the Systematic Theologian." In *The Future of Religions,* ed. Jerald C. Brauer, 80–94. New York: Harper and Row, 1966.

Tillich, Paul. *Systematic Theology.* Chicago: University of Chicago Press, 1967.

Tillich, Paul. Theology of Culture., Ed. Robert C. Kimball. New York: Oxford University Press, 1959.

Tillich, Paul. *Ultimate Concern: Tillich in Dialogue.* Ed. D. Mackenzie Brown. New York: Harper and Row, 1965.

Turner, Graeme. "Cultural Studies and Film." In *Film Studies: Critical Approaches,* ed. John Hill and Pamela Church Gibson, 193–199. Oxford: Oxford University Press, 2000.

Turner, Victor. *The Ritual Process: Structure and Anti-Structure.* Ithaca, NY: Cornell University Press, 1969.

Wall, James M. *Church and Cinema.* Grand Rapids, MI: Eerdmans, 1971.

Walsh, Frank. *Sin and Censorship: The Catholic Church and the Motion Picture Industry.* New Haven: Yale University Press, 1996.

Warshow, Robert. "The Gangster as Tragic Hero." In *The Immediate Experience: Movies, Comics, Theater, and Other Aspects of Popular Culture,* 127–133. New York: Doubleday, 1962.

Weisinger, Herbert. "The Myth and Ritual Approach to Shakespearian Tragedy." In *Theories of Myth,* vol. 5, *Ritual and Myth,* ed. Robert A. Segal, 384–408. New York: Garland Press, 1996.

Wood, Robin. *Hitchcock's Films Revisited.* New York: Columbia University Press, 1989.

Wyschogrod, Michael. "Sin and Atonement in Judaism." In *The Human Condition in the Jewish and Christian Traditions,* ed. Frederick E. Greenspahn, 120–126. Hoboken, NJ: Ktav, 1986.

Name and Subject Index

Action Films, 20, 144–52, 247
Adams, James Luther, 251n. 10
Adorno, Theodor, 31
Aeschylus, 89
Allen, Richard, 52, 256nn. 40–2
Allen, Woody, 45–6
Approaches to religion and film: theological, 17–27; Protestant-dialogical, 18–22; Roman Catholic (synthetic), 22–7; ideological, 27–32; an alternative to, 32–5
Aquinas, Thomas, 14
Aristotle, 88–90, 93, 261nn. 13–4
Arnheim, Rudolf, 49
Arvidsson, Stefan, 256n. 3
Ashby, Godfrey, 260n. 8
Asimov, Isaac, 205
Augustine, 86
Austin, Thomas, 264n. 1, 266n. 1

Bainbridge, William Sims, 40, 255n. 11
Balinese ritual, 44, 47
Barker, Martin, 138, 179, 264nn. 1–3, 266nn. 1–2
Basinger, Jeanine, 164–9, 265nn. 2–3, 5
Baudrillard, Jean, 51, 53, 256n. 37
Baudry, Jean-Louis, 50–1, 256n. 36
Bazin, Andre, 25, 49
Beck, Guy L., 260n. 6

Bell, Catherine, 80–2, 95, 104–6, 260–1nn. 2, 4, 25–29
Bergman, Ingmar, 26
Berrigan, Daniel, 29
Bhagavad Gita, 91, 222
Bible, 20–1, 30, 57–8, 77, 103, 110–1, 248–9
Bird, Michael, 25–7, 251–3nn. 1, 38, 41–4, 49, 51
Black, Gregory D., 263–4nn. 44, 46–9, 265n. 1
Bowden, John, 261n. 10
Braudy, Leo, 256nn. 32, 36, 38–9
Brauer, Jerald C., 254n. 10
Breen, Joseph, 129–30
Bresson, Robert, 26
Brooks, Kate, 266n. 2
Brown, D. Mackenzie, 254n. 8
Bryant, Darrol, 12, 251nn. 1–2
Buddhism, 37, 85, 115–6, 119–20, 122, 124–5, 127, 135, 254
Bywater, Tim, 256nn. 33–4

Calvin, John, 15, 26
Cameron, James, 171, 178, 207
Campbell, Joseph, 33, 66, 68, 217–8, 257–8nn. 12–8, 266–7nn. 3–6; and psychological interpretations of myth, 60–3

Capra, Frank, 180
Carroll, Noel, 256n. 39
Catharsis, 84, 100, 151, 170, 177–8, 200, 238; and sacrifice in theater and film, 88–94
Catholic Movie Code, 129
Catlin, George, 262n. 4
Cherry, Brigid, 227, 267nn. 1–3
Children's Films, 99, 191–201
Chinese Religions, 37
Cho Bantly, Francisca, 66, 259n. 33
Christianity, 33, 37, 40, 55, 57–58, 90, 255–6n. 30; anti-ritualism in, 79–80; and culture, 15–7; and Mircea Eliade, 65–7; and film critique, 19–27, 29, 126–32, 135; and idealism, 76, 103; and interreligious dialogue, 109–26; and sacrifice, 83–7; and secularity, 106–7; and Steven Spielberg, 199; and *Star Wars*, 222–5
Cobb, John B. Jr., 119–20, 123, 125–7, 262–3nn. 16–23, 34
Cohen, Marshall, 256nn. 32, 36, 38–9
Colette, 167
Columbus, Christopher, 110
Communism, 65, 67, 115, 223
Confucianism, 39, 254
Cooper, John C., 18, 251nn. 15–6
Coppola, Francis Ford, 159, 194, 230
Cousineau, Phil, 266n. 4
Craven, Wes, 229
Crossan, John Dominic, 25
Crowther, Bosley, 231

Dalai Lama, 120
D'Costa, Gavin, 263n. 19
Dick, Philip, 203
Dilthey, Wilhelm, 111
Doherty, Thomas, 264n. 45
Doniger (O'Flaherty), Wendy, 33, 71–4, 76–7, 256n. 1, 259–60nn. 33, 43–50, 1

Doty, William G., 74–7, 259–60nn. 52–57, 261n. 11
Dreyer, Carl, 26
Durkheim, Emile, 62, 67, 117, 258n. 20

Eisenstein, Sergei, 49
Eliade, Mircea, 27, 33, 37, 64–9, 75–6, 83, 254n. 5, 258–9nn. 24–32, 34
Enuma Elish, 69–70
Ephron, Nora, 186, 188–9

Fantasy Films. *See* Children's Films
Fascism, 58, 64–5, 67
Faulkner, William, 130
Fergusson, Francis, 89–90, 261n. 15
Ferlita, Ernest, 26–7, 253nn. 48–53
Ford, John, 143, 197
Formalism, 49–50, 104
Frazer, James George, 57, 83–4, 88–9, 256n. 2, 260nn. 3–4
Frentz, Thomas J., 257n. 11
Freud, Sigmund, 40, 58–9, 72, 83, 177, 260n. 4
Friday, Nancy, 265n. 4
Friedman, Maurice, 61, 257–8nn. 15, 18

Gangster Films, 91, 128, 139, 153–63
Geertz, Clifford, 33, 52, 60, 67, 77, 94, 105, 113, 122–3, 135, 255–6nn. 14–27, 29, 31, 258nn. 19–23, 262n. 6; definition of religion and its application to film, 41–48; on myth and sociological reductionism, 62–4
Gennep, Arnold van, 95
Genre Analysis, 137–9
Gibson, Pamela Church, 253n. 57
Gill, Sam D., 54, 112, 256n. 43, 261–2nn. 1–2, 4–5
Gilliam, Terry, 203
Girard, René, 83–8, 92, 260–1nn. 5, 12
Gire, Ken, 252n. 34
Glaser, Sheila Faria, 256n. 37

Gordon, Andrew, 266–7n. 5
Graham, Billy, 132
Greenspahn, Frederick E., 260n. 7
Gregory, Patrick, 260n. 5
Griffin, David Ray, 255n. 12
Gunning, Tom, 51, 256n. 38

Hardin, Richard F., 261n. 16
Harry Potter, 249
Harvey, John W., 254n. 3
Hauptmann, Hans, 58
Hays Office Code, 22, 129, 144, 153, 155, 165
Hays, Will, 129
Heim, Mark, 123–6, 262–3nn. 13, 34–41
Hemingway, Ernest, 130
Hengel, Martin, 261n. 10
Hick, John, 37, 115–23, 126, 254n. 6, 262–3nn. 10–2, 30
Hill, John, 253n. 57
Hinduism, 61, 71–3, 76, 85, 91, 122, 222
Hitchcock, Alfred, 157, 194, 226, 229–32, 235–40, 246, 267–8nn. 7–10
Hite, Shere, 265n. 4
Hollows, Joanne, 253–4nn. 58, 63–4, 255n. 28
Horkheimer, Max, 31
Horror Films, 92–3, 170, 196, 203–5, 226–45, 247
Hurley, Neil P., S.J., 23–5, 252nn. 35–7

Iaccino, James F., 257n. 11
Ideological Approaches to the Study of Religion and Film, 27–32, 134, 180, 216, 223, 248; alternative to, 32–5
Interreligious Dialogue, 35; and film, 126–36; theological developments in, 113–26; religion-film dialogue as, 108–13
Iser, Wolfgang, 264n. 2
Islam, 85, 106–7, 116
Italian neorealism, 50

Jackson, Kevin, 253n. 46
Jancovich, Mark, 253–5nn. 58, 63–4, 28
Jasper, David, 253n. 54
Jensen, Adolf, 69
Jesus, 25, 29, 55, 57–60, 65, 74, 87, 119–20, 149
Jewett, Robert, 19, 251–2nn. 19–23
Joffe, Roland, 29
Johnston, Robert K., 22, 252n. 33
Jones, Jim, 132
Judaism, 33, 58, 61, 65, 67, 79, 85–7, 106–7, 116, 120, 129, 135, 258
Jung, Carl, 33, 257nn. 5–10; psychological interpretations of myth, 58–62

Kellner, Douglas, 253–4n. 64, 267nn. 8–9
Kilpatrick, Jacquelyn, 265n. 2
Kitses, Jim, 264n. 4
Koresh, David, 133
Knitter, Paul, 123, 263n. 30
Kracauer, Siegfried, 25, 49, 256n. 32

Langer, Susan, 48
Las Casas, Bartolome de, 110, 118
Legion of Decency, The, 22, 130
Leitch, Thomas M., 239, 268n. 9–10
Lévi-Strauss, Claude, 20–1, 62–3, 70, 258n. 22
Lévy-Bruhl, Lucien, 62–3, 258n. 21
Lewis, C.S., 249
Lewis, Sinclair, 130
Liminality, 128, 152, 163, 168–9, 194, 213, 229, 239–40; and carnivals, 95–102
Lindbeck, George, 118, 262nn. 14–5
Lucas, George, 217–8, 225, 267n. 7, 11–2.
Lumière, Louis, 48, 50–1
Luther, Martin, 14
Lyden, John, 254n. 67, 256–7n. 4, 260n. 7, 266n. 3
Lynch, William F., 26

Mahabharata, The, 90–1
Malinowski, Bronislaw, 258n. 20
Maltby, Richard, 264n. 55, 266n. 2, 267n. 1
Marriott, McKim, 96
Marsh, Clive, 22, 34, 252–4nn. 30–2, 54, 67
Martin, Joel, 32–3, 251n. 3, 254nn. 65–6
Marx, Karl, 40, 62, 117, 249
Marxism, 110
Mass Culture theorists, 31, 46
May, John, 24–5, 27, 251–3nn. 1, 37–41, 47–9, 51
McCabe, Colin, 50, 256n. 35
McKeon, Richard, 261n. 13
McLaren, Darcee L., 259n. 51
Méliès, George, 49
Melodrama Films, 93, 164–78
Miles, Margaret, 28–31, 253nn. 54–6, 59–62, 255–6nn. 30
Mitry, Jean, 256n. 34
Morality, 23, 77, 84, 100–1, 117, 131, 158
Motion Picture Producers and Distributors of America, 129
Moyers, Bill, 60, 257n. 14, 267n. 6
Müller, Friedrich Max, 57–8
Munby, Jonathan, 154, 265nn. 4–9
Mussner, Franz, 261n. 10
Myths, 20–1, 25, 33, 45, 51, 56–78; of gangster films, 156; psychological interpretations of, 58–62; and rituals, 101–2; of romantic perfection, 190

Nationalism, 58
National Board of Censorship of Motion Pictures, 127
Native Americans, 54, 109–12, 118, 141
Nazism, 115, 130, 223
Neale, Steve, 264n. 5, 265n. 1
Niebuhr, Reinhold, 103

Niebuhr, H. Richard, 13, 16–8, 22–3, 27, 127, 251nn. 5–9, 14; *Christ and Culture*, 13–15
Nietzsche, Friedrich, 61, 257n. 14
Niven, Larry, 202

Origen, 57
Ortiz, Gaye, 252–3nn. 30, 32, 54
Ostwalt, Conrad, 12, 32, 251nn. 3–4, 254n. 65
Otto, Rudolf, 37, 67, 254nn. 3–4
Oviedo, Gonzalo Fernandez de, 110–1
Ozu, Yasujiro, 26

Palmer, Michael, 257n. 10
Pals, Daniel L., 256n. 2, 260n. 3
Panikkar, Raimundo, 120–3, 126, 263nn. 24–34
Patton, Kimberley, 259n. 44
Patton, Laurie L., 259n. 33, 260n. 1
Pinedo, Isabel Cristina, 228–30, 265n. 4, 267nn. 4–6
Pipher, Mary, 266n. 6
Plate, S. Brent, 253n. 54
Plato, 50, 57, 72, 88
Poague, Leland, 264n. 1
Porter, Jennifer E., 259n. 51
Preus, Samuel J., 255n. 12
Protestantism, 14, 80, 131; dialogical approach to film, 18–22
Psychological reductionism, 59–62
Pudovkin, V.I., 49

Rahner, Karl, 114–5, 117–8, 125–6, 262nn. 8–9
Ray, Benjamin C., 259n. 44
Read, Sir Herbert, 257n. 5
Realism, 25–6, 49–55, 102–4; applied to myths, 72–3
Reductionism, 33, 40–1, 55, 67, 108, 118; psychological (reductionism) applied

to myth, 59–62; sociological (reductionism) applied to myth, 62–4

Reiner, Rob, 186

Religion, definitions of, 36–55; Clifford Geertz's definition, 41–4; Geertz's definition applied to film, 44–8, 52–5; ideological definitions, 40–1; theological definitions, 37; Paul Tillich's definition, 38–40

Renan, Ernest, 58

Rickman, Gregg, 264n. 4

Rituals, 33–4, 44, 47, 52, 69; and the secular, 104–7; and liminality, 95–102; relation of real and ideal, 102–4

Roman Catholic, 14, 22, 29, 30, 74, 80, 114; approaches to theology and film (synthetic), 22–7; censorship of films, 128–31

Romanowski, William D., 252n. 34

Romantic Comedy Films, 179–90, 247

Rousseau, Jean-Jacques, 63

Rowling, J.K., 249

Rushing, Janice Hocker, 257n. 11

Ryan, Michael, 253–4n. 64, 267nn. 8–9

Sacrifice, 82, 239; in theater and film, 88–94; of the scapegoat, 83–7

Schleiermacher, Friedrich, 37, 254n. 2

Schrader, Paul, 26, 253n. 45

Science Fiction Films, 202–25

Scott, Bernard Brandon, 20–1, 63, 252nn. 24–9

Second Vatican Council, 22

Secularity, 12, 73, 104–7

Segal, Robert A., 61, 255n. 12, 257–8nn. 9, 13, 15, 18, 261n. 15–6

Sermon on the Mount, 30–1

Sexism, 21, 30, 93–4, 160, 179–80, 247; in *Die Hard*, 149–52

Sheed, Rosemary, 254n. 5, 258n. 24

Shelley, Mary, 205, 228

Skrade, Carl, 18, 251n. 15–6

Smith, Huston, 24

Smith, Jonathan Z., 33, 36, 67–71, 76, 102, 111, 132–4, 254n. 1, 258–9nn. 21, 35–42, 261n. 24, 262n. 3, 264n 52–4

Smith, Wilfred Cantwell, 123

Sobchack, Thomas, 256nn. 33–4

Sobchack, Vivian, 266n. 1

Sociological reductionism, 62–4

Sophocles, 88–9

Spielberg, Steven, 30, 194–6, 199–201, 230, 266n. 1

Star Trek (television series), 73–4, 204–6, 259n. 51

Stark, Rodney, 40, 255n. 11

Sterritt, David, 267n. 7

Stewart, J.S., 254n. 2

Stokes, Melvyn, 264n. 55, 266n. 2, 267n. 1

Stone, Bryan, 252n. 34

St. Paul, 19

Strauss, David Friedrich, 57, 258

Strenski, Ivan, 79, 259n. 34, 260n. 1

Swidler, Leonard, 261–3nn. 10, 18, 24

Taoism, 39, 254

Taylor, Lisa, 28, 253n. 58

Taylor, Philip M., 266n. 2

Taylor, Vincent, 260n. 9

Tearjerker Films. *See* Melodrama Films

Theological approaches to film, 17–27; alternatives to, 32–5. *See* Approaches to religion and film

Thriller Films. *See* Horror Films

Tillich, Paul, 13, 15–17, 19, 22, 24–5, 127, 251nn. 10–3, 254–5nn. 7–11; definition of religion, 38–9, 43

Tracy, David, 20

Trask, Willard R., 254n. 5, 258nn. 24–5, 28

Turner, Graeme, 253n. 57
Turner, Victor, 95–7, 101, 103, 261nn. 17–23
Tylor, Edward, 57, 256n. 2

Vedantic Hinduism, 61

Wall, James M., 19, 251n. 17–8
Walsh, Frank, 263–4nn. 42–3, 50
Warshow, Robert, 153, 265n. 3
Weber, Max, 117, 249
Weisinger, Herbert, 261n. 16

Wertmuller, Lina, 26, 27
Western Films, 20, 139, 141–5, 148, 150, 153
"Women's Films." See Melodrama Films
Wood, Robin, 267–8nn. 8, 10
Wounded Knee Massacre, 141
Wyschogrod, Michael, 85, 260n. 7

Yogavasistha, 72

Zen Buddhism, 26

Film Index

Affair to Remember, An, 167, 188
Aladdin, 192
Alien, 203
American Pie, 100
Anna Karenina, 94, 130
Annie Hall, 179
Antz, 192–3
Arrival of a Train, 48, 51

Babette's Feast, 19
Baby's Breakfast, 48
Ball of Fire, 181
Beauty and the Beast, 192
Bicycle Thief, The, 50
Birds, The, 231, 267
Blade Runner, 206
Boys Don't Cry, 94
Boys on the Side, 170
Boyz 'n the Hood, 155
Brazil, 203
Bridges of Madison County, The, 99
Buck Rogers, 217
bug's life, a, 192

Casablanca, 183
Close Encounters of the Third Kind, 224
Colossus: The Forbin Project, 205
Creature from the Black Lagoon, The, 203
Crimes and Misdemeanors, 45

Day the Earth Stood Still, The, 205–6
Dead End, 130
Dial M for Murder, 229
Die Hard, 100, 145–152, 210
Dirty Dozen, The, 100
Dirty Harry, 20
Dracula, 203, 227
Dr. Strangelove or: How I Learned to Stop
    Worrying and Love the Bomb, 205

End of the Road, 128
E.T., The Extraterrestrial, 53, 99, 194–200,
    202, 266n. 1

Fail-Safe, 205
Ferris Bueller's Day Off, 98
Fit to Fight, 128
Flash Gordon, 217
Forrest Gump, 19, 81
Frankenstein, 205, 228

Gandhi, 103
Gigi, 167
Godfather, The, 91, 156–161, 189, 247
Godfather Part II, The, 91, 156, 161–3
Gone with the Wind, 5, 93, 168, 181
Green Berets, The, 81–2
Groundhog Day, 202
Guilt of Janet Ames, The, 165–6

High Noon, 148
High Plains Drifter, 144
Home Alone, 193
Hook, 200–1

I Married a Monster from Outer Space,
     204
Independence Day, 81, 206
Invasion of the Body Snatchers, 204
It Happened One Night, 180
It's a Wonderful Life, 138, 264n. 1

James and the Giant Peach, 99
Jaws, 30
Jesus of Montreal, 28
Judge Dredd, 216

King Kong, 203, 228
Kiss, The, 127
Kitty Foyle, 165–7

Lady Vanishes, The, 231
Last Temptation of Christ, The, 28–9
Lethal Weapon, 145
Lion King, The, 192
Little Caesar, 153–4
Little Princess, The, 99
Logan's Run, 224

Magnificent Seven, The, 192
Man Who Shot Liberty Valence, The, 143
Matrix, The, 216
Midnight Cowboy, 131
Mission, The, 29
Mr. Holland's Opus, 19
Mulan, 192
Mummy, The, 228

Nine to Five, 100
North by Northwest, 231
Notorious, 231
Notting Hill, 190

Now Voyager, 169–70

101 Dalmatians, 192
On the Waterfront, 24

Pale Rider, 19, 144
Parent Trap, The, 210
Pawnbroker, The, 130
Pinocchio, 192
Planet of the Apes, 205, 207
Pocahontas, 192
Psycho, 226, 230–40, 267
Public Enemy, 153

Quiet Man, The, 197

Raiders of the Lost Ark, 30
Rear Window, 231
Red Dawn, 19
Rescuers, The, 192
Risky Business, 97
Rocky Horror Picture Show, The, 47
Romero, 30
Roxanne, 190
Runaway Bride, 189–90

Saving Private Ryan, 30
Scarface, 153–4
Schindler's List, 30, 194
Searchers, The, 142
Serendipity, 190
Seven Beauties, 26
Seven Samurai, 192
Shadow of a Doubt, 231–2
Shane, 91–2, 142
Shawshank Redemption, The, 19
Shop Around the Corner, The, 188–9
Silence of the Lambs, The, 11, 240–5
Sleepless in Seattle, 188
Sling Blade, 92
Smash-up, the Story of a Woman, 165–6
Stagecoach, 143

Star is Born, A, 166, 170, 175
Star Trek: First Contact, 205
Star Wars, Episode IV: A New Hope, 19, 216–7, 220, 223–5
Star Wars, Episode V: The Empire Strikes Back, 216–7, 221, 223–5
Star Wars, Episode VI: Return of the Jedi, 216–7, 221, 223–5
Steel Magnolias, 170
Strangers on a Train, 231

Take This Job and Shove It, 99
Teasing the Gardener, 48
Terminator, The, 205–9, 216–7, 224
Terminator II: Judgment Day, 205–6, 209–216, 217, 224
Terms of Endearment, 170
Thelma and Louise, 94, 155
Titanic, 139, 170–8, 207
To Catch a Thief, 231

To Each His Own, 168
Toy Story, 193
Trip to the Moon, A, 49
Truth About Cats and Dogs, The, 190
Twelve Monkeys, 205, 207
2001: A Space Odyssey, 205

Vertigo, 231

Wait Until Dark, 229
Waterloo Bridge, 93, 167
When Harry Met Sally, 183–190
White Heat, 155
Willy Wonka and the Chocolate Factory, 193
Wizard of Oz, The, 81, 194
Wolf Man, The, 203, 228
Workers Leaving the Lumière Factory, 48

You've Got Mail, 188–9

About the Author

John C. Lyden is Professor and Chair of the Religion Department at Dana College in Blair, Nebraska. He is the editor of *Enduring Issues in Religion*.